Crowds in the 21st Century

Crowds in the 21st Century presents the latest theory and research on crowd events and crowd behaviour from across a range of social sciences, including psychology, sociology, law, and communication studies. Whether describing the language of the crowd in protest events, measuring the ability of the crowd to empower its participants, or analysing the role of professional organizations involved in crowd safety and public order, the contributions in this volume are united in their commitment to a social scientific level of analysis.

The crowd is often depicted as a source of irrationality and danger – in the form of riots and mass emergencies. By placing crowd events back in their social context – their ongoing historical and proximal relationships with other groups and social structures – this volume restores meaning to the analysis of crowd behaviour. Together, the studies described in this collection demonstrate the potential of crowd research to enhance the positive experience of crowd participants and to improve design, planning, and management around crowd events.

This book was originally published as a special issue of *Contemporary Social Science*.

John Drury is Senior Lecturer in Social Psychology at the University of Sussex, UK. His research interests focus on crowd conflict and identity change (empowerment) and mass emergency behaviour. He also runs a module on the psychology of crowd safety management for music industry professionals at Bucks New University, UK.

Clifford Stott is a Visiting Professor at the Socio-Technical Centre at the University of Leeds, UK, and runs his own consultancy and training company. His expertise focuses on the intergroup dynamics of crowd behaviour and the implications of crowd psychology for crowd management. He has published extensively on these topics in academic journals and co-authored two books, the most recent on the 2011 riots in the UK.

Contemporary Issues in Social Science
Series editor: David Canter, University of Huddersfield, UK

Contemporary Social Science, the journal of the **Academy of Social Sciences**, is an interdisciplinary, cross-national journal which provides a forum for disseminating and enhancing theoretical, empirical and/or pragmatic research across the social sciences and related disciplines. Reflecting the objectives of the Academy of Social Sciences, it emphasises the publication of work that engages with issues of major public interest and concern across the world, and highlights the implications of that work for policy and professional practice.

The *Contemporary Issues in Social Science* book series contains the journal's most cutting-edge special issues. Leading scholars compile thematic collections of articles that are linked to the broad intellectual concerns of *Contemporary Social Science,* and as such these special issues are an important contribution to the work of the journal. The series editor works closely with the guest editor(s) of each special issue to ensure they meet the journal's high standards. The main aim of publishing these special issues as a series of books is to allow a wider audience of both scholars and students from across multiple disciplines to engage with the work of *Contemporary Social Science* and the Academy of Social Sciences.

Titles in the series:

Crowds in the 21st Century: Perspectives from contemporary social science
Edited by John Drury and Clifford Stott

Biologising the Social Sciences: Challenging Darwinian and Neuroscience Explanations
Edited by David Canter and David Turner

Crowds in the 21st Century

Perspectives from contemporary social science

Edited by
John Drury and Clifford Stott

Routledge
Taylor & Francis Group

LONDON AND NEW YORK

ACADEMY
of SOCIAL SCIENCES

First published 2013
by Routledge
2 Park Square, Milton Park, Abingdon, Oxfordshire OX14 4RN

Simultaneously published in the USA and Canada
by Routledge
711 Third Avenue, New York, NY 10017

First issued in paperback 2015

Routledge is an imprint of the Taylor & Francis Group, an informa business

British Library Cataloguing in Publication Data
A catalogue record for this book is available from the British Library

ISBN 13: 978-1-138-92291-4 (pbk)
ISBN 13: 978-0-415-63590-5 (hbk)

Typeset in Times New Roman
by Taylor & Francis Books

Publisher's Note
The publisher would like to make readers aware that the chapters in this book may be referred to as articles as they are identical to the articles published in the special issue. The publisher accepts responsibility for any inconsistencies that may have arisen in the course of preparing this volume for print.

Contents

CONTENTS

Citation Information

The chapters in this book, with the exception of Chapter 4, were originally published in the journal *Contemporary Social Science,* volume 6, issue 3 (November 2011). When citing this material, please use each article's original page numbering, as follows:

Chapter 1
Chapter 1 in this book is a revised version of the introductory article originally published in *Contemporary Social Science*, volume 6, issue 3 (November 2011), pp. 275–288. To view this article in its original format, please refer to:
http://www.tandfonline.com/doi/abs/10.1080/21582041.2011.625626

Chapter 2
The Madrid bombings and popular protest: misinformation, counter-information, mobilisation and elections aftér 11-'M
Cristina Flesher Fominaya
Contemporary Social Science, volume 6, issue 3 (November 2011) pp. 289-307

Chapter 3
Public order policing in South Yorkshire, 1984–2011: the case for a permissive approach to crowd control
David P. Waddington
Contemporary Social Science, volume 6, issue 3 (November 2011) pp. 309-324

Chapter 4
Chapter 4 in this book was first published in the *Journal of Investigative Psychology and Offender Profiling*, volume 9, issue 2 (June 2012), pp. 174-183. To cite this article, please use the following information:
Hoggett, J. and Stott, C. (2012), Post G20: The Challenge of Change, Implementing Evidence-based Public Order Policing. J. Investig. Psych. Offender Profil., 9: 174–183. doi: 10.1002/jip.1360
© 2012 John Wiley & Sons, Ltd.

Chapter 5
The crowd as a psychological cue to in-group support for collective action against collective disadvantage
Martijn van Zomeren and Russell Spears
Contemporary Social Science, volume 6, issue 3 (November 2011) pp. 325-341

Notes on Contributors

B. E. Aguirre is a Professor in the Department of Sociology and Criminal Justice, and Core Faculty, Disaster Research Center, University of Delaware, Newark, USA. He is interested in the social sciences of collective behaviour and its applications in the field of disaster sciences. He has studied evacuation and warning as well as the incident command system, among other topics.

Eric Best is a Research Assistant at the Disaster Research Center, University of Delaware, Newark, USA. He has bachelor's and master's degrees in Economics from the university. He is currently a doctoral student in the Disaster Science and Management programme at the university focusing on simulation and statistics.

David Canter is Professor of Psychology and Director of the International Research Centre for Investigative Psychology at Huddersfield University, UK.

Rose Challenger is a Researcher in Organisational Psychology at the Socio-Technical Centre, Leeds University Business School, UK. Her research focuses on understanding crowd behaviours from a systems perspective. She works with many leading organisations including the Cabinet Office and the London Metropolitan Police.

Chris Clegg is Professor of Organisational Psychology and Director of the Socio-Technical Centre, Leeds University Business School, UK. He is a Fellow of the British Psychological Society, Fellow of the British Computer Society, and Fellow of the Royal Society of Arts.

Jennifer Cole is a Research Fellow at the Royal United Services Institute. She graduated from Cambridge University in 1992 and, from an academic background in anthropology, worked in journalism and publishing before joining the Royal United Services Institute in 2007, where she heads the Emergency Management Programme. She is a military Battlefield Casualty Drills Trainer and has held both military and civilian first aid instructor qualifications.

John Drury is Senior Lecturer in Social Psychology at the University of Sussex, UK. His research interests focus on crowd conflict and identity change (empowerment) and mass emergency behaviour. The crowd events he has researched and written about include the 1990 poll tax riot, the direct action campaign against the M11 link road (London), the London bombings of 7th July 2005, and the Fatboy Slim 'Big Beach Boutique' party of 2002. He also runs a module on the psychology of crowd safety management for music industry professionals at Bucks New University, UK.

Sherif El-Tawil is Professor in the Department of Civil and Environmental Engineering, University of Michigan, Ann Arbor, USA. His general research interest lies in computational modelling of extreme events. He is especially interested in how buildings and their occupants behave when subjected to manmade and natural hazards such as seismic excitation, collision by heavy objects, and blast.

Vladimir Fedorov is a graduate student at Stanford University, California, USA. He was formerly an Undergraduate Research Assistant in the Department of Civil & Environmental Engineering, University of Michigan, Ann Arbor.

Cristina Flesher Fominaya has an MA and PhD in Sociology from the University of California, Berkeley, USA, and a BA summa cum laude in International Relations from the University of Minnesota. She has won numerous international merit awards, including the National Science Foundation Fellowship, and the German Marshall Fellowship. She was Assistant Professor in the Department of Sociology and Political Science in the Universidad Carlos III de Madrid before joining the Department of Sociology at the University of Aberdeen in 2009. She has been researching and participating in European social movements since the early 1990s. Her work has been published in Contemporary Social Science, Sociological Inquiry, Sociology Compass, International Review of Social History, South European Society and Politics, and other journals and several edited collections. She is a founder and editor of Interface Journal and is founding co-chair of the *Council for European Studies Research Network on European Social Movements.*

Kim Gill is a graduate student in the Department of Sociology and Criminal Justice, and Research Assistant, Disaster Research Center, University of Delaware, Newark, USA.

Dirk Hartmann received a PhD in mathematics in 2007. He works as a research scientist with Siemens. His interests include modelling and simulation of complex processes in industry and natural sciences. He was awarded a fellowship of the Heidelberg Junior Academy for Young Scholars and Scientists.

James Hoggett is a Senior Lecturer in Criminology at the University of the West of England in Bristol, UK.

Wolfram Klein holds a PhD in mathematics and is a research scientist with Siemens.

Gerta Köster is a Professor of Scientific Computing at Munich's University of Applied Sciences, in Germany. She studied mathematics in Munich and at the Ohio State University, USA. After receiving her PhD from the University of Munich she gathered 13 years of industrial experience as a research scientist, project and innovation manager.

Mark Lynch graduated with a Master's degree in International Security Studies from St Andrew's University, UK in 2010. He worked as a member of the National Security and Resilience Division at the Royal United Services Institute focusing on emergency response and counter-terrorism. He is currently co-Chair of the Association for the Study of Ethnicity and Nationalism's annual conference at the London School of Economics and works as a risk analyst at Aon Benfield.

Fergus Neville completed his PhD on the experience of crowd participation in the School of Psychology, St Andrews University, UK. He is currently working as a postdoctoral research fellow in the School of Medicine at St Andrews, on a project evaluating public health interventions to collective violence.

Stephen Reicher is Professor of Social Psychology at St Andrews University, UK. He has carried out research on crowd action, the construction of social categories through language and action, and political rhetoric and mass mobilisation. He is author (with Alex Haslam and Michael Platow) of *The New Psychology of Leadership: Identity, Influence and Power* (Psychology Press, 2010).

Michael Seitz graduated in computer science from Munich's University of Applied Sciences, in Germany, where he is currently employed as a research scientist.

Russell Spears is Professor of Social Psychology at the University of Groningen, the Netherlands. His research interests are in social identity and intergroup relations, including work on group-based emotions. He has published numerous papers and co-authored/co-edited *The Social Psychology of Stereotyping and Group Life* (Blackwell, 1997), *Social Identity: Context, Commitment, Content* (Blackwell, 1999), and *Stereotypes as Explanations* (Cambridge University Press, 2002).

Dr Clifford Stott is one of the most influential academic social psychologists of collective action working in Europe. His expertise focuses on the impact of intergroup dynamics upon crowd behaviour and the implications of crowd psychology for crowd management. He has published extensively in world-class academic journals and co-authored two books, the most recent on the 2011 Riots in the UK. He is currently Visiting Professor at Leeds University, UK, and at Denmark's Aarhus University, was a Visiting Fellow at Australian National University and has held posts in some of the UK's leading universities. He is Company Director of Crowd and Conflict Management Ltd, a leading edge consultancy established in 2012.

Franz Treml studied mathematics, physics and economics. He worked as a simulation expert in the area of mobile communications with Siemens. Currently he is a research scientist with Munich's University of Applied Sciences, in Germany.

David Waddington is Professor of Communications and Head of the Communication and Computing Research Centre at Sheffield Hallam University, UK, where he has been researching the policing of public order for almost 30 years. He is author of *Contemporary Issues in Public Disorder: A Comparative and Historical Approach* (Routledge, 1992) and *Policing Public Disorder: Theory and Practice* (Willan, 2007), co-author, with Karen Jones and Chas Critcher, of *Flashpoints: Studies in Public Disorder* (Routledge, 1989), and co-editor, with Fabien Jobard and Mike King, of *Rioting in the UK and France: A Comparative Analysis* (Willan, 2009).

Montine Walters is currently completing her Master's in Intelligence and International Security at King's College London, UK. She previously interned at the Royal United Services Institute within the National Security and Resilience Department. Prior to this she worked within the United Nations Office for Disarmament Affairs in New York; and has previously trained and served with the National Israeli Ambulance Service, Magen David Adom.

Martijn van Zomeren is an Associate Professor of Social Psychology at the University of Groningen, the Netherlands. He received his PhD in Social Psychology from the University of Amsterdam in 2006. His research interests revolve around the psychology of collective action, with a broad emphasis on identity, morality, emotion and efficacy processes. His work has published in major psychological journals (e.g. Psychological Bulletin, Personality and Social Psychology Review). His doctoral dissertation received the APA Division 49 2007 Dissertation Award; and he received the 2011 Jos Jaspars Early Career Award of the European Association for Social Psychology.

Foreword

Understanding people en mass has always been challenging. Should they be regarded as just the total of many individual egos, or does a crowd amount to more than the sum of its parts? Perhaps, as has often been claimed, a large number of people together in one place should be considered as less than its sum; people losing their identity and aspects of their humanity in the anonymity of the mass. These possibilities and questions connect with many different social sciences, social psychological aspects of individual and group processes, sociological concerns, communication and media studies, political implications, modelling crowd behaviour, questions of management and control, to list just the most obvious. None of these perspectives can be treated effectively in complete isolation from the others, making the study of crowds a truly multi-disciplinary endeavour.

Yet despite, or perhaps because of, the variety of different social sciences that can contribute to understanding crowds they are still a poorly studied and little understood social phenomena. Many public discussions of crowds and associated attitudes towards managing them still draw on ideas first put forward in the nineteenth century, greatly influenced by Darwinian ideas of the animal origins of human behaviour. This saw people in crowds as degenerating back to some atavistic past. It is doubtful if they were valid then, but the variety of crowds that have since been identified and the many different ways they have been observed to act certainly questions whether these ideas have any validity today.

This volume is therefore a rare compilation of original studies and examinations of crowd behaviour drawn from across the social sciences. It provides a unique range of perspectives on many different masses of people in a variety of different situations. These contributions show that crowds can be a positive force in some circumstances and that a much richer understanding of human behaviour in very large groups has significant implications for how to manage them.

With some prescience the plan for this book was set in motion before the power of protesting crowds swept across the Arab world and the August 2011 riots took place in London and some other major cities in the UK. So, like all good social science, its relevance has increased over time. The practical significance as well as the demands on theoretical development of crowdology (if I may be allowed the neologism before someone in the US comes up with it) as revealed in this volume, point to it as a viable and exciting area of research. Anyone already involved in these studies or interested in taking part in this arena will find the chapters here an invaluable starting point.

The multidisciplinary nature of the study of crowds, as well as its relevance to policy and practice, make it an obvious topic for a special issue of *Contemporary Social*

Science, the journal of the Academy of Social Science, in which it had its first incarnation. The acclaim with which that special issue was welcomed was part of the reason why it was agreed to develop it as a book. It thus provides an excellent first volume to the new book series on *Contemporary Issues in Social Science.*

Professor David Canter
Editor, *Contemporary Social Science*

Contextualising the crowd in contemporary social science

John Drury and Clifford Stott

This paper situates contemporary social scientific studies of crowd events and crowd behaviour in their historical and ideological context. The original 'crowd science' developed from definitions of 'social problems' that emerged in the late nineteenth century – in particular the concerns among the French establishment about the threat of the 'mass' to 'civilization'. This, and the surrounding intellectual context, encouraged the development of theoretical models of the crowd characterized by forms of reductionism and irrationalism. Early accounts of 'mass panic' similarly suggested that collective behaviour was irrational because it was governed by primitive bio-psychological processes. After describing these early approaches to the crowd, the paper outlines how changes in the late twentieth society, whereby those writing about the crowd were no longer necessarily 'outside' crowd events, have coincided with the development of accounts of the crowd which draw upon contemporary social scientific concepts (such as social norms, social identities, and cognition) and which assume that crowds are not alien to meaningful social and political participation, but integral to it.

The papers in this edited volume, from a range of disciplines and analysing a variety of different manifestations of 'the crowd', need to be seen in their wider context. That context comprises a series of arguments, going back more than a century, about social problems and about the theoretical tools needed to conceptualise, explain and 'solve' those social problems. The first wave of 'crowd science' was partial and grounded in the concepts and assumptions of the natural sciences. As society changed over the course of the 20th century, however, so there was greater demand among scholars for understanding and social justice rather than system justification and social control. This allowed for the development of properly social scientific accounts of crowd events and crowd behaviour, employing modern theoretical concepts such as social relations, social norms, cognition and identity, and demonstrating the meaningful relationships between crowds and broader forces and structures within society, including class and ethnicity, political and social change, nationalism and globalisation, war/terrorism, im/migration, and economic development.

If there is perhaps one feature shared by all the papers published in this edited volume, it is a commitment to situating and understanding the study of the crowd within the social sciences – whether it is sociology and social movement studies, international relations and security studies, organisational and management science, social psychology, social policy and law, criminology, or disaster studies. Yet this is not necessarily a straightforward achievement, as pressures to reductionist explanation persist, both from the broader society and from within academia itself. The crowd in whatever guise is often an object of controversy in the wider society. Consequently, there is a clear ideological function now, as there was a century ago, in attributing to the crowd some essential primitive quality explained in terms of the conceptual frameworks of the biological sciences rather than the social sciences, which sets the crowd apart from other forms of social life. Rendering the crowd a primitive, biological object, an elemental force, deprives the behaviour of its members of meaning, agency, and legitimacy. In academia, psychology's inferiority complex in relation to its 'hard science' neighbours, and the rise of cognitive science, neuroscience, evolutionary psychology and complexity science, have kept alive the fantasy of a unifying 'life science', whereby the behaviour of human crowds and all other collective phenomena – from bee swarms to social innovations – can be adequately captured by a single set of biologically grounded simple rules.

This editorial introduction contextualises the contributions to this edited volume by outlining how, in the main topic areas where the crowd has been studied – crowd 'violence'/ conflict and mass emergencies/spatial behaviour – concerns about historically specific 'social problems' within the wider society shaped the way that the crowd has been researched and theorised.

Contextualising the study of 'crowd violence'

'Crowd science' first arose in late 19th-century Europe, particularly France, as a response to urbanisation and unrest (Nye, 1975). It can be understood as part of a wider movement expressing in the realm of ideas the ruling establishment's deep-seated fear of the 'masses' (McClelland, 1989; Carey, 1992). The architecture of Paris is a monument to this fear. In the years following the revolution of 1848, the French ruling establishment sought to prevent further uprisings by commissioning Baron Haussmann to re-design the streets of the capital. He pulled down the traditional centres of revolution along with their narrow, easily barricaded streets and replaced them with long, straight, open boulevards that afforded good fields of fire for the army, along with the swift movement of troops across the city (van Ginneken, 1992). Following the collapse of the French army in the Franco-Prussian War it was the Paris commune of 1871 that represented the realisation of the European elites' worst fears; for the communards were armed, socialist in ideas, proletarian in composition and ruthless against their enemies. For three months they declared independence from the French government, which had relocated to Versailles. The commune only ended when the exiled government – re-armed by Britain and Germany – sent in troops. Over 20,000 communards died, many of whom were not involved in the fighting (Stott & Drury, in press). The new 'crowd science' emerged as an attempt to combat these 'horrors', both ideologically and practically (Barrows, 1981).

The 'crowd scientists' drew upon intellectual ideas current at the time, especially Darwinian zoology, medical science, 'race' anthropology and theories of hypnotism. Thus, Hippolyte Taine's (1876) psycho-history of the revolutions traced the supposed decay and degeneration of civilisation, as represented in the commune, to the spread of primitive emotions through 'contagion'. The Italian Scipio Sighele (1891) (cited in van Ginneken, 1992) argued that crowds were largely comprised of people who were criminal by 'nature'; hence, these individuals could be held personally responsible for their illegal actions when part of crowds. Gabriel Tarde (1901) (cited in van Ginneken,

1992), a provincial magistrate, suggested that by mere proximity people become a crowd, and hence subject to uncritical imitation and hence irrational behaviour.

One of the earliest debates in crowd theory concerned whether there was a qualitative or only a quantitative difference between individual and crowd. One school of thought argued that crowds transformed individuals (McPhail, 1991). Thus, Le Bon (1895/1968): 'Isolated, he may be a cultivated individual; in a crowd, he is a barbarian – that is, a creature acting by instinct' (p. 32). According to this approach, the individual personality was lost or 'submerged' in the crowd, to be replaced by a 'racial unconscious'. The crowd was 'like a wild beast' (McDougall, 1920, p. 64) because its behaviour was governed by a qualitatively different psychology than that of the individual.

The behaviourist Zeitgeist sweeping psychology in the 1920s involved a scepticism towards such nebulous entities as this supposed 'group mind'. Instead, the 'crowd' was said to be a nominal fiction and its behaviour explicable simply in terms of the psychology of the individuals making up that crowd. Allport (1924a) thus argued that 'the individual in the crowd behaves just as he would alone, only more so' (p. 295). He explained the violence of crowds in terms of a combination of individual predispositions (both innate and learned) and the simple stimulation of other co-present individuals, which caused basic drives to overcome the civilised values that normally controlled behaviour. He pointed out that, since minds require nervous systems, and since nervous systems exist only in individuals, then the only minds to be found in a crowd are those of the individuals within the crowd. It was simply conventional usage that served to attribute 'thingness' to crowds and indeed to other collections of individuals, including armies, football teams, revolutions and governments (Allport, 1924b). The proper approach for social science, Allport argued, was an individual level of analysis, since only individuals were real 'things'; all else were mere abstractions.

Both 'group mind' and individualist accounts shared the assumption that what needed to be explained was the tendency of the crowd to violence. However, the examples of violence that they referred to as 'evidence' – such as that of the Paris commune – took place in a social context. The violence of the communards was intimately connected with the nature of their ongoing relationships of struggle for power and freedom with other forces, such as political opponents and troops. But the early 'crowd scientists' looked at 'the crowd' as if it were an isolated specimen on a Petri dish. By neglecting the social context of crowd violence, they were inevitably drawn to the conclusion that it emanated solely from sources within the crowd itself.

What were these sources within the crowd? All agreed that violence was ultimately a function of primitive drives or instincts, whether these were located in the 'racial unconscious' or in individual dispositions. In this crucial sense, the two schools of thought were equally reductionist, for both suggested that crowd behaviour was a function of phylogenetically archaic processes: crowds tended to violence because they were atavistic.

If crowd behaviour was driven by primitive instincts and by the contagion of simple emotions, rather than by cognition, realistic beliefs, social values or conscious intentions, then it was not rational. In fact, because it was a creature of instinct and emotion rather than thought and reason, the crowd was also stupid. That stupidity led to self-defeating behaviour that needed to be suppressed, defeated or controlled if 'civilised' society were to survive.

What this attribution of irrationality and stupidity means for the place of the crowd in the wider society is made explicit in the work of Le Bon (1895/1968). In his account, the crowd could not be a meaningful political actor. The sense of power or agency that people experience when part of crowds was 'illusory'; despite the socialist slogans of crowd members, the only change they could bring about on their own (i.e. without strong leadership to direct them) was mindless destruction. The effects of crowds on society were like those of ripples on a stream; they were only transitory, and were neither meaningful nor enduring. However, while Le Bon despised and hated the crowd, he also understood that it was a political fact of life. From Le Bon onward this was now 'the age of the crowd' and the search for the 'great dictator' needed to control it had begun (McClelland, 1989; van Ginneken, 1992).

Re-contextualising 'crowd violence' as intergroup conflict

It was not until the 1950s and, especially, the 1960s that many of the ideas of 'crowd science' were challenged. Arguably, it was again the prominence of the 'violent crowd' that prompted the need for alternative, non-reductionist theoretical concepts.

First, there were the 'long hot summers' of US urban riots in 1964–1968. The first of the riots took place in Harlem, New York. A year later, the most iconic of the uprisings occurred, in Watts, Los Angeles. At the time, Watts was one of the few Los Angeles neighbourhoods where African-Americans could live. It was also a socially deprived district, with high unemployment, and a housing policy that discriminated against blacks. The police force was mostly white, and there was already a history of tension between them and the black population. In this context of grievance over social injustice, the routine arrest of one black motorist came to stand for the whole relationship between Watts residents and the establishment represented by the police. Fighting over the arrest escalated into six days of rioting. According to the official investigation, at its height up to 10,000 people took part. By the time the riots ended, 34 people had died, more than 1000 were injured and more than 600 buildings and over US$34 million-worth of property were damaged or destroyed by fire and looting (see McCone, 1965/1969).

Riots followed in many other places, including Chicago, Illinois, in 1966, and, in 1967, Newark, New Jersey, and Detroit, Michigan. Most of these events followed incidents between white police and blacks, as in Watts. All of them occurred in ghettos, and in all of them shops (many owned by whites) were looted and burned (Feagin & Hahn, 1973).

Some social scientists, who felt alarmed by what they saw as a threat to 'civilisation', harked back to the imagery, assumptions and concepts of the early 'crowd scientists'. For example, Zimbardo (1970) explicitly followed Le Bon (1895/1968) in proposing that anonymity and hence 'loss of self' was the key to this 'uncontrolled' crowd behaviour. However, for many of the social scientists that studied the urban ghetto riots, 'the social problem' was not the crowd, but deep-seated inequality and racism in US society (Allen, 1970; Feagin & Hahn, 1973; Fogelson, 1970).

The new 'civil disorder' research was able to demonstrate exactly what was wrong with the assumptions and concepts of the original wave of reductionist 'crowd science', as well as offering a platform for the development of a properly social scientific approach. Thus, for example, against methodological individualism, McPhail's (1971) statistical examination of ten reports on participation in five of the riots found that individual attributes of rioters (their individual attitudes or supposed 'disorder prone-ness') were not good predictors of participation; 'interactional environments' – the dynamic relationship with other groups – was a better explanation for who got involved. And in a withering critique, Fogelson (1971) showed that explanations in terms of the ('marginal') characteristics of the rioters were not only empirically wrong but also profoundly ideological. His survey found that the rioters were not very differ-ent from others in the ghetto. Moreover, explaining the riots in terms of the characters of the individual rioters rendered them unrepresentative and meaningless outbursts, which then allowed the white establishment to argue that society was largely fine, and that any solutions should therefore be sought in terms of enhanced law enforcement rather than political change.

The other events in the 1960s that affected the form and content of crowd research were the protests against the Vietnam War. These occurred at around the same time as the 'new social movements' were identified, the student movements became active and militant, and hence social change seemed to be in the air. While their classical equiva-lents viewed the crowd only from the outside, quite often remaining in their armchairs or studies and relying on partial secondary accounts, the social scientists of the 1960s sometimes had personal experience of being and feeling part of crowd events, through their participation in the protests and through their close connection to the student movement. It became clear that explanatory concepts inherited from a natural science model, in which the actions of crowds were rendered devoid of meaning, were not adequate to what the social scientists could see with their own eyes. Indeed, the whole 'zoological' approach to crowds, of remaining on the outside looking in at the alien 'other', was rejected, and arguments emerged in favour of approaches which enabled researchers to document crowd participants' subjective experiences, such as ethno-graphy and interviews: 'The surest road to theoretical advance in this field [of crowds and social movements] . . . is participant observation' (Milgram & Toch, 1969, p. 603).

In terms of theoretical model, one reaction against the irrationalism of 'crowd sci-ence' was to posit its diametric opposite. Gaming approaches to collective behaviour (e. g., Brown, 1965; cf. Olsen, 1965) suggested that crowd members, including the most destructive rioters, undertake actions on the basis of a calculus of losses versus gains, just as individuals supposedly do so in everyday life – at least according to economic models of 'rational man'. For example, looters decide whether or not to smash a shop window by taking into account the number of people they perceive to support them in satisfying their 'tastes' in this way versus the number who oppose them. In support of this kind of account, Berk's (1974) participant observation study of a student protest event shows the social and 'cognitive complexity' (p. 355) of participants' actions in a (divided) crowd.

The idea that crowd action was in some sense 'cognitive' (rather than simply 'emo-tional' and 'instinctive'), and that there was a psychological continuity between crowd behaviour and everyday life, represented an important step forward. But counterposing a narrow version of rationality to the irrationality posited by the 'crowd scientists' was in effect a mere re-description of the same crowd behaviour, and hence a dead-end. As Tajfel (1978a) argued, 'the dichotomy in the explanations of mass intergroup phenom-ena is not . . . between the rational and the irrational, but between the irrational and the social–cognitive' (p. 420). Further, Berk's (1974) rationalism was, just like Berko-witz's (1972) irrationalist 'frustration–aggression' account of the occurrence of civil disorder, an individualist explanation. The problem was that the simultaneous activation of hundreds or thousands of individual 'frustrations' (or 'decisions') was simply implausible as an explanation for the shared and spontaneous nature of collective behaviour (Tajfel, 1978b).

To transcend both irrationalism and reductionism, therefore, what was needed was not just a cognitive theory of crowd behaviour, but an explanation of the sociality of human cognition. One answer that has proved fruitful was to conceptualise crowds in the same way as (other kinds of) groups. The roots of this kind of analysis went back to the ideas of the Gestalt social psychologists of the 1930s, 1940s and 1950s. Thus, Muzafer Sherif (1936/1965) had shown experimentally that people interacting in small groups could produce frames of reference that become internalised, as social norms, but which are not reducible to the individual members of the group. Solomon Asch (1952) used the same kind of argument explicitly to attack reductionism. He demolished the distinction Allport (1924a) drew between 'concrete things' and 'abstract relations', showing it to be just as untenable in the natural sciences that Allport aspired to as it was in social psychology. Graphite and diamond, for example, were each composed of different patterns of relationships between the same kinds of elements (carbon atoms); and groups (relations between individuals) were phenomenologically real because they were represented as a socially structured field in the mind of each of the group members.

Interactionism was the basis of two separate approaches to the theoretical understanding of the crowd. The first of these, emergent norm theory (Turner & Killian, 1957, 1974), sought to go beyond an emphasis on crowd violence by an equal interest in explaining behaviour in 'mundane' gatherings and collective responses to emergencies and disasters. The approach was arguably hampered by inheriting a number of concepts from Blumer (1939), such as apparently uncritical social influence through 'milling' and 'keynoting' (McPhail, 1991). Yet the introduction into the study of crowd behaviour of the concept of meaning-seeking and hence social norms – shared definitions of appropriate conduct – was a crucial advance.

The second approach to the crowd that has its roots in interactionism is the social identity framework. This body of theory grew from a profound dissatisfaction with individualistic and reductionist accounts in psychology and a need to explain and engage with the most serious and pressing features of the modern era: collective atrocity, collective resistance, social structure, and social change. The first part of this project focused on intergroup relations and provided a conceptual model specifying the social psychological conditions for collective action towards social change (Tajfel & Turner, 1979). The second part of the project focused on the social psychological conditions that enable any form of collectivity: specifically, it was argued that 'social identity is the cognitive mechanism which makes group behaviour possible' (Turner, 1982, p. 21).

The social identity framework was developed explicitly into a wholly new account of crowd action by Reicher (1982, 1984, 1987), and later elaborated into a model of the emergence and escalation of crowd conflict (Drury & Reicher, 2000; Reicher, 1996a, 1996b, 2001; Stott & Drury, 2000; Stott & Reicher, 1998). In this edited volume, chapter 11 (Reicher) describes the social identity approach to the crowd in more detail, and illustrates how it can now be applied to explain a wide range of crowd phenomena, including the St Pauls urban riot of 1980, 'non-violent' direct actions against road-building, crowd cooperation in mass emergencies, and proximity seeking (or avoiding) behaviours in crowd situations. The analysis he presents makes the case for putting the crowd at the centre of the social sciences, because research on crowd actions and experiences can tell us about the social understandings of marginalised groups, about how those groups form and become empowered, and about the subjective as well as objective aspects of social change.

The arguments of social identity theorists and others, that crowd conflict needs to be analysed in terms of its intergroup, historical and political contexts, and the necessity of conceptualising crowd action in terms of 'thinking' subjects guided by social norms and identities, are taken up by three of the other contributors to this special issue.

A number of theoretical models from different disciplinary backgrounds and different starting points for enquiry have converged on the view that in order to understand crowd conflict we need to analyse the way that crowds are policed (della Porta & Reiter, 1998; Stott et al., 2007; Waddington, 1992). Waddington et al. (1989) argue that the broader structural, ideological, cultural, and historical contexts within which crowds and those policing them come to act and interpret each others' actions need to be included in such an analysis. Chapter 3 (Waddington) therefore presents a historical and comparative analysis to show that critical reactions to controversial policing tactics used at such events as the G20 protest in 2009 created pressures towards more 'permissive' policing of protests which, it is argued, are less likely to escalate conflict and undermine police legitimacy in the eyes of the public. Chapter 4 (Hoggett & Stott) complements and extends this analysis by showing how 'public order' policing has changed in relation to both public opinion and research evidence. The chapter explains the context, and barriers to full implementation, of these recent reforms to policing, and argues for an 'evidence-based approach' that requires the police to be more active in the research process.

Many contemporary social scientific approaches to crowd events reject the charge of the 'crowd scientists' that crowd empowerment is illusory and that crowds have nothing to do with politics. They also reject the division of labour between crowd events and social movements embodied in the dualism of 'collective behaviour'/ strain versus 'rational'/organised resource mobilisation. As such, these current social scientific accounts are in line with concepts and arguments developed in cultural historiography, most notably the arguments of Thompson (1971) that food riots were a meaningful form of political intervention, embodying agency and purpose, and hence enabling participants to become collective actors. Chapter 2 (Flesher Fominaya) presents a detailed ethnographic analysis of a flash mob protest following the Madrid bombings of 2004, and on the eve of the Spanish general election, to 'highlight the importance of the crowd as a political actor with agency and impact'. At the time of the events, critics tried to deny the crowd agency by suggesting that the flash mob mobilisation either had no connection to wider social movements or was simply an expression of the opposition political party's machinations. The analysis shows that in both the form of organisation and in its symbolic content – slogans, banners, chants – the mobilisation was an articulate and powerful intervention, which has also served as a model for future autonomous extra-parliamentary popular action.

Chapter 5 (van Zomeren and Spears) begins from the assumption that crowd events can be conceptualised as forms of a collective action, and follows social identity theory (Tajfel & Turner, 1979) in suggesting that collective action can overturn or challenge relations of disadvantage. Methodologically, this paper represents an important strand in both crowd research and in the social identity tradition, for it describes an experimental study. Specifically, the study tests and supports the idea that, where people share a social identity, physical co-presence may operate as a subjective source of support more for those relatively low compared to those relatively high in identification. This study suggests why, in an age where online networking makes collective action possible without physical coordination, those wishing to mobilise may still want to organise crowd events if they wish to build a movement that empowers all its members.

The concerns and debates that structured the development of research on and theories of crowd conflict are echoed in the story of the development of research on mass emergencies. As that story is less dramatic, and as its main conceptual elements have already been described, this story will be outlined only briefly.

Contextualising the study of mass emergencies and disasters

The study of crowd behaviour in emergencies and disasters began with the assumption that what needed to be explained was 'panic'. This tradition of research emerged during the First World War as a response to the perceived problem of troop in discipline during bombing raids. Many of the original studies that examined the nature and prophylaxis of 'mass panic' were published in military journals (Strauss, 1944), and the military was also a sponsor of research on civilian response to disasters and air raids (e.g., Fritz & Marks, 1954). This early military research influenced the conceptions of mass emergency behaviour held by Freud (1921) and the models of La Piere (1938; cited in Quarantelli, 2001), Schultz (1964), and Smelser (1962). For example, La Piere suggested that mass panic is caused by both the occurrence of a crisis and a lack of 'regimentation' or leadership.

Despite a number of differences of emphasis (Quarantelli, 2001), the various models of 'mass panic' have in common the same kind of assumptions of mass irrationality that characterise the early accounts of 'crowd violence'. First, there was the notion that, in an emergency, there is a false or exaggerated fear of the threat. Second, there was the claim that this exaggerated fear spreads across the crowd through emotional contagion (e.g., McDougall, 1920; Ross, 1908). Third, it was assumed that, in order to save themselves, individuals in the crowd flee in an overhasty and hence uncoordinated manner. This results in self-defeating outcomes, such as blocked exits, which mean that more people die in the act of egress than were endangered from whatever it was they were fleeing. The models are also equally reductionist in the same way as the 'classic' accounts of 'crowd violence'. Mass panic behaviour is explained in terms of primitive emotions and 'instincts' for self-preservation (Sime, 1990); it is the opposite of cognitively controlled, civilised, and socialised conduct.

Some of the earliest review evidence, from both wartime emergencies and natural disasters, undermined this picture of automatic mass irrationality, by showing that behaviour in such events was more typically reasonable and meaningful, and even calm and cooperative (Fritz & Williams, 1957; Quarantelli, 1960). An early critique in psychology was based on analogue experimental evidence that exit blocking was a function of unintended consequences of behaviours understood as reasonable from the individual's own perspective (Mintz, 1951). This analysis problematised the concept of 'panic', by making it appear redundant (Sime, 1990). However, most of the conceptual advances in this area came from sociologists not psychologists. Turner & Killian (1957) were the first to suggest that mass emergency behaviour could be understood as normative, but it was not until the 1980s that broadly normative approaches came to dominate the field of mass emergency and disaster studies (Aguirre, 2005). While there are now a variety of different norm-based approaches, all agree that mass emergency behaviour is both social (rather than antisocial or asocial) and cognitive (i.e., based on reasonable beliefs rather than non-cognitive emotions or instincts) (e.g., Canter, 1990; Drury et al., 2009; Johnson, 1987, 1988). Norm-based approaches also have implications for method. If the object of research is no longer an irrational 'other', but rather a sense-making, self-accounting, conscious actor, then research on mass emergencies should not be restricted to behavioural descriptions derived from archives or simulations but should also include analyses of survivors' accounts (e.g., Donald & Canter, 1990).

This kind of account of crowd behaviour in mass emergencies has three further implications that are discussed by contributors to this edited volume.

The first implication is to do with blame. 'Mass panic' functions as a blame-deflecting device (Chertkoff & Kushigian, 1999; Sime, 1990); a tragedy can thus be explained in terms of the 'natural' tendency of crowds to panic rather than the negligent actions of those professionally responsible for venue safety or event management. But if 'mass panic' is simply a disaster myth (Jacob, Mawson, Payton, & Guignard, 2008), then the social aspects of crowd safety and crowd management become foregrounded as objects of investigation in their own right. Chapter 6 (Challenger and Clegg) presents a socio-technical analysis of three crowd disasters: the Hillsborough football stadium (1989), the King's Cross underground fire (1987), and the Bradford City stadium fire (1985). The analysis suggests that, in each case, a combination of different factors at different levels – including organisational goals and cultures, technology and leadership – together explain how the tragedy came to occur. The kind of analysis presented by Challenger and Clegg moves attribution for disasters away from the supposedly inherent problems of the crowd to deficiencies in management and planning. This must be a positive development, for it suggests that crowd disasters are preventable through improvements to planning, rather than something that 'just happens' from time to time due to the psychology of the crowd.

A second implication of contemporary social scientific accounts of mass emergency behaviour is that crowds can be conceptualised as sources of resilience. This thesis is explored in a security context in Chapter 7 (Cole, Walters & Lynch). The chapter begins from two premises, based on evidence from emergencies such as the London or '7/7' bombings. From the study of the professional response side, it is observed that emergency medical services might be unable to attend to a mass emergency in time or in sufficient numbers to intervene effectively. The second premise is the wealth of evidence that, far from panicking, crowds in emergencies are frequently able to respond intelligently and in a coordinated and effective manner to their collective predicament – acting as first responders, in fact. Putting these two points together, Cole et al. argue that the resilience of crowds, and hence of the public as a whole, needs more official recognition and resourcing.

A third implication of current models has to do with design and engineering. Computer modelling of crowd flow is a hugely important global industry, which contributes to decisions in the design of public space and in emergency planning. There is a long-standing discussion over the extent to which there is adequate communication between social scientific theory and modelling (Sime, 1995). This discussion is still at a very preliminary stage, it would seem.

Take spatial behaviour in crowds. Research on crowding began from the assumption that proximity to others in a crowd was inherently aversive and even a source of social pathology (Novelli, 2010). This picture was complicated by the findings that 'personal space' varies by culture, gender and other demographic factors; and the fact that people often seek out conditions of density (Freedman, 1975). Recent research demonstrates that variability in crowding behaviours and experiences, both between and within people, is a function of shared social identity, which itself varies according to social context (Novelli et al., 2010; see also Reicher, in this volume). An implication of this argument is that a crowd could in principle be made up of a single psychological group (in which case mutual proximity is desired among members), multiple groups (in which case there is both avoidance and attraction) or no groups (proximity is avoided where possible). How can we begin to capture this conceptually and hence in applied settings? Chapter 8 (from Neville & Reicher) draws a crucial distinction between, on the one hand, having a particular group identity and, on the other, being aware that others in the crowd share this same group identity. As they show in interview and survey questionnaire analysis gathered at football matches, a protest march and a music festival, this distinction has important implications for both experience and behaviour. We enjoy and embrace others in the crowd literally as well a figuratively much more when we share an identity with them.

This volume also includes two chapters that seek to apply ideas about 'groupness' in crowd setting to computer modelling. Chapter 9 (by Köster, Seitz, Treml, Hartmann & Klein) presents a model of crowd egress that draws on the social scientific research literature on small group spatial behaviour within crowds. They show empirically that modelling at the level of individuals and subgroups, rather than treating the whole crowd as an aggregate of particles, has implications for the speed and efficiency of egress behaviour. This may in turn have implications for emergency evacuations; specifically, people who see themselves as a group will try to move as a unit in relation to those around them. The authors highlight the extent to which models often employ the designer's intuitions, rather than evidence from social scientific research, and therefore call for greater cooperation between social scientists and modellers.

Chapter 10 (Aguirre, El-Tawil, Best, Gill & Federov) complements Köster et al.'s analysis by pursuing the theme of the gap between existing modelling approaches and current knowledge in social science in more detail. The paper begins with a critical review of current agent-based models of building evacuation. As Aguirre et al. point out, while the consensus in social science is that mass emergency egress from fires is explicable in terms of social norms, values, leadership, group identification and so on, there is a tendency among modellers to revert to the discredited concept of panic. The observation is an extremely important one, for it demonstrates that explanations that reduce crowd phenomena to primitive and irrational forces are still alive and indeed highly influential in some circles that are apparently cut off from the impact of contemporary social scientific research and theory. Aguirre et al. substantiate their argument for a social-level explanation by presenting evidence in the form of different versions of a computer simulation of the infamous 'Station nightclub fire'; this demonstrates that a group behaviour model fits the pattern of evidence better than an individualistic model of the type implicit in many existing simulations.

Conclusion

This brief historical sketch of the development of social scientific studies of the crowd has illustrated two things. First, the wider social context – the nature and definition of 'social problems' – has on occasion served to push the crowd to the forefront of research and theorising. Second, the power structure in society and the social position of theorists has shaped the types of concepts and categories employed, with reductionist and irrationalist accounts particularly prominent in those times and places when 'the crowd' is seen as a threat to the existing order.

After the 1920s, the crowd disappeared from most social science textbooks (Reicher & Potter, 1985). Up till then, it was at the heart of debates around the 'master problem' – that of the individual-group relation (Allport, 1962). However, the incorrigible return of 'the crowd' to contemporary social life – whether in the form of the student protests of autumn 2010, the recent 'Arab spring', the massive protest demonstration over public sector cuts, and the wave of urban riots in London, Manchester and other cities in August 2011 – suggests very strongly that it is premature to regard theoretical discussion of this topic as completed or the topic itself as ephemeral. The appearance of this edited volume containing so many and varied social scientific analyses of the crowd, and the interest we received from contributors wishing to be involved, is also testament to the abiding importance of the crowd to the understanding of and participation in contemporary society.

Thanks to the following reviewers: Colin Barker, Robin Woolven, Richard Amlôt, Hugo Gorringe, Tom Postmes, Andrew Livingstone, Alex Haslam, Mehdi Moussaid, Paul Langston, Michael Rosie, Mike King, Alex Hirschfield, Anthony Mawson, Michael Schmitt, Nick Hopkins, David Novelli, Simon Teun, Britta Osthaus, Pat Tissington, Keith Still, Dominic Elliot and Lynn Hulse.

References

Aguirre, B. E. (2005) Commentary on 'Understanding mass panic and other collective responses to threat and disaster': emergency evacuations, panic, and social psychology, Psychiatry, 68, 121–129.

Allen, V. L. (1970) Towards understanding riots: some perspectives, Journal of Social Issues, 26, 1–18.

Allport, F. H. (1924a) Social psychology (Boston, MA, Houghton Mifflin Co.).

Allport, F. H. (1924b) The group fallacy in relation to social science, Journal of Abnormal and Social Psychology, 19, 60–73.

Allport, F. H. (1962) A structuronomic conception of behaviour: individual and collective, Journal of Abnormal and Social Psychology, 64, 3–30.

Asch, S. E. (1952) Social psychology (Englewood Cliffs, NJ, Prentice-Hall).

Barrows, S. (1981) Distorting mirrors: visions of the crowd in late nineteenth-century France (New Haven, CT, Yale University Press).

Berk, R. (1974) A gaming approach to crowd behaviour, American Sociological Review, 39, 355–373.

Berkowitz, L. (1972) Frustrations, comparisons and other sources of emotional arousal as contributors to social unrest, Journal of Social Issues, 28, 77–91.

Blumer, H. (1939) Collective behaviour, in: R. E. Park (Ed.) Principles of sociology, (New York, NY, Barnes & Noble), pp. 219–288.

Brown, R. (1965) Social psychology (New York, NY, Free Press).

Canter, D. (1990) Studying the experience of fires, in: D. Canter (Ed.) Fires and human behaviour (London, David Fulton), pp. 1–14.

Carey, J. (1992) The intellectuals and the masses (London, Faber & Faber).

Chertkoff, J. M. & Kushigian, R. H. (1999) Don't panic: the psychology of emergency egress and ingress (Westport, CT, Praeger).

della Porta, D. & Reiter, H. (Eds) (1998) Policing protest: the control of mass demonstrations in Western democracies (Minneapolis, MN, University of Minnesota Press).

Donald, I. & Canter, D. (1990) Behavioral aspects of the King's Cross underground fire, in: D. Canter (Ed.) Fires and human behaviour (2nd edn) (London: David Fulton).

Drury, J., Cocking, C. & Reicher, S. (2009) Everyone for themselves? A comparative study of crowd solidarity among emergency survivors, British Journal of Social Psychology, 48, 487–506.

Drury, J. & Reicher, S. (2000) Collective action and psychological change: the emergence of new social identities, British Journal of Social Psychology, 39, 579–604.

Feagin, J. R. & Hahn, H. (1973) Ghetto riots: the politics of violence in American cities (New York, NY, Macmillan).

Fogelson, R. M. (1970) Violence and grievances: reflections on the 1960s riots, Journal of Social Issues, 26, 141–163.

Fogelson, R. M. (1971) Violence as protest: a study of riots and ghettos (New York, NY, Anchor).

Freedman, J. L. (1975) Crowding and behaviour (San Francisco, CA, W. H. Freeman).

Freud, S. (1921) Group psychology and the analysis of the ego, In: Civilization, society and religion (Harmondsworth, Penguin), pp. 91–178.

Fritz, C. E. & Marks, E. S. (1954) The NORC studies of human behavior in disaster, Journal of Social Issues, 10, 26–41.

Fritz, C. E. & Williams, H. B. (1957) The human being in disasters: a research perspective, Annals of the American Academy of Political and Social Science, 309, 42–51.

Jacob, B., Mawson, M. A., Payton, M. D. & Guignard, J. C. (2008) Disaster mythology and fact: Hurricane Katrina and social attachment, Public Health Reports, 123, 555–566.

Johnson, N. R. (1987) Panic at 'The Who Concert Stampede': an empirical assessment, Social Problems, 34, 362–373.

Johnson, N. R. (1988) Fire in a crowded theatre: a descriptive investigation of the emergence of panic, International Journal of Mass Emergencies and Disasters, 6, 7–26.

Le Bon, G. (1968) The crowd: a study of the popular mind (Original work published 1895) (Dunwoody, GA, Norman S. Berg).

McClelland, J. S. (1989) The crowd and the mob: from Plato to Canetti (London, Unwin Hyman).

McCone, J. A. (1969) Violence in the city: an end or a beginning? A report by the Governor's Commission on the Los Angeles Riots, in: R. M. Fogelson (Ed.) The Los Angeles riots (New York, NY: Arno) (Original work published 1965). Accessed online at: http://www.usc.edu/libraries/archives/cityinstress/mccone/.

McDougall, W. (1920) The group mind (New York, NY, G. P. Putnam's Sons).

McPhail, C. (1971) Civil disorder participation, American Sociological Review, 38, 1058–1073.

McPhail, C. (1991) The myth of the madding crowd (New York, NY, Aldine de Gruyter).

Milgram, S. & Toch, H. (1969) Collective behavior: crowds and social movements, in: G. Lindzey & E. Aronson (Eds) The handbook of social psychology. Volume 4 (2nd edn) (Reading, MA, Addison Wesley).

Mintz, A. (1951) Non-adaptive group behavior, Journal of Abnormal and Social Psychology, 46, 150–159.

Novelli, D. (2010) The social psychology of spatiality and crowding. Unpublished DPhil thesis. University of Sussex, Falmer, Brighton. Available online at: http://sro.sussex.ac.uk/6275/1/Novelli%2C_David_Lee.pdf

Novelli, D., Drury, J. & Reicher, S. (2010) Come together: two studies concerning the impact of group relations on 'personal space', British Journal of Social Psychology, 49, 223–236.

Nye, R. A. (1975) The origin of crowd psychology: Gustave Le Bon and the crisis of mass democracy in the third republic (London: Sage).

Olsen, M. (1965) The logic of collective action: public goods and the theory of groups (Cambridge, MA: Harvard University Press).

Quarantelli, E. L. (1960) Images of withdrawal behavior in disasters: some basic misconceptions, Social Problems, 8, 68–79.

Quarantelli, E. L. (2001) Panic, sociology of, in: N. J. Smelser & P. B. Baltes (Eds) International encyclopedia of the social and behavioral sciences (New York, NY, Pergamon), pp. 11020–11023.

Reicher, S. (1982) The determination of collective behaviour, in: H. Tajfel (Ed.) Social identity and intergroup relations (Cambridge, Cambridge University Press).

Reicher, S. (1984) The St Pauls riot: an explanation of the limits of crowd action in terms of a social identity model, European Journal of Social Psychology, 14, 1–21.

Reicher, S. (1987) Crowd behaviour as social action, in: J. C. Turner, M. A. Hogg, P. J. Oakes, S. D. Reicher & M. S. Wetherell (Eds) Rediscovering the social group: a self-categorization theory (Oxford, Blackwell), pp. 171–202.

Reicher, S. (1996a) Social identity and social change: rethinking the context of social psychology, in: W. P. Robinson (Ed.) Social groups and identities: developing the legacy of Henri Tajfel (London: Butterworth), 317–336.

Reicher, S. (1996b) 'The Battle of Westminster': developing the social identity model of crowd behaviour in order to explain the initiation and development of collective conflict, European Journal of Social Psychology, 26, 115–134.

Reicher, S. (2001) The psychology of crowd dynamics, in: M. A. Hogg & R. S. Tindale (Eds) Blackwell handbook of social psychology: group processes (Oxford, Blackwell), pp. 182–208.

Reicher, S. & Potter, J. (1985) Psychological theory as intergroup perspective: a comparative analysis of 'scientific' and 'lay' accounts of crowd events, Human Relations, 38, 167–189.

Ross, E. A. (1908) Social psychology: an outline and source book (New York, NY, Macmillan).

Schultz, D. P. (Ed) (1964) Panic behavior: discussions and readings (New York, NY, Random House).

Sherif, M. (1965). The psychology of social norms (New York, NY: Octagon) (Original work published 1936).

Sime, J. D. (1990) The concept of 'panic', in: D. Canter (Ed.) Fires and human behaviour (2nd edn) (London: David Fulton), pp. 63–81.

Sime, J. D. (1995) Crowd psychology and engineering, Safety Science, 21, 1–14.

Smelser, N. J. (1962) Theory of collective behaviour (London, Routledge & Kegan Paul).

Stott, C., Adang, O., Livingstone, A. & Schreiber, M. (2007) Variability in the collective behaviour of England fans at Euro 2004: 'hooliganism', public order policing and social change, European Journal of Social Psychology, 37, 75–100.

Stott, C. & Drury, J. (2000) Crowds, context and identity: dynamic categorization processes in the 'poll tax riot', Human Relations, 53, 247–273.

Stott, C. & Drury, J. (In press) A picture of the pathology of the mass: exploring the politics and ideology of 'classic' crowd psychology, in: A. A. Romero (Ed.) Archaeology for the masses: theoretical and methodological approaches to a neglected identity category (Oxford, British Archaeological Reports).

Stott, C. & Reicher, S. (1998) Crowd action as inter-group process: introducing the police perspective, European Journal of Social Psychology, 28, 509–529.

Strauss, A. L. (1944) The literature on panic, Journal of Abnormal and Social Psychology, 39, 317–328.

Taine, H. (1876) The French Revolution: the origins of contemporary France (vol. 1) (J. Durand, Trans.) (London: Daldy, Ibister & Co.).

Tajfel, H. (1978a) Differentiation between social groups: studies in the social psychology of intergroup relations (London: AP).

Tajfel, H. (1978b) Intergroup behaviour: individualistic perspectives, in: H. Tajfel & C. Fraser (Eds) Introducing social psychology (Harmondsworth: Penguin).

Tajfel, H. & Turner, J. (1979) An integrative theory of intergroup conflict, in: W. G. Austin & S. Worchel (Eds) The social psychology of intergroup relations (Monterey, CA: Brooks/Cole), pp. 33–48.

Thompson, E. P. (1971) The moral economy of the English crowd in the eighteenth century, Past and Present, 50, 76–136.

Turner, J. C. (1982) Towards a cognitive redefinition of the social group, in: H. Tajfel (Ed.) Social identity and intergroup relations (Cambridge: Cambridge University Press), pp. 15–40.

Turner, R. H. & Killian, L. M. (1957) Collective behavior (Englewood Cliffs, NJ, Prentice-Hall).

Turner, R. H. & Killian, L. M. (1972) Collective behavior (2nd edn) (Englewood Cliffs, NJ, Prentice-Hall).

Van Ginneken, J. (1992) Crowds, psychology, and politics 1871–1899 (Cambridge, Cambridge University Press).

Waddington, D. (1992) Contemporary issues in public disorder: a comparative and historical approach (London: Routledge).

Waddington, D., Jones, K. & Critcher, C. (1989) Flashpoints: studies in public disorder (London, Routledge).

Zimbardo, P. G. (1970) The human choice: individuation, reason and order versus de-individuation, impulse and chaos, in:W. J. Arnold &D. Levine (Eds) Nebraska symposium on motivation 1969 (Lincoln, NE, University of Nebraska).

The Madrid bombings and popular protest: misinformation, counter-information, mobilisation and elections after '11-M'

Cristina Flesher Fominaya

Department of Sociology, University of Aberdeen, Aberdeen, UK

This article analyses the '13-M' flash mob protests following the 11-M terrorist bombings in Madrid and immediately preceding the Spanish General Elections of 14 March 2004. The Governing Popular Party's insistence that ETA were the main suspects, despite contradictory evidence, led to a widespread perception that they were deliberately misleading the public for electoral purposes. This sparked the indignation and mobilisation of thousands of citizens on 13 March, in an illegal unprecedented 'flash mob' protest. Contrary to the two main explanations in the literature, I argue that the 13-M protests were neither purely spontaneous manifestations of public opinion, nor the result of Socialist Party machinations. Autonomous social movement activists used cell phones and the internet to mobilise previously established networks for a protest that quickly spread as critiques and demands they were making resonated with an important segment of public opinion. Drawing on ethnographic, primary and secondary data, this analysis provides an inside look at the mobilising structures and motives behind an important protest and adds to our understanding of political flash mobs in the 21st century.

Introduction

One week before the Spanish general elections of 14 March 2004, polls were predicting a win for the ruling Popular Party (PP) (*El País*, 2004a). Since the PP's campaign had revolved primarily around the fight against Basque separatist terrorism (ETA), and the PP presented themselves as the best party to stop terrorist attacks in Spain, when ten bombs exploded on four trains on the morning of 11 March, just three days before the elections, it seemed very likely the PP would win by a much larger majority than expected, regardless of who was responsible for the bombings. Terrorist bombings generally translate into support for incumbent governments (Olmeda, 2005; Moreno, 2005). Yet on 14 March, the PP lost the election, and the PSOE (Spanish Socialist Workers Party) presidential candidate was voted into office with the greatest number of votes ever in Spain's democracy. What actually happened between the bombings of 11-M and the vote on 14-M? Numerous hypotheses have been advanced, but one key factor was the mobilisation of former abstainers to vote (Torcal & Rico, 2004; Michavila, 2005; van Biezen, 2005). Most analysts attribute the PP's loss to some combination of the following factors: anger against the government's insistence that ETA was behind the attacks despite early contradictory evidence, and the resurgence of the PP's unilateral support of the War on Iraq as an electoral issue as the result of the bombings.[1]

On 13 March, the day before the election, activists and members of the public took to the streets in the thousands, first congregating in front of the PP headquarters demanding the truth about the attacks, then spreading throughout the city centre of Madrid. These protests were historically unprecedented in two ways: one, in that any political manifestation is illegal on the 'day of reflection', and there had never been protests on this day; and two, because it was the first case of a political 'flash mob' or smart mob protest in Spain.

'Flash mob' is a term that originally referred to social experiments and countercultural movements to reclaim public spaces (Salmond, 2010) through the use of creative 'happenings' involving music, dance or theatre. Rheingold (2003) coined the term 'smart mob' to denote a flash mob with an intelligent, defined goal. I use the term 'political flash mob' because it retains a key feature of these protests, which is they are organised at very short notice to respond to what is seen as an urgent or crisis situation. Political flash mobs are considered important examples of how information and communication technologies (ICTs) can be used to mobilise protests in repressive political contexts, especially where there is limited freedom of press or access to alternative media such as the Philippines in 2001 or Venezuela in 2002 (Rafael, 2003; Rheingold, 2003). Even in consolidated democracies where access to pluralistic media is considered the norm, use of flash mobs is a way of reacting to surveillance, infiltration and repression. The key frame of the 13-M protest was that the government was not providing citizens with the truth and was engaged in a media blackout; the fact that the protests were clearly illegal; the urgent sense that the government must be made to 'come clean' before the elections the next day; and the use of SMS text messages as the primary means of mobilising make the 13-M protests an important case study of a political flash mob.

Understanding the motives that led thousands of citizens to take to the streets on the day of reflection, in clear violation of the law, should be of key interest to scholars seeking to interpret the unexpected electoral results. Yet a review of analyses of the 14-M elections shows that little attention is paid to the protests. Torcal & Rico (2004) highlight the importance of the strategic vote of IU and other small party supporters who voted for the PSOE to punish the PP, but do not mention the 13-M protests. In reference to 13-M, Chari

(2004, p. 957) writes of 'questions from both opposition parties and citizens, demanding transparency in the investigation' but makes no reference to the protests as an expression of those demands, nor does he link the pressure of the protests to the PP's decision finally to announce 'the arrest ... of four people associated with Al-Qaeda', contradicting their prior insistence on ETA's responsibility. Van Biezen (2005, p. 102) writes that on 13-M 'Spaniards took to the streets again', implying a routine, spontaneous response. Although Blakeley (2006, p. 342) highlights the importance of the 13-M protests, he writes that 'evidence suggests that they were entirely spontaneous and were organised through mobile phones'. Burkitt (2005, p. 693) sees the protests as a 'howl of grief and rage directed at the government, that in the course of three days, brought it down'. This 'spontaneous' thesis dominates the literature, and leaves the impression that the protests sprung 'de novo' from the ether, unmediated by any pre-existing networks or organisational framework. In addition, these accounts downplay the historically unprecedented nature of the protests and downplay their political importance. An important exception is Olmeda (2005), who argues that the protests were carefully planned. He raises the question as to whether or not the Socialist party or IU party was connected with the protest organisation and concludes that this is possible because some activists reported receiving robotic messages whose cost surpassed that affordable to young SMS users. Although Olmeda gives more credit to social movement organisation, particularly through the use of movement websites, he also inclines toward the 'party machinery' thesis. For its part, the PP maintains that the 13-M mobilisations in front of their party headquarters were orchestrated by the PSOE and mobilised public opinion against them, costing them the election (Francescutti *et al.*, 2005). The PSOE deny any such allegation.

The present analysis of the 13-M political flash mob should be of key interest to scholars seeking to understand the relation between the use of new ICTs, flash mob mobilisations and democratisation processes, including the impact of these protests on electoral outcomes (Hermanns, 2008). 13-M was neither a totally 'spontaneous' manifestation of rage and grief nor a result of PSOE machinations. It was initially organised by a nucleus of activists who drew on contacts developed through previous mobilisations, used new ICTs to disseminate the call, and made a conscious decision to engage in civil disobedience on the day of reflection, making the protests historically unprecedented in Spain. The strength and importance of the protests, however, extend far beyond the social movement network that initiated them, and reflect public support for the protest's critique. Exit polls indicate one in five Spaniards had the bombings in mind when they voted (Tremlett, 2006); *what* those who voted against the PP were thinking and feeling is illuminated by understanding the emotions and motivations of those who took to the street. These motives are not as unified and straightforward as they might seem at first glance.

Methods

At the time of the 13-M protest, I had already been integrated in Madrid's social movement networks as an ethnographic researcher for two years. In addition to participant observation of the protest itself, and conversations with activists in a number of university and social movement forums, analysis is drawn from the following social movement listserves and internet sites: *Indymedia Madrid*; *Indymedia Barcelona*; *Nodo50.org Madrid*; *La Haine*; *Lista Madrid*, and *a-infos.org*; three other private activist listserves; and scholarly and activist accounts as cited. I also followed radio (Cope and Cadena SER) and television news, and read the following newspapers (11–14 March 2004): *ABC, Madrid*; *El Mundo, Madrid*; *El Mundo.es*; *El Pais, Madrid*; *La Jornada.com, Mexico*; *La Razón, Madrid*; *Le Monde, Paris*; *Metro Directo, Madrid*; *The Guardian, UK*; and *20 Minutos, Madrid*. The newspapers and radio span from right to left in political orientation, whereas the social movement listserves only represent autonomous/left forums. Because the protests were illegal, no names or other identifying characteristics are provided for non-published sources. I have chosen representative emails and quotes drawn from these sources. The signs and slogans analysed here are those I observed and recorded between 6 and 10 p.m. at the original nucleus of the protest (Genova 13, Madrid), after which the protests spread to other areas of the city.

Frame analysis is used to understand ways actors actively and strategically engage in the production of interpretations of events in order to mobilise supporters, demobilise antagonists and convince observers of the worthiness of their cause (Snow & Benford, 1988). Entman (1993) defines framing as 'to select some aspects of a perceived reality and make them more salient in a communicating text, in such a way as to promote a particular problem definition, causal interpretation, moral evaluation, and/or treatment recommendation' (p. 52). Frame analysis is therefore useful in analysing political discourse, including political flash mob slogans and demands. I present all the signs and slogans in Table 1 and classify them into eight key frames that emerge from the data.

The analysis below is organised chronologically and traces the progression of opinion and feeling within the social movement networks and the public as drawn from this data set.

11-M

The official story[2]

7:39 a.m. 11 March 2004, Madrid: ten bombs exploded on four trains killing 192 people and injuring 1847. While most people immediately assumed ETA was responsible, ETA experts expressed doubt because the scale, target and absence of warning was inconsistent with ETA's usual modus operandi.[3] At 10:50 a.m. police discovered a van containing copper detonators of a kind not used by ETA and a Koranic tape. Despite this evidence, at 1:15 p.m. Minister of the Interior Ángel Acebes declared that 'The government has no doubt ETA is responsible.' Acebes' 8:00 p.m. press statement confirmed that ETA continued to be the main suspect, but he also announced the discovery of the van with the Koranic tape. But he added, 'I want to stress however, that the terrorist organisation ETA is still the priority suspect

Table 1.   Frame analysis of slogans and signs, 13-M Protest, 13 Génova Street, Madrid

Frames	Slogans/signs[a]
Demand for truth/critique of the Popular Party (PP)	Liars
	Who did it?[a]
	You do know the truth
	Our president is a lying shit
	Enough lies
	We're not leaving without the truth
	In Europe they already know
	The entire world already knows
	We want the truth before we vote
	Less police and more information
	Don't manipulate our dead
	Enough manipulation
	Where is your dignity?
	Don't play with the dead
	The rest of the world already knows[a]
	Manipulation of information = manipulation of the vote[a]
	If ETA lies, they always lie[a]
	We aren't stupid[a]
	No more manipulation[a]
Anti-war	We said NO to the WAR
	Your war, our dead
	The bombs of Iraq, explode in the trains
	Aznar guilty, you are responsible
	Let's see what happens now, with the war at home
Critique of the mass media	Let's see if you put us on Channel 1
	Enough manipulation
	Television, manipulation
	We want Urdaci to come out
	Urdaci put us on TV
	Tomorrow you'll say there were only 5 or 6 of us here
Democracy	They call it a democracy but it isn't
	Oay Oay Oay, it's a dictatorship of the PP
	Resign, government resign
	Tomorrow we vote, tomorrow we throw you out
	Your whore mother will vote for you
	Tomorrow we'll throw them out, if we all vote
	We are the people, don't be afraid
	They don't represent us
	Assassins who? Democracy where?
	We're reflecting, oh yes, we are reflecting

(Continued)

Table 1   Continued

Frames	Slogans/signs[a]
	Join us, don't look at us [to the police and the people inside PP headquarters who would approach the upstairs window]
Alternative political discourse	This is where the PP votes will go [mini toilet][a] Neither ETA, nor Al-Qaeda, nor the PP We were also at yesterday's march
General critique of the PP	ETA no, lies either This is what we get for having a fascist government Aznar and company, abuse of power and arrogance We want Franco to come out [of PP headquarters]
Peace	These are our weapons [holding hands up in the air]
Grief/solidarity	Peace[a] Not all of us are here, 200 of us are missing Atocha, brothers, we don't forget We were also at yesterday's march

Note: [a]Signs are distinguished by an asterisk as opposed to slogans which are chanted.

according to the Guardia Civil and the police forces, but I have instructed them not to overlook any line of investigation . . . .'

The response of the social movements and public opinion: confusion, grief

The overwhelming emotion within the autonomous/leftist social movement network was much the same as among the public: grief, anger at the terrorists and confusion as to 'who did it'. Roig & López's (2005) analysis of alternative web-based media shows that on the morning of 11-M many political and social organisations published communiqués condemning ETA for the bombings without waiting for confirmation or evidence.

Divisions appeared early within Madrid's autonomous/left social movement network as revealed in a meeting called to discuss the response of the social movements to the bombings and how they were being handled by the government. According to activists present, the meeting was marred by division over the appropriate response to President Aznar's call for a public demonstration. One activist said:

> It was depressing. I was disgusted. There were people who were saying: Well, depending on who was behind the attacks I'll march or not. I was furious. Who cares? Do we have to have a common political position to march in solidarity with the victims? . . . There is no common plan. We'll meet tonight at 6 and go together, we'll wear black and carry candles. We'll walk in silence. There is not much point in doing anything else, this is so much bigger than any group, than any of us. We just need to be on the streets.

Part of the resistance to the official protest march was due to the slogan announced for the banner: 'With the victims, with the constitution, against terrorism.' In an election campaign marked strongly by the PP's discursive dichotomy between the constitution (good) and nationalist claims for increased autonomy (bad and anti-constitutional), this slogan was interpreted as a strategy to use the bombings to campaign for the elections. One email posted to a listserve summed up these feelings:

> My horror at the massacre doesn't impede my ability to recognize the leeches that try to gain something from it. The same rage turns into disgust at the spectacle of how they try to benefit from tragedy. Do I have to be in favor of the constitution to be against the assassination of hundreds of workers, students and normal people? Is this a pre-requisite?

12-M

Government and media action

By 12 March foreign newspaper reports that Al-Qaeda had claimed responsibility for the attack began to filter through to part of the public. There was an important shift in national newspaper headlines too, with all major papers removing ETA from the headlines, but reporting the government's insistence that 'all signs point to ETA'.[4]

During the course of the day, police discovered three unexploded bombs and a detonator, which were linked to an Al-Qaeda supporter. Despite this new evidence, the official story did not change. At his 6 p.m. press statement Minister Acebes confirmed that 'ETA is the number one suspect, and there is no reason for this not to be so. No other line of investigation will be overlooked.' At 8 p.m. Cadena SER, the radio station with the largest audience share (over 4 million listeners), reported that investigators were claiming all evidence pointed to a radical Islamic group, which shed doubt on the transparency of Acebes' official statements.

Public reaction: doubt, anger, and a demand for the truth

As the initial overwhelming grief began to lessen slightly, the anger within the autonomous/leftist social movement network intensified. Emails poured in on the listserves with expressions of grief, rage and, perhaps most importantly, with links to international press reports attributing the bombings to Islamic fundamentalists. One email read:

> *We are being hoodwinked and manipulated!*
>
> Acebes, Aznar and the rest of the fanatical Spanish nationalists would like to choose at their whim the culprits of the bombings in Madrid in accordance with their 'patriotic' interests. But they can't because RESPONSIBILITY FOR THE ATTACKS HAS ALREADY BEEN CLAIMED!! Now it's a question that they cannot hide from us, nor the terrible implications this has for a government that has been a lackey to Bush's imperialism. If you haven't received the news yet, here's a translation from the AFP newswire in which Al-Qaeda takes responsibility, in terms that will set even the most temperate reader's hair on end .... 'AL-QAEDA CLAIMS MADRID, ISTANBUL BOMBINGS'.

All the major activist listserves carried the news that ETA had denied responsibility for the attack.

There was still indecision about whether to participate in the mass demonstration called by the government for that evening, as reflected in this email:

> Today everyone is almost begging to know who did this, to know who could be capable of this. But today it doesn't matter. Tomorrow and the day after it will matter and it will have different consequences depending on who did it. . . . Today isn't a day for slogans, nor for political epithets against anybody, and so, instead of the understandable reactions of demanding responsibility and attacking this or that politician, the best answer we can give is our silence. Let our silence unite us, and the best homage is to carry a candle in memory of all those people.

Many people resolved their ambivalence about marching by taking to the streets and marching in parallel to the official march given their feelings that the slogan of the march and the insistence on attributing blame to ETA was manipulative.

Neither silence nor unity characterised the demonstrations of approximately 11 million Spaniards who marched in the pouring rain that evening. The strong divisions in public opinion, although glossed by the media, were exceedingly clear.[5] Although much of the crowd carried anti-ETA slogans, there was an insistent repetition of chants and slogans crying 'Who was it? Who was it?' and 'Before we vote we want the truth', also expressed on signs held aloft by demonstrators. In Madrid, an elderly woman chased after the Minister of the Interior as he left the demonstration, crying 'Who was it? We want the truth before we vote on Sunday!' (Tele5 Newshour, 13 March 2005).

Although an exhaustive analysis of media coverage during these days is beyond the scope of this paper, the coverage was partial at best, with television coverage in particular focusing almost exclusively on the anti-ETA demonstrators and ignoring the insistent chanting of 'Who was it?' (*Quien ha sido?*). Footage of the woman chasing the Minister of the Interior was only shown on Tele5 (more critical of the PP) on the following day, 13-M.

Perhaps more compelling than the coverage itself is the testimony from journalists. On 14 March, the newspaper *Metro Directo* reported that the foreign press in Madrid had filed a complaint against the government for engaging in 'inadmissible behaviour' by pressuring and tricking them into supporting the ETA thesis. Other accusations and evidence of partisan manipulation of news were reported (*20 Minutos*, 2004b; *El País*, 2004a, 2004b; Cadena SER, 12 March 2004).

13-M

Mobilisation

By morning, Minister Acebes, while admitting that other lines of investigation were open, was still affirming ETA was the main suspect. At 2:30 p.m. he stated, 'No member of the security police force has informed me that Al-Qaeda is behind the attacks.' Cadena SER News, however, reported that sources from the National Center of Intelligence had a 99% certainty that a radical fundamentalist Islamic group was behind the attacks, and that ETA was no longer the prime suspect.

By this point activists and members of the public were confronted with divergent accounts of the identity of the perpetrators, between official statements (ETA), divergent national media accounts (ETA/Al-Qaeda) and foreign news (Al-Qaeda). There were also differences between official statements regarding evidence and Cadena SER. These divergent interpretations led to a serious questioning of the media's objectivity and the government's transparency and fuelled a great deal of anger.

By the morning of 13-M, the feeling of outrage was the overwhelming emotion characterising the tone of activist emails and communication. Activists called each other, trying to come up with some way to express their anger and to demand that the government come clean about the evidence they had regarding the responsibility for the attacks. Five activists met in a café in Madrid and decided to send out a call for a protest in front of the PP headquarters at 6 p.m. One had close ties to a political party (IU), another was an IU militant but identified more strongly as an activist than as a party sympathiser, and the other three were unaffiliated with any party. All five were active anti-globalisation and/or anti-war activists. They set a time and place for the protest, and drew on contact lists from former movement campaigns, primarily the Transatlantic Social Forum, set up to protest the meeting of heads of state during the Spanish presidency of the European Union in 2002, and the protests against the invasion of Iraq and the *Prestige* disaster in 2003.[6]

The original text message read:

> 'Aznar sitting pretty?[7] They call it a day of reflection and Urdaci is working?[8] Today, March 13, at 18:00, at the PP headquarters, c/Genova, 13. No political parties. 'We want to know the truth.' Pass it on.[9]

It initially circulated through activist networks but quickly spread far beyond the original nucleus. The phone companies reported a 20% increase in SMS messages on that day (*20 Minutos*, 2004a). Increase in Internet use throughout this period has also been documented (Olmeda, 2005). The message was also posted on major alternative media web pages and was passed on through activist listserves.

At 6 p.m. I was one of 20 people standing in front of PP headquarters, facing a line of riot police vans. BBC, CNN, Antena 3 and Cadena SER press trucks were also parked out in front, offering potential protection against riot police. As the crowd grew to about 60, riot police formed a cordon, and some of them began to push. One policeman walked purposefully towards the crowd, asked to see the identity cards of people in the front line, and began to jot down the numbers. In one spontaneous but synchronised move the crowd whipped out national identity cards and held them in the air. The message was clear: if you write down one ID number, you write them all down. The policeman reflected, desisted and walked back across the street to the entrance of the headquarters. More people began to arrive, a steady trickle that turned into a flow, eventually reaching between 3000 and 5000 people.[10] People began to shout out slogans, which were picked up by the rest of the crowd:

Who did it?

Enough manipulation!
More democracy, less repression
Television, manipulation
Liars, Liars, Liars

The mood was very tense, and rumours of an imminent police charge rippled through the crowd. No one moved. A man handed out pieces of paper, purportedly from 'The family members of the victims of 11-M'. Although its origin is unclear, whoever wrote it mirrored the feelings people in the crowd expressed that day:

13-3-04

The families of the victims of the terrorist attack of 11-M are outraged by the manipulation that the government is engaging in with the information of this attack.

It goes without saying that we believe that ETA is a group of assassins, and that all of its members should be tried and imprisoned. But to attribute an attack to them that they didn't commit only serves to strengthen them.

In the entire world, from the first hours of 11-M, it was known that this attack was perpetrated and claimed by terrorist groups linked to Al-Qaeda.

To try and make the Spanish people believe that this had nothing to do with the war in Iraq is shameful, manipulative and crooked, especially in elections. It is also a cruelty to us, those directly affected.

The covering up of information about such a grave incident is without precedent in Spain's democracy, and adds outrage to our immense sorrow.

NO MORE BLOOD, NO MORE MANIPULATION, NO MORE LIES

To those of you who have access to the media, we request that you disseminate this text.

FAMILIES OF THE VICTIMS OF 11-M

The crowd became increasingly heterogeneous as time went on, elegant elderly women and men mixed in with younger 'scruffier' looking people. As more people arrived, the crowd began to relax a bit. It became less likely that the police would charge, and the press did not leave. The chanting did not stop. People were sending messages on their mobiles, and holding up their phones for people to hear what was happening. Activists were keenly aware that the protest was unprecedented and illegal. As time passed and voices grew hoarse, the crowd began to feel a bit more light-hearted. The protest felt cathartic as the crowd collectively released anger and sorrow, in the company of friends and strangers.

There was also a strong feeling of creativity and spontaneity, which contrasted sharply with the regimented prearranged sloganising of most protest marches in

Madrid, as people shouted out different slogans. If people liked them, they would be picked up. Some provoked laughter, like the one asking General Francisco Franco to come out of the PP headquarters. In addition to the majority of signs which read 'Peace' (PAZ), there were many hand-painted signs in the crowd. Someone lifted a mini toilet in the air with a sign attached reading 'This is where the PP votes will go'.

Periodically messages calling for a minute's silence would pass through the crowd ('At 7:15, a minute of silence, pass it on'). At the designated time people would lift their hands up in the air, palms facing front, and hold a minute's silence for the victims. The mood would instantly become very sober and many people wiped tears from their cheeks. Later in the evening a new call to protest travelled from cell phone to cell phone: 'At midnight in Sol. Pass it on'. Protests also broke out in front of PP headquarters in Barcelona, Santiago de Compostela, Valencia, Bilbao, Palencia and Palma de Mallorca, among other cities.

At 6.30 p.m. Cadena SER began broadcasting coverage of the protests. The main channels were not covering the protests live, but had covered them very briefly in the news programmes,[11] but Localia, a local television station, was showing uninterrupted coverage of the protest from CNN. At 9:30 p.m., the PP presidential candidate, Mariano Rajoy, made a statement broadcast on the major television and radio channels. He accused the PSOE of orchestrating the protests and denounced the protests as 'illegal and illegitimate', affirming that their sole purpose was to 'coerce the will of the electorate on the day of reflection, when all demonstrations are against the law so that the electoral process can unfold fairly'. He ordered 'the citizens who are gathered' to 'cease their behaviour and conclude this antidemocratic act of pressure on tomorrow's elections'. He said that the protests rumoured for midnight in Sol should be called off. He concluded with a call to the vote (TVE Channel 1, 13 March, 2004). While the PP was undoubtedly under extreme pressure, Rajoy's statement was a strategic error, since more people took to the streets following it, and the protests spread far beyond the PP headquarters and the Puerta del Sol, continuing until 3 a.m.

Making sense of the protests

The 13-M protests offer a rather unique opportunity to understand the motivations and emotions of the protesters, because unlike most protest demonstrations in Spain the slogans and signs were not the result of negotiations between party, union and movement group members, but instead reflected the feelings of those present. The slogans are presented in Table 1.[12]

Analysing the themes present in the slogans and signs, we can see eight main frames projected by the protesters:

1. Critique of PP/demand for truth: anger at the PP for a lack of transparency, accusations that the PP deliberately lied, and a demand for the truth about who was responsible for 11-M.

2. Anti-war: a resurgence of anti-war frames. Crucial here is the connection between PP's support for the war and bombings and blaming of the PP for making Spain a target.
3. Critique of the mass media: for manipulating information in favour of political party interests, for uncritically acting as a mouthpiece for the government, and for ignoring or downplaying the voices of protest against the government's repeated projection of the ETA thesis.
4. Democracy: a call for the vote as a means of punishing the PP ('throwing them out'), and a tension between a critique of the existing democracy and support for democracy as a value.
5. General critique of the PP: slogans that characterize the PP as being a fascist party, linked to Franco and which carries on with his censorship activities.
6. Alternative political discourse: a rejection of the binary set up by the PP, 'Anti-terrorism = Support for PP', and a rejection of PP 'ownership' of terrorism as a political issue.
7. Peace: a desire for peace/antimilitarism.
8. Grief/solidarity: an expression of grief for and solidarity with the victims.

Some slogans can be understood as overlapping between frames: 'We were also at yesterday's march', for example, represents an attempt to portray the protesters as aligned with the victims (solidarity frame), but also attempts to project an alternative political discourse in that it is a rejection of government (PP) 'ownership' of terrorism as a political issue. Also closely linked are the critique of government withholding or manipulation of information and the conventional media's complicity and support for it. The general critique of the PP, which characterises the party as 'fascist', can also be seen as connected to the democracy frame. Comments from people in the crowds drew explicit connections between Franco-era censorship and the PP's handling of information during the two days following 11-M, which was seen as a grave attack on civil liberties. Historical memory clearly marked the understanding of the protest.

These slogans show that the overwhelming themes of the protest were anger caused by the belief that the PP deliberately lied about the responsibility for the attack, which was linked to a call for the punishment vote to throw them out of office. Therefore the 'demand for the truth' frame was closely linked to the 'democracy' frame. Although it is impossible to quantify the number of times each slogan was repeated, one of the most insistent was simply the repeated chanting of 'Liars, liars, liars'. There is no presentation of an alternative 'socialist' discourse (any slogan directly linked to PSOE propaganda or electoral discourse) nor was there any explicit expression of support for the PSOE or for IU.

14-M: election day

Election morning dawned to find anti-PP political graffiti all over different polling stations and PP headquarters, and one PP headquarters had been burned in Galicia. Newspaper headlines read: 'All signs point to Al-Qaeda' (*El País*), 'First arrests link massacre to Islamic terrorism' (*El Mundo*) and 'The government and the PP accuse the PSOE of encouraging the harassment of (PP) headquarters all over Spain' (*ABC*).

Analysing the vote

Voter turnout was exceptionally high, at 77% (versus 68.7% in 2000). The PP only lost about 700,000 votes with respect to the previous elections. The PSOE won almost 3 million more votes than in 2000, also helped by 2 million young first-time voters. Also central to the victory of the PSOE was the mobilisation of the former abstainers' vote. One sector of former abstainers who voted represents voters already sympathetic to the PSOE but had not voted in the previous elections. But the punishment vote seems to have been crucial. The loss of four of five seats by left party IU suggests that the strategic/punishment, as opposed to the ideological vote, was also important, where supporters of IU or other small parties voted for the PSOE to ensure the defeat of the PP.

The importance of the strategic punishment vote and the mobilisation of abstainers is supported by qualitative evidence from the Madrid social movement network, which suggests that many autonomous activists who do not vote on principle were moved to vote in this election. A typical feeling was a text message one activist sent around stating: 'How revolting! I'm going to vote'. Another activist reported the bizarre sight of Anarchist Youth members, who never vote on principle, debating between the strategic vote (for the PSOE) and the ideological vote (for IU). 'It will be many years before we see anything like *that* again!' he exclaimed. Typical activist emails called for people to 'vote for anyone but the PP' (see also Sampedro & Martínez, 2005). While it is unclear what proportion of abstainers these young activists make up, it is clear that the unusual circumstances following the bombings compelled them to vote when they otherwise would not have.

Analysts of the vote disagree somewhat about which factors were decisive in the outcome. Sanz & Sánchez-Sierra (2005) argue that the bombings brought dissatisfaction with the PP's foreign policy and authoritarian style of governance to the fore. They cite post-election polls that show two out ten Spaniards believed the bombings were linked to Aznar's support for the invasion of Iraq. However, evidence from the 13-M protests lends support to the analysis of Van Biezen (2005, p. 102) who contends that although anger over the invasion of Iraq and the *Prestige* disaster resurfaced after 11-M, it is doubtful these issues alone would have mobilised the former abstainers' vote. The overwhelming sentiment of the 13-M protesters was outrage due to their belief that the 11-M victims' deaths were being manipulated for electoral purposes and that the government and sympathetic media were deliberately lying to win the election. Although these concerns were clearly linked to the issues of the PP's support for the war in Iraq and the targeting of Spaniards as a result, they were secondary to the issue of government misinformation.

Conclusions

Analysing the 13-M flash mob protests using ethnographic data provides two contributions. First, it allows for a correction of two contradictory speculative claims made about the protests by scholars and parties: that they were completely spontaneous or that they were orchestrated by the PSOE. Second, frame analysis of the protests sheds light on quantitative analysis of the unexpected electoral outcome.

It is clear that the protests of 13-M were not simply spontaneous manifestations of public opinion. The original call to protest was initiated from a small nucleus of activists who drew on contact lists developed through previous movement campaigns and provided coordination by choosing a specific target (the PP headquarters) and a time to meet. The decision to take the risk of protesting on the day of reflection, in a context of repression and limited space for civil disobedience, also reflected increasing support within the network for civil disobedience in part as a result of experience of engaging in civil disobedience in the protests against the *Prestige* disaster and the invasion of Iraq (see also Alcalde *et al.*, 2005). The support for the call, however, far surpassed the strength of the local social movement network. The rapid circulation of the text message beyond the network was due in great part to the already existing youth social networks who use SMS as a means of communication, and whose decision to participate depended on the already high level of trust and confidence they had in the members of their SMS network (Francescutti *et al.*, 2005). There is also evidence that the exact meaning of the original SMS was not clear to those outside the social movement network, reflecting its endogamic nature: activists erroneously assumed 'everyone' would get the message (Francescutti *et al.*, 2005). Once the protest was covered on television, especially following Rajoy's statement, participation spread to the general public.

Neither was the protest orchestrated by PSOE militants. Despite the involvement of one activist very close to IU, the protests were organised autonomously, at least initially. The protests did not reflect increased support for the PSOE (or even IU) among autonomous activists, as is made clear by this activist article (re)posted on various alternative web pages:

A Little More Space. ZP[13] (Zapatero) You're Next.[14]

... Are we living in an SMS democracy? Are we going to internalize the reactionary discourse that assumes the PP lost because of the 'illegal and illegitimate' mobilizations on Saturday? Let's calmly analyse the new scenario. A few hours after the attack the panorama couldn't have been worse. Had the butchery in Madrid been the work of ETA, an absolute majority for the PP would have been almost automatic. ... Getting an absolute majority of the PP off our backs is a blast of oxygen to the movement, especially with the PSOE obliged to play tightrope walker in parliament. ... The protest (on Saturday) was amazing and promising. But let's not congratulate ourselves, nor attribute ourselves more than the little weight we have. The PP lost because of the bombings and their subsequent lies and manipulation, not because of what happened in the streets. It looks like the informal networks left over from the remains of anti-globalization resistance ... can still give a fright ... thanks to the new technologies ... Now let's see if the PSOE says NO TO WAR or NO TO *THIS* WAR. See you on the streets. ZP, you're next. Unity. Action. Autonomy.

The little weight given to the mobilisations by the PSOE and the insistence by the PP that they were orchestrated by the PSOE and IU reflect the dominance of party politics in Madrid's political field. Party politicians genuinely find it inconceivable that protests, especially of that magnitude, can be organised without the backing of a party or union. Neither the PP's insistence on a PSOE plot and the PSOE's insistence that the protests were completely spontaneous give any credit to the agency of social movement networks. Ironically, intellectuals on the right gave more weight to the effects of the protest (perhaps preferring that to a critical analysis of the Popular Party's handling of the crisis). Typical is the following excerpt from an ABC editorial:

> the resentful faction of the left … has renewed their predilection for a sort of living room coup-d'état with branch offices in the street, especially in Genova Street in Madrid. It was a perfect symbiosis of lies and violent direct action whose supposed ends were to find electoral profit from terror and the delegitimation of a victory of the PP in the ballot boxes. (Sánchez Cámara, 2004)

One of the few examples of positive credit for the protests came from Manuel Saco, a columnist for local daily paper *20 Minutos*, who wrote: 'I think it was the mobilization via mobile phone messages that pulled the truth about the attacks from them' (Saco, 2004).

Despite the unprecedented nature of the 13-M protests, they did not reflect an increase in the capacity of response of the Madrid autonomous/left network to other issues of concern for them. Divisions, fragmentation and a weak resource base continue to characterise the Madrid network. Autonomous social movements in Madrid have a particularly difficult time carving out space for themselves between the two cleavages that divide Spanish politics: left/right and state nationalism/autonomous nationalism. Identifying neither with the right nor with the institutionalised left, and with no form of nationalism leaves the movement in a marginal position in a city dominated by national party politics (Flesher Fominaya, 2007). Activists felt that despite the divisions evident in the meeting on the day of the attacks, their ability to mobilise on such short notice, using only cell phones, Internet, and mouth-to-mouth communication was an uplifting and encouraging experience. But it took an unprecedented traumatic 'spark' and a particular response from the government and media to set off the mobilisation.

This analysis restores agency to the social movement networks that organised them but, unlike Burkitt (2005), does not claim a *direct* effect of the protest on the elections. It does, however, highlight the importance of the crowd as a political actor with agency and impact. Frame analysis of the slogans contributes additional information on the motivations and emotions of the crowd that were directed explicitly to the elections, and are likely to have influenced them. If Saco (2004) is right, and the protests 'pulled' the truth from the governing party on the eve of the election, then this is another effect of the protest on the elections. As such, this analysis helps illuminate quantitative analyses of the election based solely on poll data.

The analysis presented here also offers a theoretical contribution to scholars seeking to understand the relation between the use of new ICTs, political flash mobs and democratisation processes. This analysis raises the question of the 'spontaneity' of political flash mobs and other protest events and calls for more theoretical refinement of the concept. If by spontaneity we mean acts of civil disobedience that are organised at short notice, using new ICTs and bypassing hierarchical organisational structures, then 13-M was 'spontaneous'. The frames analysed here are useful as a reflection of protester opinion precisely because they were unmediated by political movement and party structures. But the use of the word 'spontaneous' as used in many of the analyses cited here denies the importance of pre-existing social movement networks in the mobilisation and downplays the agency and importance of the protest. As Melucci (1995) argued too much analysis takes protest events as the starting point, rather than the end point. More research needs to be done that makes clear the connections between latent movement networks and visible protest events. Given that the protests were illegal, the appearance of the small original nucleus of protesters facing riot police at 6 p.m. implies pre-existing solidarity and trust built up through movement collective identity processes (Pfaff, 1996). We also need to guard against technological over-determinism. While the existence of SMS messaging has clear implications for mobilisation, not least the ability of activists to bypass traditional leadership and decision-making structures, and reach a large number of people quickly and cheaply, the protest itself was the result of two days of intensive face-to-face, phone and email communication, before the call to protest was launched via SMS.

Despite their 'temporary' nature, political flash mobs can also have long-term and unintended consequences. At the time of writing (June 2011), thousands of people, mostly youth, fill the central plazas of Spain on the eve of regional and local elections, once again deliberately defying the ban on political mobilisation on the day of reflection. They call their protest '15-M' in a clear allusion to 13-M and they are demanding increased democracy and transparency from political leaders.[15] The influence of 13-M, which set the precedent for defying the ban, is clearly felt in these protests which are making headlines around the world and have spread to other countries. Ironically, on this occasion the election resulted in a sweeping victory for the PP across Spain, which is unlikely to be the outcome these leftist/autonomous protesters would have wished for.[16]

This analysis of 13-M documents a transition from shock to grief to confusion to anger. 13-M therefore also highlights the need for attention to emotions in social movement analysis (Jasper, 2011) as the trauma of the bombings and the subsequent emotions are central to understanding this protest event and the election outcome.

Finally, I want to highlight the importance of political flash mobs as a means of countering increased surveillance and repression of social movements in a post-9/11 security context (Flesher Fominaya & Wood, 2011) while at the same time not romanticising the possibilities of new ICTs: security forces can and do bring down cell phone networks as a means of social control, even in democratic countries. I hope this analysis of the 13-M protest helps illuminate the motives, mobilising structures, and consequences of political flash mobs, a new kind of 21st-century crowd that will undoubtedly continue to form an important part of the global political landscape.

Acknowledgements

The author is grateful to Celia Valiente for her comments on an original draft of this article, written in 2004. Thanks also to John Drury, Laurence Cox, and the anonymous reviewers for their feedback and suggestions. This research was supported by the German Marshall Fund and the John L. Simpson Foundation.

Notes

1. Michavila (2005) argues that in fact a confluence of a latent desire for a change in government, the emotional response caused by the attacks, a punishment of the government for their involvement in Iraq and the reinforcement of these factors by the manipulation of information by both the government *and* against the government account for the vote. For a journalistic chronicle of the government's contradictions in information provided following the bombings, see Magán (2004).
2. This is a very brief account. For hour-by-hour coverage of Cadena SER during these days, including Popular Party Minister of the Interior Acebes' statements, see http://www. cadenaser.com/static/especiales/2005/sonidos11_14/index.html/. For frame analysis of government and opposition messages as transmitted through the media, see Olmeda (2005). For a detailed analysis of the government and media responses to the bombings during this three-day period, see Sampedro *et al.* (2005).
3. I was working at a conference at the Universidad Complutense, Madrid, on the morning of the bombings. That morning's speaker was an expert on ETA terrorism, and he made all of these observations at 9 a.m. on 11 March 2004.
4. For a full analysis of the changes in mass media coverage over this period, see Sampedro *et al.* (2005).
5. The acute division in public opinion over responsibility for the bombings reflects the deep left–right cleavage in Spain.
6. The *Prestige* was an oil tanker that spilled fuel off the coast of Galicia in November 2002. The PP was harshly criticised in some sectors for their slow response and poor handling of the spill, which sparked a powerful social movement campaign called *Nunca mais* (Never Again).
7. The original expression is '*de rositas*', which means to be in an advantageous position, or to be 'off the hook', to 'get away with' something, and not to have to pay for your crimes. In this case Aznar's 'crimes' can mean supporting the Invasion of Iraq against the will of the overwhelming majority of Spaniards (86–91%), or deliberately misleading the public as to the perpetrators of 11-M.
8. Urdaci was Director of TVE, Channel 1. News directors of public television are generally considered to be handpicked by the ruling government and partial to whichever party is currently in office. Urdaci was no exception, and under his direction there have been complaints and protests by reporters that they are unable to report the news faithfully, especially regarding Iraqi War coverage and the *Prestige* disaster. An action was brought against TVE for deliberately misleading the public during the coverage of the general strike of 20 June 2003. The judge ruled against TVE, and they had to broadcast an apology. The line 'they call it a day of reflection and Urdaci is working?' refers to the fact that no political propaganda is legal the day before the election, and if he is reading the 'news' he is in violation of the law since he supposedly engages in propaganda for the PP.
9. Some versions said: In silence for the truth. Later more messages were sent round. One read: Information intoxication. Al-Qaeda claims responsibility in Arab media. The government denies it. Pass it on.

10. Estimates from police, media and activist sources.
11. Two identical 1 minute 35 second segments were aired on TVE Channel 1, considered to be most favourable to the PP, and Channel 5, more critical of the PP, aired one 3 minute 9 second segment.
12. Many of these rhyme in Spanish, and many are sung to popular tunes.
13. ZP is President Zapatero's nickname.
14. Anon. (2004).
15. The protests are also a direct response to the economic crisis in Spain and the perceived lack of leadership in addressing its consequences. The multiple manifestos circulated by the protesters show a clear anti-capitalist or anti-neo-liberal orientation (for example, http://www.democraciarealya.es/).
16. Hermanns (2008) shows that flash mobs can have constructive or destructive consequences, as with the case of Thai opposition in 2006 that brought down the government and led to a military coup.

References

20 Minutos (2004a) 'Pasalo': el poder de los SMS, *20 Minutos*, 12 March, 4.
20 Minutos (2004b) Cacerolada en TVE contra Urdaci, *20 Minutos*, 16 March, 3.
Alcalde, J., Sádaba, I. & Fco. Sampedro, V. (2005) Del no a la guerra al 13M: ciclo de movilizaciones y comunicación alternativa, in: V. Sampedro (Ed.) *13-M multitudes on-line* (Madrid, Catarata), 126–151.
Anon (2004) *Indymedia ACP.* Available online at: http://acp.sindominio.net.article.pl?sid=04/03/15/1659215&mode=thread&threshold=0/.
Blakeley, G. (2006) It's politics, stupid! The Spanish General Election of 2004, *Parliamentary Affairs*, 59(2), 331–349.
Burkitt, I. (2005) Powerful emotions: power, government and opposition in the 'war on terror', *Sociology*, 39, 679–695.
Chari, R. S. (2004) The 2004 Spanish election: terrorism as a catalyst for change? *West European Politics*, 27(5), 954–963.
El País (2004a) Instituto Opina, *El País*, 7 March.
El País (2004b) Conato de plante en 24 horas, *El País*, 15 March, 93.
El País (2004c) La Fundacion Buesa acusa a TVE de 'utilizar la memoria de víctimas de ETA', *El País*, 15 March, 93.
Entman, R. M. (1993) Framing: toward clarification of a fractured paradigm, *Journal of Communication*, 43(4), 51–58.
Flesher Fominya, C. M. (2007) Autonomous movement and the Institutional Left: two approaches in tension in Madrid's anti-globalization network, *South European Society and Politics*, 12(3), 335–358.
Flesher Fominaya, C. M. & Wood, L. (2011) Repression and social movements, *Interface: A Journal For and About Social Movements*, 3(1), 1–11.
Francescutti, P., Baer, A., Mª García de Madariaga, J. & López, P. (2005) La noche de los móviles: medios, redes de confianza y movilización juvenil, in: V. Sampedro (Ed.) *13-M multitudes on-line* (Madrid, Catarata), 64–85.
Hermanns, H. (2008) Mobile phones as democratic tools, *Politics*, 28(2), 74–82.
Jasper, J. (2011) Emotions and social movements: twenty years of theory and research, *Annual Review of Sociology*, 37, 285–303.
Magán, L. (2004) Tres días de marzo: las contradicciones en la información del Gobierno sobre el 11-M, *El País.com*, 27 March. Available online at: http://www.elpais.com/articulo/espana/dias/marzo/elpepunac/20040327elpepinac_24/Tes (accessed 1 April 2004).
Melucci, A. (1995) The process of collective identity, in: H. Johnston & B. Klandermans (Eds) *Social movements and culture* (Minneapolis, MN, University of Minnesota Press), 41–63.

Michavila, N. (2005) *Guerra, terrorismo y elecciones: incidencia electoral de los atentados Islamistas de Madrid*. Working Paper No. 13/2005 (Madrid, Real Instituto Elcano).

Moreno, L. (2005) The Madrid bombings in the domestic and regional politics of Spain, *Irish Studies in International Affairs*, 16, 65–72.

Olmeda, J. (2005) *Fear or falsehood? Framing the 3/11 attacks in Madrid and electoral accountability*. Working Paper No. 24/2005 (Madrid, Real Instituto Elcano).

Pfaff, S. (1996) Collective identity and informal groups in revolutionary mobilization: East Germany in 1989, *Social Forces*, 75(1), 91–118.

Rafael, V. (2003) The cell phone and the crowd: messianic politics in the contemporary Philippines, *Public Culture*, 15(3), 399–425.

Rheingold, H. (2003) *Smart mobs: the next social revolution* (Cambridge, Perseus).

Roig, G. & López, S. (2005) Del desconcierto emocional a la movilización política: redes sociales y medios alternativos del 11m al 13m, in: V. Sampedro (Ed.) *13-M multitudes on-line* (Madrid, Catarata), 152–197.

Saco, M. (2004) Corren Rumores, *20 Minutos*, 16 March, 4.

Salmond, M. (2010) The power of momentary communities: locative media and (in)formal protest, *Aether: Journal of Media Geography*, V.A., 90–100.

Sampedro, V., Alcalde, J. & Sádaba, I. (2005) El fin de la mentira prudente. Colapso y apertura de la esfera pública, in: V. Sampedro (Ed.) *13-M multitudes on-line* (Madrid, Catarata), 198–245.

Sampedro, V. & Martinez, M. (2005) Primer voto: castigo político y descrédito de los medios, in: V. Sampedro (Ed.) *13-M multitudes on-line* (Madrid, Catarata), 25–63.

Sánchez Cámara, I. (2004) La izquierda atapuerca, *ABC*, 15 March, 3.

Sanz, A. & Sánchez-Sierra, A. (2005) *Las elecciones generales de 2004 en España: política exterior, estilo de gobierno y movilización*. Working Papers Online Series, Estudio/Working Paper 48/2005 (Madrid, Universidad Autónoma de Madrid). Available online at: http://www.uam.es/centros/derecho/cpolitica/papers.htm) (accessed 1 July 2006).

Snow, D. & Benford, R. D. (1988) Ideology, frame resonance and participant mobilization, *International Social Movement Research*, 1, 197–219.

Torcal, M. & Rico, G. (2004) The 2004 Spanish General Election: under the shadow of Al-Qaeda? *South European Society and Politics*, 9, 107–121.

Tremlett, G. (2006) *Ghosts of Spain* (London, Faber & Faber).

Van Biezen, I. (2005) Terrorism and democratic legitimacy: conflicting interpretations of the Spanish elections, *Mediterranean Politics*, 10(1), 99–108.

Public order policing in South Yorkshire, 1984–2011: the case for a permissive approach to crowd control

David P. Waddington

Sheffield Hallam University, Sheffield, UK

The Metropolitan Police Service's handling of the anti-G20 demonstration on 1 April 2009 attracted widespread public criticism and indignation. Mass media coverage of the event emphasised how police officers had reacted to protesters in a sometimes violent and allegedly indiscriminate manner, and had resorted to the now familiar and controversial tactic of 'kettling' demonstrators into a confined space before detaining them for several hours. Media reports initially echoed police briefings in disclosing that the death of a male passer-by, unintentionally caught up in the event, was due to natural causes. Video footage of the incident subsequently contradicted this account, suggesting that the fatality resulted from an unprovoked attack by a police officer. Reports prepared by Her Majesty's Chief Inspector of Constabulary have since called on the police to adopt a more permissive approach to managing political protest, predicated on a commitment to facilitating the right to protest. This paper lends weight to arguments in favour of such an approach by highlighting the experience during the last 28 years of South Yorkshire Police, a force which has not only revised its practical and philosophical approach to handling public dissent, but also developed a more open attitude in its dealings with the media in a bid to restore public confidence and staff morale, following nationwide controversy around the Orgreave mass picket of 1984 and the Hillsborough stadium tragedy of 1989.

Introduction

In April 2009, the United Kingdom hosted the international G20 summit in London. The Metropolitan Police Service's (MPS) policy for managing the accompanying protest activity incorporated the controversial technique known variously as 'kettling', 'corralling' or 'containment'—a tactic designed to curtail the mobility (and potential to engage in disorder) of participating groups. The main anti-G20 demonstration, occurring in the capital on 1 April, was characterised by scenes of violence in which participants objected to what they obviously perceived as police attempts to nullify their protest. In one incident, a man collapsed shortly after an altercation with police and died en route to hospital. It later emerged that the person concerned, Mr Ian Tomlinson, had been a passer-by unwittingly caught up in police lines while trying to return home via his usual route (Greer & McLaughlin, 2010; Rosie & Gorringe, 2009).

Initial reporting of the event focused on the sporadic violence that did occur—most notably, the vandalism inflicted on a branch office of the Royal Bank of Scotland (Rosie & Gorringe, 2009, p. 10). Ian Tomlinson's death was mentioned but did not immediately arouse controversy. This was undoubtedly because a press briefing by the MPS asserted that Mr Tomlinson had died of 'natural causes' and made no reference to any intermediate encounter with police officers. Newspaper reports were consistent with this version of events, even echoing the MPS's disclosure that officers trying to revive the stricken man had been pelted by a screaming mob (Rosie & Gorringe, 2009, p. 10).

However, by 3 April, the press discussion of police tactics had become decidedly more sceptical. *The Guardian* and *The Times* newspapers each contained critical commentaries on police kettling tactics, maintaining how, at the very first hint of trouble, demonstrators (including women and children) had become trapped inside a police cordon and told that under no circumstances would they be allowed to leave (Rosie & Gorringe, 2009, p. 11). Mounted police and dog handlers had been deployed in order to ensure that containment was effective, and that protesters were eventually provoked into violence as the police dealt harshly and indiscriminately with anyone refusing to comply (Rosie & Gorringe, 2009, p. 12). Worse still followed for the MPS when, days later, *The Guardian* published video evidence showing how a completely passive Ian Tomlinson had been struck and sent sprawling by a baton-wielding officer, and that claims of police attempts to resuscitate him while under attack by protesters were entirely disingenuous (Rosie & Gorringe, 2009, pp. 12–13).

Subsequent reports by the House of Commons Home Affairs Committee (HAC) (2009) and by Her Majesty's Chief Inspectorate of Constabulary (HMCIC) (2009a, 2009b) lent further credence to claims that police tactics had been overzealous and undifferentiating, and had constituted a major cause of violence in themselves. Such reports freely acknowledged the extent to which events at the G20 and the resulting media outcry had adversely affected public perceptions of police legitimacy—primarily, by calling into question their tactical approach to handling major political protests, and by highlighting the MPS's dishonesty in its briefings of the press.

This crisis of legitimacy and methodology has obvious precedents in the experience of South Yorkshire Police (SYP), following the immensely controversial roles they played in the miners' strike of 1984–1985 and the Hillsborough stadium disaster of April 1989. The force's uncompromising and allegedly heavy-handed treatment of local striking miners and their families, particularly during confrontations outside the Orgreave coking plant, and in their mishandling of the crowd congestion which resulted in 96 deaths at the 1989 FA Cup semi-final between Liverpool and

Nottingham Forest, has had a longstanding and negative effect on legitimacy and morale (Mawby, 2002; Scraton, 2004; Waddington *et al.*, 1989).

This paper focuses, in close detail, both on the nature and implications of these crises for SYP, and on the way in which the force has since adapted its crowd-control philosophy and tactical and strategic orientations in a conscious attempt to repair its image, reputation and relationship with its constituent communities. The paper will draw a parallel between SYP's handling of events at Orgreave and Hillsborough and the bungled attempts at impression management which followed, and the tactics and strategies employed by the MPS both during and in the aftermath of the G20 protest. It will then conclude by emphasising that the practical and philosophical adjustments undertaken by SYP in the wake of the Orgreave and Hillsborough debacles chime with the recommendations set out in the HMCIC reports, and therefore lend further weight to the argument in favour of a more open and permissive approach to the police management of public protest and dissent.

Care will be taken throughout to ensure that, although the primary focus of analysis is that of events occurring in South Yorkshire, due consideration is paid to the relevance of developments at national and, indeed, international level, and of their implications for trends and transitions in the nature of public order policing. Indeed, in order to fully understand the main reasons for the uncompromising and often severe conduct displayed by SYP towards the miners and their supporters (especially at Orgreave) during the 1984–1985 dispute, it is imperative that we begin by appreciating the nature and consequences of an earlier picket-line confrontation, coincidentally occurring at another coking works (the Saltley Depot in Birmingham), during the national miners' strike of 1972. As we shall now see, it was the reading of the police 'capitulation' to so-called flying pickets by the Conservative government under the premiership of Ted Heath, the outcome of a subsequent miners' strike of 1974, and the resultant transformation of civil contingency arrangements for dealing with national 'crises' of this nature, which had a profound bearing on the manner in which the Orgreave pickets were dealt with by police officers.

The spectre of Saltley Gate

The pivotal events at Saltley took place during a seven-week stoppage by the National Union of Mineworkers (NUM), which lasted from 9 January to 25 February 1972 and led to a complete shutdown of the nation's 269 collieries (Turner, 2008, p. 12). The NUM membership was demanding a £9 a week rise on their average pay of £25 and, whilst coal stocks were reportedly high, the miners used the innovative and highly effective strategy of despatching 'flying pickets' to prevent coal being admitted to power stations (Pelling, 1976, p. 281). It was in relation to this practice that, on 10 February, an event occurred at Saltley which was to haunt contingency planners for another decade (Jeffrey & Hennessy, 1983, p. 236). There, hundreds of NUM members had been engaged in a six-day struggle with police to prevent the movement of fuel from what was, by now, the nation's last major stockpile.

Much has been made of the part played by the future NUM President, the Barnsley-born Arthur Scargill, in ensuring the closure of the depot (Beckett, 2009; Beckett & Hencke, 2009). Though only a relatively lowly branch official at this time, Scargill nonetheless helped to mastermind the Saltley operation, and it was he who orchestrated the concerted pressure applied to police lines. Scargill was also instrumental in persuading 15,000–20,0000 Birmingham trade unionists to 'sympathetically' join his NUM colleagues on the Saltley picket line on 10 February, in solidarity against the scores of awaiting police officers (Scargill, 1974).

The numerical presence and sheer collective determination of the mass picket soon made it impossible for any lorry to approach or leave the plant; and fearing the possibility of serious injury, or even death, the Chief Constable of the West Midlands police, Sir Derrick Capper, asked the Depot Manager to close the gates (Beckett, 2009, p. 82). This activity was duly carried out in full view of the television cameras, with the upshot that 'the incident was made into a symbolic public surrender of the police to the power of the mass pickets' (Clutterbuck, 1981, p. 23).

The Heath government capitulated forthwith, immediately designating the miners a 'special case' and conceding a pay rise well in excess of the limits imposed by their hitherto strict incomes policy. More important still was the symbolic or psychological impact of the police 'surrender' at Saltley. Within Heath's own Conservative cabinet, his Secretary of State for Education and future prime minister in her own right, Mrs Margaret Thatcher, had also calculated the implications of the Saltley debacle:

> For me, what happened at Saltley took on no less significance than it did for the Left. I understood, as they did, that the struggle to bring trade unions properly within the rule of law would be decided not in the debating chamber of the House of Commons … but in and around the pits and factories where intimidation had been allowed to prevail. (Thatcher, 1995a, p. 218)

McCabe & Wallington (1988, p. 239) emphasise that: 'Contingency planning since 1972 has been directed towards mitigating the consequences of industrial strength exercised in the direct, Saltley manner.' Heath decided in 1972 to commission a review of the nation's civil contingency arrangements. This resulted in the establishment of the so-called Civil Contingencies Unit (CCU or 'Cuckoo'), a body equivalent in rank to a Cabinet Committee, which would henceforward be responsible for liaising with Chief Constables, military leaders and other government departments to offset the effects of any future stoppages in the essential industries (Hain, 1986, p. 127).

Meanwhile, in an attempt to resolve the serious deficit in police mutual aid provision highlighted by events at Saltley, the Association of Chief Police Officers (ACPO) and the Home Office decided, independently of any public debate or consultation with police authorities, to set up a National Reporting Centre (NRC) within Scotland Yard, whose remit would be to coordinate police mutual aid provision in the event of possible or actual large-scale public disorder (Kettle, 1985, p. 23).

A series of events spanning the next three years were also to have a crucial impact on reforms of the police system for responding to future public order crises. The most immediately significant of these was the decision by the NUM to impose an overtime ban (as of 12 November 1973) in defiance of a 7% limitation on pay increases under

'Stage III' of the Heath government's statutory income policy. Heath levelled a string of accusations that the NUM was intent on bringing down his government but these only served to harden the miners' attitudes (Allen, 1981, p. 235). Thus, at the end of January 1974, the union's membership voted by 81% to go on strike on 10 February. Heath responded pre-emptively on 7 February by calling a General Election three weeks hence, based on the slogan 'Firm Action for a Fair Britain' (Allen, 1981, p. 283).

The election resulted in a 'hung parliament', i.e. with no party having an outright majority of seats. Following an abortive attempt to forge a coalition with the Liberals, Heath resigned as Prime Minister, leaving the way for the Labour Party, under Harold Wilson, to form a minority government (Allen, 1981, p. 284). A repeat General Election on 10 October 1974 secured Labour a wafer-thin majority of three seats (and an overall total of 319). The Conservatives then staged a leadership contest in February 1975, in which Ted Heath was defeated by Thatcher (Allen, 1981).

The latter had evidently already taken heed of the political implications of the 1974 miners' strike, considering that:

> It was a frightening demonstration of the impotence of the police in the face of such disorder. The fall of Ted Heath's government after a general election precipitated by the 1973–4 miners' strike lent substance to the myth that the NUM had the power to make or break British Government, or at the very least the power to veto any power threatening their interests by preventing coal getting to the power stations. (Thatcher, 1995b, pp. 340–341)

Following Thatcher's election as Leader of the Opposition, the Conservative Party immediately began to consider how they might handle a future confrontation with the NUM, once they were returned to office. On 27 May 1978, *The Economist* magazine leaked a confidential Conservative Party document (the so-called Ridley Report) which purported to be the blueprint of a possible strategy for 'taking on' the miners. This document advised a future Conservative government to prepare for strike action by:

- Stockpiling coal reserves at power stations.
- Having a contingency plan for importing coal.
- Introducing dual oil- and coal-fired burning in power stations.
- Reducing social security benefits for strikers and their families.
- Setting up mobile police squads to thwart flying pickets, and obtaining sufficient numbers of 'reliable' non-union drivers who would be prepared to breach the picket lines (Waddington, 1992, p. 100).

The Conservatives were re-elected in 1979. Two years into Thatcher's term of office as Prime Minister, rioting occurred in several major English cities. These represented only one of four separate instances in which the NRC had been activated since its inception. In the relevant period, 30,000 officers were deployed to eight forces requiring mutual aid (Kettle, 1985, p. 25). Resulting improvements in the training and coordination of officers, and the provision of better equipment, meant that, by

1984, police forces nationwide were able to call upon 416 well-drilled mobile police support units totalling 13,500 officers (Kettle, 1985, pp. 29–30).

Writing one year prior to the 1984–1985 miners' strike, Jeffrey & Hennessy (1983, pp. 236–237) observed that the Saltley showdown with the miners was 'a demon still to be exorcised in the contingency planning community'. This was all due to change in the course of the year-long dispute on the issue of pit closures, which was embarked on by the majority of NUM members working in the key administrative 'Areas' of the industry (notably, Yorkshire, Durham, Scotland, Kent and South Wales), though not in Nottinghamshire and some parts of the North Derbyshire and Midlands Areas, where miners continued to work normally (Waddington *et al.*, 1991).

The NUM National Executive's decision not to call a national strike ballot of its members was seized on by a largely unsympathetic mass media and politicians of all parties as part of a 'virulent ideological onslaught' which championed the 'right to work' whilst castigating the strike as illegitimate and unconstitutional: Mrs Thatcher herself branded the NUM (alongside IRA terrorists and 'subversive' local governments) as part of the 'enemy within', thereby encouraging the harshest possible policing of the picket lines (Waddington, 1992, p. 104). Far from asserting their independence in the face of implicit and explicit forms of governmental pressure, chief constables in strike-bound areas of the country were outspoken in publicly endorsing the Cabinet's perspective (McCabe & Wallington, 1988, p. 134). All told, therefore:

> it became impossible for the police as a whole to avoid a distortion of priorities and for individual police officers it became more and more difficult to disentangle fact from prejudice in assessing those whom they were sent to police. (McCabe & Wallington, 1988, pp. 134–135)

The Battle of Orgreave and its legacy

Initially, conflict between the police and striking miners focused on the pit gates of Nottinghamshire and neighbouring coalfield Areas where flying pickets appealed to fellow NUM members to support their industrial action. However, South Yorkshire soon emerged as the epicentre of strike violence. There were major set-piece confrontations between miners and police outside NUM Executive Meetings in Sheffield city centre on 12 and 19 April (Waddington *et al.*, 1989). Neither of these achieved the severity or notoriety of subsequent clashes between police and pickets, in late May and early June, as the latter sought to deter convoys of coke leaving the Orgreave Coking Plant on the outskirts of Sheffield, whilst the former were keen to avoid any repetition of (and, preferably, exact revenge for) what had happened at Saltley (Waddington *et al.*, 1989).

The contrast between police attitudes at Saltley and those prevailing at Orgreave was evident virtually from the start when, on 27 May, Scargill (by now elevated to the position of NUM National President) was unceremoniously bundled to the floor by police officers, an outcome that would have been unthinkable just over 12 years earlier (Waddington *et al.*, 1989, p. 84). Outraged, Scargill quickly appeared on television news broadcasts, calling on the miners and their supporters to turn

Orgreave into 'another Saltley' (Waddington, 1992, p. 105). The following day was Bank Holiday Monday, but when hundreds of pickets duly assembled the day after that, they came up against resolute contingents of police officers, drafted in from 11 separate forces:

> One crowd of pickets was prevented from getting within a mile of the gates by lines of police officers, while a second group, who had managed to assemble earlier opposite the gates, was charged by police horses and dog handlers. When the convoys of coke lorries arrived, any attempt at picketing was rendered ineffectual: whenever serious pushing was exerted against police lines, snatch squads were instantly deployed. Sensing the futility of their actions, some miners threw stones. This was answered by the production of full-length riot shields and, as the throwing intensified, mounted horses with baton-wielding riders were sent in. (Waddington, 1992, p. 105)

The treatment meted out to pickets appeared vengeful and undifferentiating, prompting retaliatory volleys of stones and other missiles by men now united in anger and indignation due to the fact that their 'right to picket' was being so flagrantly denied (Waddington et al., 1989, pp. 84–86).

The most serious day of such violence occurred on 18 June, when 93 arrests were made as 10,000 pickets faced up to 4000 police. According to Mawby, images of the so-called Battle of Orgreave, including television news broadcasts of a police officer 'repeatedly aiming blows at a cowering picket', constitute an 'enduring legacy, symbolising the breakdown of order and the relationship between police and miners during the strike' (Mawby, 2002, p. 112). Mawby quotes from a television interview in which the then Chief Constable of South Yorkshire, Peter Wright, acknowledged how the truncheoning incident captured on film was a public relations setback for the force, insofar as it 'gave credibility to all other statements of police misbehaviour which were rife' (Mawby, 2002, p. 112).

Mawby's account does not adequately convey the extent to which violent police conduct at Orgreave appears to have been premeditated, or the degree to which the so-called battle was so patently one-sided. News coverage of the events of 18 June lent credence to police claims that any aggression by officers had been meted out only in response to the riotous behaviour of the pickets, and that the fighting had 'ebbed and flowed' as befitted an 'equal contest' of such nature (Masterman, 1985; Waddington, 1992). However, academic analyses—and, more especially, evidence produced at the subsequent High Court trials of 14 pickets alleged to have 'rioted' on 18 June—seriously questioned the veracity of such an interpretation (Jackson & Wardle, 1986).

East et al. (1985, pp. 309–310) claim that the mass presence of miners at Orgreave was the result of a carefully orchestrated police roadblock strategy which was used, not for the customary purpose of *preventing* access to the plant, but on this occasion to *encourage it*: 'In fact it would seem that the police intended that Orgreave would be a "battle" where, as a result of their preparation and organisation, they would "defeat" the pickets.' Defence solicitors at the Orgreave trials made reference to a secret ACPO Tactical Options Manual which showed that many aspects of the police conduct exhibited on 18 June (e.g. the use of police horses to scatter the crowd, the frightening and provocative beating of truncheons on riot shields, and the use of short-shield units to 'incapacitate' missile-throwers or ringleaders by striking them about the arms, legs and torso) were intrinsic to official policy (East *et al.*, 1985, p. 312; McCabe & Wallington, 1988, pp. 49–50). This suggested that, far from being purely reactive, as media reports had indicated, police aggression at Orgreave was actually *calculated and proactive*.

This inference was given further credence by the production, as part of the case for the defence, of the official police video of the day's events on 18 June, the only visual record of what happened in its entirety. The film not only cast doubt on the plausibility of police statements of evidence—including the key recollections of the Assistant Chief Constable who commanded the police operation—but also showed how the 'violent but unequal' struggle on the day in question had actually been instigated by the police:

> There is little evidence of serious stone-throwing before the first police advance. ... But as the official police film of the encounter makes clear (contrary to the image of much of the media coverage), there were no 'scenes of violence' before mounted officers rode into the pickets and drove them away from the picket line. Only after they had been attacked in this way did the pickets retaliate. Then barricades were built and set alight and missiles hurled at the advancing police. In the end, however, the pickets were no match for them. They abandoned the field on that day and never again attempted battle at Orgreave. (McCabe & Wallington, 1988, pp. 76–77)

McCabe and Wallington maintain that: 'For the police it was a victory—but a dangerous one', in light of television coverage of their 'violent treatment of fleeing miners' (p. 77). Following their 'defeat' at Orgreave, striking miners focused their attention on picketing their own pits in response to the National Coal Board's 'back to work' campaign (Green, 1990, p. 43). Meanwhile, the police's mastery of the NUM's 'flying picket' strategy gave impetus to their own policy of escorting strike-breakers back into the mines—a practice deemed reprehensible by the generally pro-strike communities of South Yorkshire, whose residents knew that it was impossible, in the absence of the wider workforce, for the handfuls of returning miners to be given any productive work to do. It was therefore evident to them that the police were giving 'systematic priority to achieving the objectives of one party to an industrial dispute, to the detriment of normal police services, through a mistaken assessment of their priorities or in response to pressure, or both' (McCabe & Wallington, 1988, p. 132). Thus,

> Immense ill-will was generated, especially in those closely knit mining communities where feelings of solidarity were outraged by the return of individual miners often not themselves resident in the immediate community. The consequent influx of pickets and police was a high price, paid by the community, for the individual's exercise of his freedom to go to work. The ill-will against the police was undoubtedly compounded by inexcusable conduct by some police officers, but the very exercise of providing police protection was enough. (McCabe & Wallington, 1988, p. 132)

In many such communities, e.g. Maltby (Rotherham) and Grimethorpe (Barnsley), local residents complained of siege-like conditions being imposed on them by marauding police units, principally from the Metropolitan and Greater Manchester constabularies who, having been billeted nearby, entered such villages in search of revenge and retribution (Waddington *et al.*, 1989). Deep-seated feelings of alienation were compounded by the Chief Constable of South Yorkshire's refusal to soften his approach in the face of the local democratic pressure applied by his Police Committee (Spencer, 1985), while anti-police sentiments were vindicated and reinforced both by the collapse of the Orgreave 'riot' trial and the force's subsequent out of court settlement in 1991 of £500,000 in damages to 39 miners arrested on 18 June, who had sued them for 'assault, wrongful arrest, malicious prosecution and false imprisonment' (Milne, 1995, p. 24). Thus, as Mawby justifiably maintains, a huge rift was created between SYP and the county's mining communities: 'Whilst nationally the strike is regarded as a key stage in the politicisation of the police service, at a local level in South Yorkshire its lasting effect was on the relationship between local people and local police' (2002, p. 114).

The Hillsborough Stadium disaster and its aftermath

In much the same way that confrontations between miners and police had served to undermine relations between SYP and large areas of its constituency, so too did the Hillsborough stadium disaster of 15 April 1989 have an enduring and catastrophic effect on public confidence in the force and on corresponding perceptions of its legitimacy.

This tragedy occurred in the context of an FA (Football Association) Cup semi-final between Liverpool and Nottingham Forest, occurring at the neutral venue of Sheffield Wednesday's Hillsborough football ground. The Leppings Lane end of the stadium (positioned behind one of the two goal-lines) had been allocated exclusively to Liverpool supporters but, with the kick-off fast approaching, many of them had still not passed through the turnstiles and taken up their places on the terracing (Scraton, 1999, p. 282).

All too quickly, a dangerous crush developed in which police on horseback struggled to break free and many fans experienced difficulty breathing. A senior officer present therefore radioed the SYP match commander, Chief Superintendent David Duckenfield, who, having had his attention drawn to closed-circuit television pictures available in the police control box located inside the stadium, acceded to his colleague's request to throw open an exit gate in a bid to relieve the pressure. Some 2000 fans immediately spilled down a 1-in-6 gradient tunnel and into two central spectator pens positioned behind the goal, which were already packed full of Liverpool supporters:

> With twice the number of people on the steps, compression was immediate. Faces were jammed against the perimeter fence, people went down underfoot and then, near the front of pen 3, a barrier collapsed resulting in a tangled mass of bodies. (Scraton, 1999, p. 282)

The match commander failed initially to appreciate the severity of the situation and, therefore, had no reason to redirect junior colleagues who were still following instructions not to open perimeter gates into the pens unless told otherwise by a senior officer. The resulting delay compounded the unfolding tragedy. Despite the heroic efforts of those fans who employed advertising hoardings as makeshift stretchers on which to rush the hapless victims down the pitch into the Sheffield Wednesday gymnasium, no fewer than 96 people died (Scraton, 1999).

In his immediate briefing of the Football Association's Chief Executive, Chief Superintendent Duckenfield, alleged that the catastrophe had occurred as a result of Liverpool supporters collectively forcing their way through the forbidden exit gate, thereby creating the fatal 'inrush' cost so many lives. As Scraton (2004) points out, 'Within minutes this version of events was broadcast worldwide. ... Thus, Liverpool fans were responsible for the deaths of "their own" (p. 184). The lens of hooliganism was firmly in place.' This distortion of the truth was accentuated by subsequent off-the-record police briefings which soon formed the foundation of press reports that hooligan Liverpool supporters had threatened and attacked emergency personnel who were in the process of treating victims, and even urinated on police officers who were providing mouth-to-mouth resuscitation to stricken civilians (Jemphrey & Berrington, 2000, p. 285).

A subsequent judicial inquiry (Taylor, 1989) laid the blame for the disaster squarely at the feet of senior match-day officers, who had 'frozen' on the day and failed to exhibit the 'qualities of leadership to be expected of their rank'. Chief Superintendent Duckenfield was singled out for particular criticism on the grounds that his decision-making capacity appeared to have collapsed and that he had falsely attributed blame for the disaster to the Liverpool supporters. The following December, SYP acknowledged its culpability by paying out damages to the bereaved (Scraton, 2004, pp. 188–189). However, the failure by various governmental legal bodies to take punitive action against individual officers or SYP per se has left relatives of the victims campaigning to this day for justice to be done (e.g. BBC News, 2009).

Post-Hillsborough developments

The combined impact of the Orgreave and Hillsborough debacles was undoubtedly profound. According to Mawby (2002), 'the image of SYP was tarnished and the force turned its gaze inwards, battening down the hatches and treating outsiders such as the media with great suspicion. The force had arguably reached its nadir' (p. 116). A key point of transition was the retirement of Peter Wright in May 1990 and the appointment as his successor of the Oxford-educated Richard Wells, a former Deputy Assistant Commissioner from the Metropolitan Police with 26 years' experience in media, community relations, training and operational command. Unquestionably, Mr Wells was taking over a force 'which was beleaguered and dispirited. [It] was demoralized as a result of a series of events which had damaged its reputation, confidence and integrity' (Mawby, 2002, p. 116). Thus, as the Chairman of the South Yorkshire Police Authority explained at the time, their main purpose in appointing Mr Wells was to 'win back public support and to restore confidence in the police' in the wake of the miners' strike and Hillsborough (quoted in Mawby, 2002, p. 116).

Wells duly set about this task by attempting to transform SYP's image, culture and identity. Following a countywide consultation exercise involving both the general public and members of his own organisation, he eventually produced a new document, a *Statement of Force Purpose and Values*, which established a novel philosophy regarding the way that SYP would henceforward discharge its duties and conduct itself:

> It exhorts staff to strive to act with 'integrity', to be 'honest, courteous and tactful' and to 'use persuasion, common sense and good humour'. It emphasizes also that staff should display honesty, humanity and compassion, be willing to listen, to try new ways of working and to admit failings. It is, in sum, a statement which both provides guidance to members of SYP and also gives people expectations concerning how they will be treated in their dealings with the force. (Mawby, 2002, p. 119)

Mawby helpfully provides an example of the way in which the force philosophy was incorporated into its methods of managing public order, by focusing on SYP's handling of a demonstration later that month in Sheffield city centre by Reclaim the Streets (a coalition of environmentalist and environmental groups). A previous Reclaim the Streets demonstration held earlier that year in Leeds had been confrontational, due largely to the uncompromising approach of West Yorkshire Police, who physically prevented the protesters from erecting a makeshift 'sound system' out of scaffolding in the middle of the street. In his briefing to the 60 SYP officers involved in the operation, the Gold commander urged them to act 'in a professional manner in accordance with our statement of purpose and values' (quoted in Mawby, 2002, p. 160). Generally speaking, the command team called on colleagues to 'police the event in an unobtrusive and relaxed manner' and 'to adopt a non-aggressive, "softly, softly" approach. Officers were instructed *not* to try and prevent the erection of scaffolding. Instead, they should just 'let it happen and don't sully the name of South Yorkshire Police' (Mawby, 2002, p. 160). The upshot was that the event was almost universally peaceful.

A corresponding shift was detectable in terms of SYP's policy of communicating via the media. The deliberately 'closed approach' characterising force–media relations in the immediate wake of Hillsborough was supplanted by one of 'openness and honesty' in an attempt to 'rebuild the external image and internal identity of the force and to seek to re-legitimate it' (Mawby, 2002, p. 186). Mawby detects that, whilst the force's image and self-assuredness had substantially improved by the time he finished his fieldwork, such progress continued to be hampered by the legacy of Hillsborough (Mawby, 2002). The resulting need for ongoing commitment to the core statement and reparation of community relations is further evident in a study, by Waddington (Waddington, 2007, 2011a; Waddington & King, 2007) of SYP's handling of protest accompanying the G8 Justice and Home Affairs Ministerial Meeting in Sheffield in June 2005.

Waddington's analysis acknowledges how, in the wake in the wake of confrontations between police and protesters at the 1999 World Trade Organisation summit meeting in Seattle, North American and European police forces have resorted to a broadly similar range of tactical approaches for dealing with 'transgressive' (unruly and uncooperative) protesters, which Noakes & Gillham (2006) refer to as *strategic incapacitation*. Finding themselves increasingly faced with 'non-hierarchical' ('leaderless') groups whose 'transgressive', anti-systemic protest repertoires defy cooperation, the police have resorted with increasing regularity to such tactics as the creation of no-protest zones, the use of containment ('kettling'), preventative arrests and surveillance to selectively disable and, arguably, repress collective dissent. This trend is exemplified by the fortification mentality surrounding the protection of the Internationally Protected Persons (IPPs) attending world summit meetings (Noakes & Gillham, 2006). Increasingly, such IPPs have been 'shielded' and/or isolated to such an extent that accompanying protest activity has been rendered ineffectual (Waddington, 2007).

There was a distinct possibility that this might also have happened in Sheffield. Here, however, the force recognized an obligation to resist steadfastly Sheffield City Council's preference for a 'zero tolerance' approach with regard to any forms of planned protest. The latter was not only nervous about ensuring the safety and security of the visiting dignitaries (including the future French President, Nicolas Sarkozy) and their entourages, but was also very eager to project Sheffield as tourism and conference centre of potential world renown. Ultimately, a compromise was achieved whereby demonstrators were allowed to congregate in special protest compounds that were close enough to the summit venues to enable them to let their feelings be heard but not close enough to enable any acts of violence to occur. The Chief Constable of SYP emphasized in interview that his Gold strategy for the event involved giving equal priority to 'facilitating the lawful business of the summit' and 'facilitating lawful protest'. Local political sensibilities were obviously fundamental to this approach—as was his adherence to the force's post-1980s philosophy:

> This is why, in fact, I don't believe in having a national public order police. I take the decisions about public order in the G8 in the light of the fact that I'm still going to be here the day after. I've been here the year before, so I've had time to meet the community, talk to leaders, get to know the MPs a bit, get to know the councillors, appear in front of them and tell them what I'm gonna do, and make my decisions on the basis of very firm local roots. *Because we do remember the legends of the NUM dispute and the stories of the Metropolitan Police and we are all very anxious to put those legends to bed.* (quoted in Waddington, 2007, p. 149, original emphasis)

Aside from a minor incident in which a small number of anarchists were thwarted in their attempt to penetrate police lines surrounding a ministerial meeting, the only notable instance of disorder occurred when police corralled some two hundred people who suddenly engaged on an impromptu march away from the 'approved' protest site and used 'snatch squads' to make a total of seven arrests. This specific intervention was subsequently criticised by marchers as an unnecessary, though uncharacteristic, over-reaction by police support units drafted in from Greater Manchester to patrol the periphery of the protest (Waddington, 2007, p. 158). Interview respondents were generally complementary about the tolerant and accommodating attitude exhibited by SYP during the three days of the protest, which was in stark contrast to the uncompromising stance adopted by Derbyshire police at the forum of G8

Environment and Development Ministers, held three months earlier in Derby (Waddington, 2007, pp. 139, 158–159).

This continuing shift towards a more permissive style of public order policing was further apparent in SYP's handling of a more recent protest organised by the 'Sheffield Anti Cuts Alliance' (SACA) outside the two-day Liberal Democrats' Spring Party Conference in Sheffield in March 2011. Following the 'Lib Dem's' formation of a Coalition Government with the Conservatives after the 2010 General Election, the party had attracted nationwide public and political criticism for jointly endorsing a programme of massive public spending cuts and approving a large increase in student higher education fees—a policy it had pledged itself opposed to in the run-up to the election (BBC News, 2010). The resulting sense of betrayal was keenly felt in Sheffield, a city with two major universities and a high dependency on public sector employment, and in which Mr Clegg was MP for Sheffield Hallam (e.g. *Sheffield Telegraph*, 10 December 2010).

By this time, many of the recommendations set out in the 'Adapting to Protest' reports had been incorporated into the revised Association of Chief Police Officers, Association of Chief Police Officers in Scotland, and National Police Improvement Agency (ACPO/ACPOS/NOIA) (2010) *Manual of Guidance on Keeping the Peace*, a document signed off by the Chief Constable of South Yorkshire in his capacity as ACPO Lead for the Uniformed Operations Business Area. Interviews undertaken with senior SYP officers responsible for the force planning and management of the anti-Lib Dem protest (Waddington, 2011b) show how their thinking was primarily influenced by:

- The now familiar preoccupation with enhancing the city's commercial and tourist potential.
- SYP's recent tradition of tolerating protest.
- Various prescriptions set out in 'Keeping the Peace' (notably, those advocating a commitment to facilitating protest, operating a 'no surprises' approach to police–protester interaction, and meeting legal obligations under the European Convention on Human Rights to safeguard lives, property and the right to peacefully protest).
- The social psychological and practical rationales (namely, the Elaborated Social Identity Model and Swedish Dialogue Policing approach, respectively) which extensively underpin the Adapting to Protest recommendations for best practice (Stott, 2009).

Finally, and not surprisingly, the Chief Constable's formal role within ACPO was recognised by SYP officers as an additional symbolic incentive to conform to principles embodied in the *Manual of Guidance*.

As part of its commitment to balancing such considerations, SPY chose to erect a protective 6–8 feet high, concrete-based, steel-mesh barrier around the conference venue of Sheffield City Hall. One purpose of this barrier was to promote the safety and security of conference delegates while facilitating the right to peaceful protest. A secondary reason for its existence was that it would help to eliminate the opportunity for police and protesters to come directly into contact and engage in confrontation. In keeping with the principles and modes of best practice established by proponents of the ESIM and Dialogue Policing model, SYP deployed an ad-hoc 15-person Police Liaison Team (PLT), comprising trained negotiators and officers who had been specially selected on the basis of acknowledged communication skills. The specialist negotiators were given the task of liaising with protest organisers prior to the conference in a bid to explain and justify the police approach, gather relevant information regarding the likely numbers and motives of participants, allay any possible concerns the organisers might raise, and do their best to accommodate the objectives of the protest.

Then, during the two days of the demonstration, all members of the PLT (who were clearly recognisable in their 'soft hats' and pale blue tabards) mingled amidst the crowd, good-naturedly working in conjunction with a Social Media Cell to communicate police intentions to the public, rectify possible misperceptions on both sides, and occasionally provide 'risk assessments' to the remotely located Silver Command team regarding the current moods of the crowd and its actual or possible reactions to particular forms of police activity (McSeveny & Waddington, 2011).

The overall effectiveness of this 'Operation Obelisk' can be gauged by the fact that, during the two days of protest (involving gatherings of 800 and 5000 people), there was only one arrest, which occurred when a demonstrator ignited a flare and scaled the security barrier, whereupon he was briskly, though not forcibly, led away by awaiting officers. Interviews undertaken afterwards with representatives of SACA and the National Union of Students endorsed the general impression of ten participant observers of the protest that SYP had been exceedingly tolerant of behaviour that may well have been perceived as 'over-boisterous' on other occasions, and that they seemed genuinely intent on facilitating protest (McSeveny & Waddington, 2011; Waddington, 2011b).

Conclusions

A host of recent reports (HAC, 2009; HMCIC 2009a, 2009b) were openly critical of what they clearly regarded as the potentially provocative, and arguably repressive, police public order tactics employed in relation to the anti-G20 demonstration in London on 1 April 2009. Such reports were equally disapproving of the blatantly disingenuous way in which the MPS tried to suppress the true details of the circumstances in which Mr Ian Tomlinson had died as a result of unprovoked police violence.

The Chief Inspector of Constabulary's (HMCIC, 2009b) review of public order policing heralds a potentially new approach to the policing of such events. His report sensibly recognises that police crowd control interventions are liable to cause or, possibly, aggravate conflict whenever they appear unreasonable and/or indiscriminate according to those present. It emphasises the need for police officers to be more accountable to the public (e.g. by clearly displaying their identification numbers); for them to communicate more effectively and sympathetically with protesters who are temporarily trapped in 'kettles'; and, above all, for them to do their utmost to facilitate *meaningful* protest.

This paper has provided a clear endorsement of such recommendations. It has shown how at Orgreave in particular SYP were spurred on by a hostile and stigmatising climate of opinion against the miners (and, in all probability, by the need to exact revenge for the humiliation incurred at Saltley) into perpetrating undifferentiating acts of violence and flouting the right to picket. Such activities were notably absent from the examples provided from 1997 and 2011, in which SYP were clearly committed to facilitating the objectives of those gathered in protest. There are clearly important parallels to be drawn between the political fallout arising from the MPS's handling of the anti-G20 protest and the self-inflicted damage incurred by SYP as a result of the Orgreave and Hillsborough debacles. In both cases, tremendous harm was done to the reputations and public standing of these forces due not only to the misconduct of their officers, but also to corresponding attempts to divert responsibility onto the victims of such actions.

The type of measures advocated by the HMCIC reports clearly resonate with the strategic orientation now favoured in South Yorkshire, where a more accommodating and less confrontational approach to crowd management appears to be reaping dividends, both in terms of achieving orderly expressions of protest and in the gradual restoration of public confidence in the police. It therefore seems reasonable to suggest that in their future attempts to win back public faith in the police's impartiality and to avoid future confrontation, the MPS and other British forces would be well advised to adopt the kind of strategic and tactical approach recently implemented in Sheffield.

References

Allen, V. L. (1981) *The militancy of British miners* (Shipley, Moor Press).

Association of Chief Police Officers, Association of Chief Police Officers in Scotland, and National Police Improvement Agency (ACPO/ACPOS/NOIA) (2010) *Manual of guidance on keeping the peace* (Wyboston, National Police Improvement Agency).

BBC News (2009) Hillsborough justice bid goes on, BBC News, 14 April. Available online at: http://news.bbc.co.uk/1/hi/england/7998231.stm/.

BBC News (2010) Nick Clegg regrets signing anti-tuition fees pledge, BBC News, 11 November. Available online at: http://www.bbc.co.uk/news/uk-politics-11732787/.

Beckett, A. (2009) *When the lights went out: what really happened to Britain in the seventies* (London, Faber & Faber).

Beckett, F. & Hencke, D. (2009) *Marching to the fault line: the 1984 miners' strike and the death of industrial Britain* (London, Constable).

Clutterbuck, R. (1981) *The media and political violence* (2nd edn) (London, Macmillan).

East, R., Power, H. & Thomas, P. A. (1985) The state v the people: lessons from the coal dispute, *Journal of Law and Society*, 12(3), 305–319.

Green, P. (1990) *The enemy without: policing and class consciousness in the miners' strike* (Buckingham, Open University Press).

Greer, C. & McLaughlin, E. (2010) We predict a riot? Public order policing, new media environments and the rise of the citizen journalist, *British Journal of Criminology*, 50(6), 1041–1059.

Hain, P. (1986) *Political strikes: the state and trade unionism in Britain* (New York, NY, Viking).

Her Majesty's Chief Inspectorate of Constabulary (HMCIC) (2009a) *Adapting to protest (interim report)* (London, HMIC).

Her Majesty's Chief Inspectorate of Constabulary (HMCIC) (2009b) *Adapting to protest: nurturing the British model of policing* (London, HMIC).

House of Commons Home Affairs Committee (HAC) (2009) *Policing of the G20 protests: eighth report of the Session 2008–09* (London, The Stationery Office (TSO)).

Jackson, B. & Wardle, T. (1986) *The Battle for Orgreave* (Brighton, Vanson Wardle).

Jeffrey, K. & Hennessy, P. (1983) *States of emergency: British governments and strikebreaking since 1919* (London, Routledge & Kegan Paul).

Jemphrey, A. & Berrington, E. (2000) Surviving the media: Hillsborough, Dunblane and the press, *Journalism Studies*, 1(3), 469–484.

Kettle, M. (1985) The National Reporting Centre and the 1984 miners' strike, in: B. Fine & R. Millar (Eds) *Policing the miners' strike* (London, Cobden), 23–33.

Masterman, L. (1985) The Battle of Orgreave, in: L. Masterman (Ed.) *Television mythologies: stars, shows and signs* (London, Comedia/Routledge).

Mawby, R. C. (2002) *Policing images: policing, communication and legitimacy* (Cullompten, UK, Willan).

McCabe, S. & Wallington, P. (1988) *The police, public order and civil liberties: legacies of the miners' strike* (London, Routledge, Chapman & Hall).

McSeveny, K. & Waddington, D. P. (2011) Up close and personal: the interplay between information technology and human agency in the policing of the 2011 Sheffield anti-Lib Dem protests, in: B. Akhgar & S. Yates (Eds) *Intelligence management (knowledge driven frameworks for combating terrorism and organised crime)* (New York, NY, Springer), 199–212.

Milne, S. (1995) *The enemy within: the secret war against the miners* (London, Pan).

Noakes, J. A. & Gillham, P. F. (2006) Aspects of the 'new penology' in the police response to major political protests in the United States, in: D. della Porta, A. Peterson & H. Reiter (Eds) *The policing of transnational protest* (Aldershot, Ashgate), 97–115.

Pelling, H. (1976) *A history of British trade unionism* (Harmondsworth, Penguin).

Rosie, M. & Gorringe, H. (2009) What a difference a death makes: protest, policing and the press at the G20, *Sociological Research Online*. Available online at: http://www.socresonline.org.uk/14/5/4.html/.

Scargill, A. (1974) The new unionism (interview with Robin Blackburn). *New Left Review*, 24(July/August), 3–35.

Scraton, P. (1999) Policing with contempt: the degrading of truth and denial of justice in the aftermath of the Hillsborough disaster, *Journal of Law and Society*, 26(3), 273–297.

Scraton, P. (2004) Death on the terraces: the contexts and injustices of the 1989 Hillsborough disaster, *Soccer and Society*, 5(2), 183–200.

Sheffield Telegraph (2010, December 10) Students vent fury on Clegg, *Sheffield Telegraph*. Available online at: http://www.sheffieldtelegraph.co.uk/news/local/students_vent_fury_on_clegg_1_2846763

Spencer, S. (1985) The eclipse of the police authority, in: B. Fine & R. Millar (Eds) *Policing the miners' strike* (London, Lawrence & Wishart), 34–53.

Stott, C. (2009) *Crowd psychology and public order policing: an overview of scientific theory and evidence. Submission to the HMIC of Policing of Public Protest Review Team* (Liverpool, University of Liverpool).

Taylor, Rt. Hon Lord Justice (1989) *The Hillsborough Stadium disaster, 15 April 1989: interim report*. Home Office Cmnd 765 (London, HMSO).

Thatcher, M. (1995a) *The path to power* (London, HarperCollins).

Thatcher, M. (1995b) *The Downing Street years* (London, HarperCollins).

Turner, A. W. (2008) *Crisis? What crisis? Britain in the 1970s* (London, Aurum).

Waddington, D. P. (1992) *Contemporary issues in public disorder: a comparative and historical approach* (London, Routledge).

Waddington, D. P. (2007) *Policing public disorder: theory and practice* (Cullompten, UK, Willan).

Waddington, D. P. (2011a) Policing the British G8 protests: a contextualized analysis, in: T. D. Madensen & J. Knutsson (Eds) *Preventing crowd violence* (London, Lynne Rienner), 95–114.

Waddington, D. P. (2011b) A 'kinder blue': analysing the police management of the Sheffield anti-'Lib Dem' protest of March 2011. Unpublished paper (Sheffield, Sheffield Hallam University).

Waddington, D. P., Jones, K. & Critcher, C. (1989) *Flashpoints: studies in public disorder* (London, Routledge).

Waddington, D. P. & King, M. (2007) The impact of the local: police public order tactics and strategy during the G8 Justice and Home Affairs Ministerial Meeting in Sheffield, England, June 2005, *Mobilization*, 12(4), 417–430.

Waddington, D. P., Wykes, M. & Critcher, C. (1991) *Split at the seams? Community, continuity and change after the 1984-5 coal dispute* (Milton Keynes, Open University Press).

Post G20: The challenge of change, implementing evidence-based public order policing

James Hoggett[a]* and Clifford Stott[bc]

[a] *University of the West of England, Frenchay Campus, Bristol, UK*
[b]*CCM Consultancy*
[c]*Section of Sports Science, Aarhus University, Denmark*

In the wake of the 2011 'riots', public order policing tactics in England and Wales have once again been brought into question. Yet, the riots came two years since police regulatory authorities in the UK called for fundamental reforms to the policing of public order. Questions are raised about why the change called for appears to have been so slow and what can be done to assist reform. This paper suggests that developing an evidence- based policing approach within the field of public order policing to inform police decision-making would provide the answers. By doing so, the paper addresses some of the possible barriers to implementing evidence-based policing in public order and calls for police academic partnership to overcome these to make 'change' an ongoing reality.

THE 2011 RIOTS AND A CRISIS OF POLICING

The large-scale urban 'disorder' throughout England early in August 2011 posed a serious challenge for understanding how crowds behave and how they should be policed. In particular, in the midst of the crisis the British Prime Minister David Cameron suggested the use of distance weaponry such as water cannon and plastic baton rounds. The implication was that these should be seen as available tactics for a police force under fire for somehow 'going soft' on the rioters. Sir Hugh Orde, President of the Association of Chief Police Officers, robustly rejected these as 'the wrong tactic, in the wrong circumstances' and that 'excessive force will destroy our model of policing in the long term' (Orde, 2011). None the less, the Prime Minister during a subsequent speech in his constituency of Witney pointed out how the riots reflected the need for fundamental police reforms.

Urban unrest and the 'crisis' it poses for policing are not a new phenomenon. For example, as recently as 2009, Nick Hardwick, Chair of the Independent Police Complaints Commission (IPCC), speaking after the death of a member of the public during the G20 protests in London in April 2009 demanded tougher political accountability. He warned that the police should remember that they were 'the servants not the masters' of the people (Hinsliff & Syal, 2009). Indeed, the G20 protests in London and the subsequent inquiries and reports can be viewed as somewhat of a watershed in public order policing in mainland UK. Arguably, the most important outcome of which was the commissioning and publication of the report 'Adapting to Protest—Nurturing the British Model of Policing' by Her Majesty's Inspectorate of Constabulary (HMIC, 2009).

The report identified that the time was right to fundamentally reform public order policing within England and Wales so that it was capable of adapting to the 'changing face' of protest in the 21st Century. However, its focus on change was framed by a commitment to a stability of underlying philosophy; 'how best should the police as a service adapt to the modern day demands of public order policing while retaining the core values of the British policing model' (HMIC, 2009, p. 5). The report also recognised that the changes it recommended could 'only happen with the consistent and transparent support of local authorities, professional bodies and the Home Office' (HMIC, 2009, p. 13). In making this statement, the report identifies a key assertion of this paper; that is, in order to adapt and develop, public order policing must work in stronger partnership with science to develop an evidence-based approach.

Evidence-based policing

Sherman (1998) identified how the profession of medicine was based upon a commitment to strong scientific evidence and that a similar approach would prove invaluable for the professionalisation of policing. Sherman (1998) noted that, 'of all the ideas about policing, one stands out as the most powerful force for change: police practices should be based on scientific evidence about what works best' (p. 2). In short, evidence-based policing (EBP) is an approach that uses peer-reviewed and scientifically validated research to guide and evaluate policy and practice.

It seems self evident that such an approach may have a lot to offer the police. However, research suggests that the development of an evidence-based approach is not straightforward (Austin, 2003; Chancer & Mclaughlin, 2007; Foster & Bailey, 2010; Murji, 2010). Bullock and Tilley (2009) identify three reasons why. First, there can be disputes about the nature of evidence. Second, there can be issues concerning the availability of evidence. Third, there can be organisational constraints (such as cultural resistance) that may prevent or slow implementation.

THE NATURE OF EVIDENCE

Within the EBP literature, there has been much debate about what constitutes evidence (Davies, Nutley, & Smith, 2000; Hollin, 2008; Nutley, Walter, & Davies, 2002; Sherman, Farrington, Welsh, & Mackenzie, 2002; Tilley, 2009). Initially, experimental methods were recognised as the most suitable way of providing the necessary scientific rigour from which to determine effective police practice (Sherman, 1984, 1992, 1998; Sherman et al., 2002). At first glance, public order policing may therefore not appear to be an arena particularly suited to an EBP approach as scientific enquiry on the policing of crowds has been derived from a diverse range of methods, contexts, disciplines, and countries (Button & Brierley, 2002; De Lint, 2005; Della Porta, & Reiter, 1998, Jefferson, 1990; Sheptycki, 2005; Stott, Adang, Livingstone, & Schrieber, 2007, 2008a; Stott, Livingstone, & Hoggett, 2008b; D. Waddington, 2007; PAJ Waddington, 1994b).

A central barrier for an EBP approach may therefore be that the background science lacks the epistemological coherence and consistency needed for the approach to become established within the UK. However, this issue of 'suitable' or 'acceptable' evidence in EBP mirrors wider ontological and epistemological debates within the philosophy of social science. These debates have traditionally focused on the issue of the 'incommensurability' between the different dominating paradigms (e.g. Kuhn, 1970; Von Wright, 1971). More recently, however, these distinctions and incompatibilities have begun to be questioned and addressed, particularly within the social sciences (e.g. Campbell & Fiske, 1959; Waszak & Sines, 2003; Johnson & Onwuegbuzie, 2004; Brannen, 2005). The nature of the evidence debate in EPB therefore reflects one of the central problems of all scientific enquiries, that of epistemological uncertainty.

By recognising that this uncertainty always exists, the police—like science itself—need to understand that this does not prevent anyone from utilising scientific knowledge. Evidence-based practice is not some kind of panacea for uncertainty, a bipolar decision between 'truth' and 'falsity'. Rather, EBP is an approach that couples the best currently available evidence and theory with operational practice but at the same time develops capability to test these theories within police operational practice by using widely accepted techniques of scientific inquiry. In other words, the development of evidence-based public order policing is not just a matter of mapping what science already knows onto public order police practice but also working with scientists on an ongoing basis to develop new knowledge gathered through scientific method.

THE AVAILABILITY OF EVIDENCE

The second barrier to EBP is a potential lack of scientific theory and evidence; a barrier that this paper will assert is not present in the domain of public order policing. A range of sociological and criminological research has examined the policing of labour disputes, political protests, environmental movements, and sporting events among other types of crowds (e.g. Della Porta & Reiter, 1998; PAJ Waddington, 1987, 1993a, 1993b, 1994a, 1994b; Waddington, Jones, & Critcher, 1989; Waddington, 2007). P. A. J. Waddington (1998) emphasises that crowd events are seldom policed solely on the basis of stringent pre-planning or rigid adherence to a single set of tactical and strategic options. Public order operational deployment usually involves a variety of contingency plans that consider different geographical spaces, categorisation of those present, and other temporal and dynamic developments.

Nonetheless, the literature identifies substantial historical changes in policing practices and policy in North America and Europe since the Second World War (McCarthy & McPhail, 1998; Hall & De Lint, 2003). Changes that reflect movement from reactive policing grounded in the threat and use of force—what is generally termed as an 'escalated force' model—to a more preventative consent-based approach that relies initially on communication and facilitation—or what is generally termed a 'negotiated management' model (McPhail, Schweingruber, & McCarthy, 1998). Moreover, there is general consensus that the policing of crowd events in Western Europe and Northern America have moved away from a reliance on overt force (Della Porta & Reiter, 1998; Waddington & King, 2005).

King and Waddington (2004) suggest that this trend in public order policing in the West is the result of growing police recognition that police actions can negatively impact on crowd behaviour whereby it is possible to identify 'what may loosely be described as an apparent increase in police sensitivity concerning the possible impact of their actions' (King & Brearley, 1996, p. 102). In other words, there is a growing understanding and recognition within police forces of the dynamics through which their interactions with crowds can increase disorder and that such knowledge may be leading to changes in operational practice (King & Waddington, 2004, 2005; Waddington & King, 2005).

Within psychological research on crowd dynamics, the potentially escalatory role that police action may have has long been identified (Drury & Reicher, 2000; Reicher, 1996a; Stott & Drury, 2000, Stott, Hoggett, & Pearson, 2012). Central to this research is the Elaborated Social Identity Model (ESIM) of crowd behaviour (Drury & Reicher, 2000; Reicher, 1996b; Stott & Reicher, 1998a). Drawing from social identity (Tajfel & Turner, 1979) and self-categorisation (Turner, Hogg, Oakes, Reicher, & Wetherell, 1987) theories, ESIM proposes that collective behaviour during a crowd event is made possible through the shared salience among crowd participants of a common and socially determined identity (Reicher, 1982, 1984, 1987).

Both the form and content of a crowd's identity is viewed as context dependent and therefore can and does change as a function of the intergroup interactions that occur during a crowd event (Drury & Reicher, 2000). As such, ESIM research is based upon a rejection of the 'classic' and 'irrationalist' crowd psychology of Le Bon (1895) and Allport (1924). However, this programme of research has also identified how these 'irrationalist' theories are still relevant today because of the following: (1) they often underpin the perceptions of those who are charged with controlling crowds; (2) they may potentially be counterproductive because such ideological positions lead to practices that initiate and escalate 'disorder' through a kind of self-fulfilling prophecy (Drury, Stott, & Farsides, 2003; Stott & Reicher, 1998b; Hoggett & Stott, 2010a, 2010b); and (3) such irrationalist theories saw a resurgence as explanations for the 2011 riots (Reicher & Stott, 2011).

Clearly then, there is a substantial body of research in this domain that suggests that the availability of evidence is not a substantive barrier to EBP in public order. Moreover, in light of the August disorder, the case can be made that such evidence is urgently needed so that informed police decision-making can combat widely accepted and inaccurate discourses about crowd behaviour. Indeed, research in this area has begun to identify how an understanding of this theory and evidence can be usefully integrated into 'police knowledge' in ways that do this by significantly improving police crowd management strategies and tactics.

On the basis of the ESIM, Reicher et al. (2004, 2007) developed four specific principles for crowd policing—termed education, facilitation, communication, and differentiation. In terms of education, Reicher et al. (2004, 2007) suggest that it is of great practical importance to understand the social identities (cultural norms, sensitivities, intentions) of the crowd so that police tactics can be tailored towards the facilitation of those aspects of a crowd identity that are consistent with democratic principles and practices. Moreover, they suggest that a comprehensive communication strategy should run through all phases and all aspects of a crowd event, especially when police use of force is judged necessary. Finally, Reicher et al. (2004) suggest that the central component to any crowd policing strategy should be the avoidance of the undifferentiated use of force.

Whilst for brevity, these principles have not been covered here in detail; they raise important questions about how tactically such strategic intentions can be implemented. The most compelling example can be found at the 2004 European Football Championships in Portugal (Euro 2004). For the Championship, ESIM principles and a tactical model developed by Stott and Adang (2003a, 2003b) were used to inform the security policy for the tournament of one of Portugal's two main police forces, the Polícia de Segurança Pública (PSP). The PSP have jurisdiction for all Portugal's main cities and were therefore responsible for all match venues involving the England team. In line with Adang and Stott (2004), the strategic policing approach developed was graded, dynamic, information-led, and non-confrontational. If problems did emerge, the policy was to first identify and validate the risk before specifically targeting those responsible through the information-led use of force.

The success of the tournament in terms of the absence of collective 'disorder' among fans is now widely acknowledged in policy circles throughout Europe (Stott & Pearson, 2007). For example, the Police Cooperation Working Party of the Council of the European Union developed its recommendations for policing football matches with an international dimension in line with the Euro 2004 model of good practice. The value of these principles has also been recognised by the Association of Chief Police Officers (ACPO) in their 'Manual of Guidance for Keeping the Peace' (2010). Finally, the HMIC (2009) report into G20 included an entire chapter on the relevance of understanding crowd dynamics and incorporating such principles into public order strategy and tactics (chapter 4, pp. 85–92). What Euro 2004 demonstrates therefore, is that an EBP approach to public order policing is both possible and productive.

Given that such a wealth of evidence is available, this raises the question of why an EBP approach is not being more actively developed to assist public order policing in England and Wales? Indeed, it seems pertinent to refer once again to Sir Hugh Orde who stressed the importance and challenge of retaining a 'model of policing, premised on human rights and the minimum use of force. We police with consent and must be professional, proportionate, fair and justifiable to the public at all times' (Orde, 2011). Such challenges are never going to be easily met, and it is our assertion that given the realities facing public order policing in the current socio-economic climate, an EBP approach is not just desirable but essential.

ORGANISATIONAL CONSTRAINTS

Given that there is no substantive case for barriers to EBP in terms of the nature and availability of evidence, what then of organisational resistance?

On the one hand, the importance of and need to utilise science to assist change has been recognised to some extent by the HMIC (2009) report. This is particularly so as it relates to police training. For example, two of their key recommendations relate directly to this issue. Recommendation four: public order training states that 'the Association of Chief Police Officers and the National Policing Improvement Agency should work together to ensure consistency of content and accreditation of public order training programmes across the police service' (p. 16). Recommendation five: public order command training states that 'public order command training should be significantly enhanced to provide explicit guidance to officers on communication strategies before, during and after public order policing events and ensure police understanding and management of crowd dynamics' (p. 17).

In light of these recommendations, some change has begun to occur. For example, new command courses have been developed for strategic (gold), tactical (silver), and operational (bronze) commanders that take into account the scientific research on crowd dynamics (Stott, 2011; HMIC, 2011). Additionally, the National Policing Improvement Agency (NPIA) and the National Centre for Applied Learning Technologies (NCALT) have sought to remedy the theory practice imbalance within training (Stott, Gorringe, & Rosie, 2010).

Additionally, the HMIC (2011) provides a number of case studies that suggest that some of their recommendations may be feeding into operational practice. For example, one of the core proposals of the 2009 report was the formation of protest liaison officers (PLOs) to assist in communicating with the crowd. Subsequently, in 2010, the Thames Valley Police made extensive use of 'PLOs' during the policing of the 'Big Blockade' (protests organised by 'Trident Ploughshares' at the Atomic Weapons Establishment [AWE], Aldermaston). During this protest, the role of the PLOs was to negotiate with groups in the crowd in order to understand their intentions and the nature of their protest. Commanders at the event reported that this enabled them to avoid using a more confrontational approach when attempting to gain compliance with police directives (HMIC, 2011, p. 27).

However, whilst such developments appear to be positive, there remains little in the way of systematic independent evaluation of these kinds of developments. A problem made even more pressing by the HMIC (2011) report that points towards failures with implementing core recommendations from adapting to protest. For example, the report highlights the series of student protests in London in November and December 2010 that involved serious disruption and disorder and notes 'as the scenes in London during the student protests of November and December show, filtering peaceful protestors from violent criminality in a timely way remains a huge operational challenge' (HMIC, 2011, p. 23).

Given these challenges, we argue that simply developing practice based on police interpretations of evidence and theory is not sufficient for change nor is it strictly adopting an EBP approach. What is needed is fuller and greater partnership with science. For example, it is important to recognise that 'in-house' changes often lack a broader perspective and critical analysis that greater collaborative EBP approaches could offer. Without such partnership, evidence and theory are potentially being taken on board without the required understanding of how it should be applied. As Innes (2010) argues, whilst researchers generate findings, they remain largely removed from designing interventions or evaluating their implementation in practice. The problem being that 'such arrangements do not aid in developing a disciplined and focussed attention upon the key issues identified by the research data. Nor do they help resist the political influences that can often skew the way in which evidence is spun and implemented' (Innes, 2010, p.129)

This is in no way to place the blame at the feet of either the police or public order researchers but to highlight the pressing need for the continued and coherent development of police academic co-operation and partnership. This is especially important during the early stages of such change to counter any cultural and political resistance. This is because as Stott et al. (2010) identify, 'the HMIC recommendations are only beginning to feed into policing practice and there is a very real danger that knee-jerk reactions to events of this nature [the Millbank student protests] could undermine that process' (p. 17). In light of the recent urban unrest of August 2011 and subsequent calls for a radical overhaul of public order policing, this is a particularly prophetic point.

In conclusion, this paper suggests that the nature and availability of evidence are not substantial barriers to developing an EBP approach in public order. On the one hand, problems around the nature of evidence simply reflect the epistemological concerns of the social sciences more generally. As such, 'evidence' is no panacea but a foundation for beginning to understand how to approach the problems of sustaining democratic forms of public order policing. On the other, the availability of theory and evidence in this field of inquiry is extensive. Indeed, this research has already begun to provide practical examples of how EBP can be used in the management of crowds.

The key barrier appears to be organisational. It is not that EBP requires the simple absorption of existing knowledge. Rather, policing itself needs to generate the capacity for knowledge development. By working in closer partnership with science practitioners in this area, police officers can be developed into experts who not only make decisions informed by social science research but also develop the capacity to inform and test these decisions scientifically.

However, this may not be a quick or easy process. This is because the police and academia have very different work practices that create situations in which both party's prioritise their view as superior to those of the other. As Canter (2008) eloquently notes, the problem is that both parties perceive themselves as the one-eyed king in the kingdom of the blind. Until a formal and equal relationship between the police and academia is created, inherent tensions will remain a practical barrier to success. For example, the police tend to focus on immediate, practical, and pressing issues. They work to short time frames, and this leaves little space for examining the merits of different types of approaches or developing strategies that reflect a wider knowledge base as public order researchers can do. As Sherman (1998) noted, most police practices are still shaped by local custom, opinions, theories, and subjective impressions. EBP challenges this and emphasises the need to make science a core part of police officers education, culture, and training. Developing partnerships with the academic community is a vital first step in this.

The recent urban unrest and the subsequent political and public discourses calling for the greater use of police force highlight that such an approach is badly needed. In this way, EBP can be used to resist the often salient political pressures that can interfere with operational policing (Cronin & Reicher, 2006; PAJ Waddington, 1994a). By doing so, public order practice and decision making can move away from personal preference and unsystematic experience towards those based on the best available scientific evidence. In other words, EBP could be used as a tool for the professionalisation of policing more generally. The continuing challenge for change for both the police and academic researchers therefore is to develop collaborations that improve both parties' knowledge and understanding of public order policing. In turn, this knowledge can be utilised to help implement and evaluate practice rather than simply policy. By doing so, in the future, events such as the G20 protests or the recent urban unrest may become a less-bruising experience for all parties involved (Glass, 2010). Evidence-based public order policing may thus provide the most suitable answer to the question posed by the HMIC (2009) report 'how best should the police as a service adapt to the modern day demands of public order policing while retaining the core values of the British policing model' (p. 5).

Note from the Publisher

This chapter was first published in the *Journal of Investigative Psychology and Offender Profiling*, volume 9, issue 2 (June 2012) and is reproduced with kind permission by Wiley-Blackwell. Please refer to the Citation Information page at the start of this book for more information and full details on how to cite this article.

REFERENCES

Adang, O., & Stott, C. (2004). Preparing for Euro 2004: Policing international football matches inPortugal. Unpublished report for the Portuguese Public Security Police.

Allport, F. (1924). Social psychology. Boston, MA: Houghton Mifflin.

Association of Chief Police Officers (ACPO). (2010). Manual of guidance on keeping the peace.

Austin, J. (2003). Why criminology is irrelevant? Criminology and Public Policy, 2(2), 557–664.

Brannen, J. (2005). Mixing methods: The entry of qualitative and quantitative approaches into the research process. International Journal of Social Research Methodology, 8(3), 173–184.

Bullock, K., & Tilley, N. (2009). Evidence-based policing and crime reduction. Policing: A Journal of Policy and Practice, 4(2), 381–387.

Button, M., Johnb, T., & Brierley, N. (2002). New challenges in public order policing: the professionalization of environmental protest and the emergence of the militant environmental activist. International Journal of the Sociology of Law, 30, 17–32.

Campbell, D. T., & Fiske, D. W. (1959) Convergent and discriminant validation by the multi-trait-multi-method matrix. Psychological Bulletin, 56, 81–105

Chancer, L., & McLaughlin, E. (2007). Public criminologies: Diverse perspectives on academia a policy. Theoretical Criminology, 11(2), 155–173.

Canter, D., & Žukauskiene, R. (ed.), (2008). Psychology and law bridging the gap. London: Ashgate Publishing.

Cronin, P., & Reicher, S. (2006). A study of the factors that influence how senior officers police crowd events: On SIDE outside the laboratory. British Journal of Social Psychology, 45, 175–196

Davies, H., Nutley, S., & Smith, C. (eds.) (2000). What works? Evidence-based policy and practice in public services. Bristol: Policy Press.

Della Porta, D., & Reiter, H. (1998) Policing protests: The control of mass demonstrations in Western democracies. Minneapolis, Minnesota: University of Minnesota Press.

De Lint, W. (2005). Public order policing: A tough act to follow?. International Journal of the Sociology of Law, 33/4: 179–199.

Drury, J., & Reicher, S. (2000). Collective action and psychological change: The emergence of new social identities. British Journal of Social Psychology, 39, 579–604.

Drury, J., Stott, C., & Farsides, T. (2003). The role of police perception and practices in the development of 'public disorder'. Journal of Applied Social Psychology, 33(7), 1480–1500.

Foster, J., & Bailey, S. (2010). Joining forces: maximising ways of making a difference in policing. Policing: A Journal of Policy and Practice, 4(2), 95–103.

Glass, D. (2010). The London G20 protests: A bruising experience? Policing: A Journal of Policy and Practice, 4(2), 160–162.

Hall, A., & De Lint, W. (2003). Policing labour in Canada. Policing and Society, 13, 219–234.

Her Majesty's Inspectorate of Constabulary. (2009). Adapting to protest—Nurturing the British model of policing.

Her Majesty's Inspectorate of Constabulary. (2011). Policing public order—An overview and review of progress against the recommendations of Adapting to Protest and Nurturing the British Model of Policing.

Hinsliff, G., & Syal, R. (2009) IPCC chief slams tactics of G20 police at demo. Guardian (online) 10 August. Available from: http://www.guardian.co.uk/politics/2009/apr/19/ipcc-police-g20-protests. (Accessed 10August 2011).

Hoggett, J., & Stott, C. (2010a). The role of crowd theory in determining the use of force in public order policing. Policing and Society, 20(2), 223–236.

Hoggett, J., & Stott, C. (2010b) Crowd psychology, public order police training and the policing of football crowds. Policing: An International Journal of Police Strategies and Management, 33(2), 218–235.

Hollin, C. (2008). Evaluating offender behaviour programmes: Does only randomisation glitter? Criminology and Criminal Justice, 8(1), 89–106.

Innes, M. (2010). A 'mirror' and a 'motor': Researching and reforming policing in an age of austerity. Policing: A Journal of Policy and Practice, 4(2), 127–134.

Jefferson, T. (1990). The case against paramilitary policing. Milton Keynes: Open University Press.

Johnson, R. B., & Onwuegbuzie, A. J. (2004). Mixed methods research: A research paradigm whose time has come. Educational Researcher, 33(7), 14–26.

King, M., & Brearley, M. (1996). Public order policing: Contemporary perspectives on strategy and tactics. Leicester: Perpetuity Press

King, M., & Waddington, D. (2004). Coping with disorder? The changing relationship between police public order strategy and practice—A critical analysis of the Burnley riot. Policing and Society, 14(2), 118–137.

King, M., & Waddington, D. (2005). Flashpoints revisited: a critical application to the policing of anti-globalisation protest. Policing and Society, 15(3), 255–282.

Kuhn, T. S. (1970). The structure of scientific revolutions. (2nd Ed.) Chicago: University of Chicago Press.

Le Bon, G. (1895, translated 1947). The crowd: A study of the popular mind. London: Ernest Benn.

McCarthy J. D., & McPhail, C. (1998). The institutionalization of protest in the United States. In

Meyer, D. S., & Tarrow, S. (Eds.) The social movement society: Contentious politics for a new century. New York: Rowman and Littlefield.

McPhail, C., Schweingruber, D., &McCarthy, J. (1998). Policing protest in the United States: 1960–1995. In D. Della Porta, & H. Reiter (Eds.) Policing protests: The control of mass demonstrations in Western democracies. Minneapolis, Minnesota: University of Minnesota Press.

Murji, K. (2010) Introduction: Academic–police collaborations—Beyond 'two worlds'. Policing: A Journal of Policy and Practice, 4 (2), 92–94.

Nutley, S., Walter, I., & Davies, H. (2002). From knowing to doing: A framework for understanding the evidence into practice agenda. Research unit for research utilisation discussion paper 1. St. Andrews: University of St. Andrews.

Orde, H. (2011). Water cannon make for good headlines—and bad policing. The Independent (online) 16 August. Available from: http://www.independent.co.uk/opinion/commentators/ sir-hugh-orde-water-cannon-make-for-good-headlines-ndash-and-bad-policing-2335676.html. (Accessed 16 August 2011)

Reicher, S. D. (1982). The determination of collective behaviour. In H. Tajfel (Ed.) Social identity and intergroup relations. Cambridge, UK: Cambridge University Press.

Reicher, S. D. (1984). The St. Pauls 'riot': An explanation of the limits of crowd action in terms of a social identity model. European Journal of Social Psychology, 14, 1–21.

Reicher, S. D. (1987). Crowd behaviour as social action. In Turner, J., Hogg, M., Oakes, P., Reicher, S., & Wetherell, M. (Eds.), Rediscovering the social group: A self-categorisation theory. Oxford, UK: Blackwell.

Reicher, S. (1996a). The crowd century: Reconciling theoretical failure with practical success. British Journal of Social Psychology, 35, 535–553.

Reicher, S. (1996b). The Battle of Westminster: Developing the social identity model of crowd behaviour in order to explain the initiation and development of collective conflict. European Journal of Social Psychology, 26, 115–134.

Reicher, S., & Stott, C. (2011). Mad mobs and Englishmen. London: Constable and Robinson.

Reicher, S., Stott, C., Cronin, P., & Adang, O. (2004). An integrated approach to crowd psychology and public order policing. Policing: An International Journal of Police Strategies and Management, 17(4), 558–572.

Reicher, S., Stott, C., Drury, J., Adang, O., Cronin, P., & Livingstone, A. (2007). Knowledge based public order policing: Principles and practice. Policing: A Journal of Policy and Practice, 1, 403–415.

Sheptycki, J. (2005). Policing political protest when politics go global: Comparing public order policing in Canada and Bolivia. Policing and Society, 15, 327–352

Sherman, L. W. (1984). Experiments in police discretion: Scientific boon or dangerous knowledge? Law and Contemporary Problems, 47(4), 61–81

Sherman, L. W. (1992). Policing domestic violence: Experiments and dilemmas. New York: Free Press.

Sherman, L. W. (1998). Evidence based policing. Washington D.C: Police Foundation.

Sherman, L. W., Farrington, D. P., Welsh B. C., & Mackenzie D. L. (Eds.), (2002). Evidence-based crime prevention. London: Routledge.

Stott. (2011). Crowd dynamics and public order policing. In T. Madensen, & J. Knutsson (Eds.), Preventing crowd violence. London: Lynne Reinner Publishers Inc.

Stott, C., & Adang, O. (2003a). Policing football matches with an international dimension in the European Union: Understanding and managing risk. Unpublished Report to the UK Home Office.

Stott, C., & Adang, O. (2003b). Crowd psychology and public order policing. Paper presented PSP Euro2004 Strategy meeting, Instituto Superior de CieciasPoliciais e SegurancaInterna, Lisbon.

Stott, C., Adang, O., Livingstone, A., & Schrieber, M. (2007). Variability in the collective behaviour of England fans at Euro 2004: Hooliganism, public order policing and social change. European Journal of Social Psychology, 37, 75–100.

Stott, C., Adang, O., Livingstone, A., & Schreiber, M. (2008a) Tackling football hooliganism: A quantitative study of public order, policing and crowd psychology. Psychology, Public Policy, and Law, 14(2), 115–141

Stott, C., & Drury, J. (2000). Crowds, context and identity: Dynamic categorisation processes in the poll tax riot. Human Relations, 53, 247–273.

Stott, C., Gorringe, H., & Rosie, M. (2010) HMIC goes to Millbank. Police Professional, Issue 232.

Stott, C., Hoggett, J., & Pearson, G. (2012). 'Keeping the peace' social identity, procedural justice and the policing of football crowds. British Journal of Criminology, 52(2), 381–399.

Stott, C., Livingstone, A., & Hoggett, J. (2008b). Policing football crowds in England and Wales: A model of good practice? Policing and Society, 18, 1–24.

Stott, C., & Pearson, G. (2007). Football hooliganism, policing and the war on the English disease. London: Pennant Books.

Stott, C. & Reicher, S.. (1998a). How conflict escalates: The intergroup dynamics of collective football crowd violence. Sociology, 32, 353–377.

Stott, C., & Reicher, S. (1998b). Crowd action as intergroup process: Introducing the police perspective. European Journal of Social Psychology, 26, 509–529.

Tajfel, H., & Turner, J. C. (1979). An integrative theory of intergroup relations. In Worchel, S., & Austin, W. G. (Eds.), Psychology of Intergroup Relations, Monterey CA: Brooks-Cole.

Tilley, N. (2009). Sherman vs. Sherman: Realism vs. rhetoric. Criminology and Criminal Justice, 9(2), 135–144.

Turner, J., Hogg, M., Oakes, P., Reicher, S., & Wetherell, M. (1987). Rediscovering the social group: A self-categorisation theory. Oxford, UK: Blackwell.

Von Wright, G. H. (1971). Explanation and Understanding. London: Routledge.

Waddington, D. (2007). Policing public disorder: Theory and practice. Cullompton: Willan Publishing.

Waddington, D., Jones, K., & Critcher, C. (1989). Flashpoints: Studies in public disorder. London: Routledge.

Waddington, D., & King, M. (2005). The disorderly crowd: from classical psychological reductionism to socio-contextual theory—The impact on public order policing strategies. The Howard Journal, 44, 490–503.

Waddington, P. A. J. (1987). Towards paramilitarism? Dilemmas in the policing of public order. British Journal of Criminology, 27(1), 37–46.

Waddington, P. A. J. (1993a). Dying in a ditch: The use of police powers in public order. International Journal of the Sociology of Law, 21, 335–353

Waddington, P. A. J. (1993b). The case against paramilitary policing considered. British Journal of Criminology, 33(3), 353–373.

Waddington, P. A. J. (1994a). Coercion and accommodation: Policing public order after the Public Order Act. The British Journal of Sociology, 45(3), 367–385.

Waddington, P. A. J. (1994b). Liberty and order: Public order policing in a capital city. London: UCL Press.

Waddington, P. A. J. (1998). Controlling protest in contemporary historical and comparative perspective. In D. della Porta, & H. Reiter (Eds.), Policing protest: The control of mass demonstrations in Western democracies. Minneapolis, Minnesota: University of Minnesota Press.

Waszak, C., & Sines, M. (2003). Mixed methods in psychological research. In A. Tashakkori, & C. Teddlie (Eds.), Handbook of mixed methods in social and behavioural research (pp. 557–576). Thousand Oaks, CA: Sage.

The crowd as a psychological cue to in-group support for collective action against collective disadvantage

Martijn van Zomeren[a] and Russell Spears[b]

[a]Department of Social Psychology, University of Groningen, Groningen, the Netherlands;
[b]School of Psychology, Cardiff University, Cardiff, UK

Collective action against collective disadvantage is an important socio-psychological phenomenon that represents a powerful pathway to social change. One key conclusion from the psychological literature on collective action is that a strong subjective sense of *social identity* is almost a necessity for disadvantaged group members to become motivated to undertake collective action against collective disadvantage. We propose, however, that even those individuals who may not identify strongly with their group might engage in collective action when they are in a crowd. This is because one core feature of the crowd, the *physical co-presence of in-group members*, conveys a psychological cue to in-group support for collective action against collective disadvantage. This is particularly relevant for lower identifiers, because, unlike higher identifiers, they do not view themselves as similar to other group members and thus do not *expect* in-group support. As a consequence, expectations of in-group support and therefore interest in collective action should increase for lower identifiers when they are in a crowd. We tested this idea in a psychological experiment in which higher and lower identifiers with a disadvantaged group were randomly assigned to a physical co-presence or control condition. Results showed indeed that the physical co-presence of in-group members increased only lower identifiers' expectations of in-group support and their interest in collective action against collective disadvantage. We discuss the theoretical and practical implications of these results.

Collective disadvantage refers to any disadvantage that is structurally or incidentally imposed on a group, and thus typically includes low-status and/or low-power groups. It includes ethnic and gender discrimination, but also arises in contexts of increases in national or local taxes, increased tuition fees for students, and national or local government decisions to build a factory in one's neighbourhood (van Zomeren *et al.*, 2008a, 2011a). Collective action, defined as any action that individuals undertake to improve the group's position (van Zomeren & Iyer, 2009), is an important and agentic potential response to collective disadvantage because it can foster or enforce social change (e.g. demonstrations, strikes, riots; Klandermans, 1997). Over the last decades psychological theorising and research has converged on at least one important conclusion. *Social identity*, defined as that part of the self that is derived from one's membership in social groups together with the emotional and value significance thereof (Tajfel & Turner, 1979), is almost a precondition for collective action against collective disadvantage (for reviews, see Drury & Reicher, 2009; Haslam, 2004; Klandermans, 1997; and Van Zomeren *et al.*, 2008a). Indeed, psychological research demonstrates that individuals' motivation to undertake collective action strongly depends on whether they subjectively identify with their group and thus see themselves as similar to fellow group members on identity-relevant dimensions.

Important though this insight may be, many individuals within a disadvantaged group are likely to be *lower identifiers* who, most of the time at least, see themselves as unique individuals who do not perceive fellow group members as similar to themselves. This may explain why demonstrations typically attract only a small percentage of the full mobilisation potential (Klandermans, 1997), and why it is so notoriously difficult to convert passive sympathisers, never mind other group members into active protesters (Klandermans & Oegema, 1987; Oegema & Klandermans, 1994). One important theoretical question is therefore how lower identifiers become motivated to undertake collective action. Whereas previous work has focused on lower identifiers' personal instrumental motivations (e.g. Kelly & Breinlinger, 1995; van Zomeren *et al.*, 2008b), in this article we focus on the potency of the crowd to convey, through *the physical presence of in-group members*, psychological cues to in-group support to those who are in most need of them: lower identifiers with the group. We tested this idea in a laboratory experiment.

The psychology of social identity and collective action

Social identity theory (Tajfel & Turner, 1979) provides a strong social–psychological explanation of collective action. It posits that under particular socio-structural conditions (i.e. when there is hope and scope for social change, and group boundaries are closed; Tajfel, 1978), individuals' social identity becomes a psychological platform on which motivations to achieve social change through collective action can emerge. The more strongly individuals identify with their disadvantaged group, the stronger their motivation to undertake collective action (e.g. Ellemers, 1993). Self-categorisation theory (Turner *et al.*, 1987; Turner, 1991, 1999), which developed out of social identity theory, complements this view by detailing the psychological process through which individuals self-categorise (i.e. come to view themselves as group members). In this tradition, self-categories are viewed as social, historical, and ideological constructs (Reicher, 1987). These categories can become salient through chronic accessibility (e.g. gender among highly identified women), but also in response to group-related events (e.g. women confronted with gender discrimination). Thus, a social identity perspective conceptualises the self as a subjective and dynamic process that explains how individuals view themselves and their social world (i.e. as a group member or as a unique individual).

With this theoretical background in place, we note that psychological research has tended to operationalise these different levels of self by focusing on those who identify more weakly or strongly with a group (Ellemers et al., 1999; Leach et al., 2008; Turner, 1999; Veenstra & Haslam, 2000). Indeed, the well-established link between group identification and participation in collective action against collective disadvantage implies that higher identifiers are more likely to participate in collective action than lower identifiers. Meta-analytic evidence derived from psychological studies of collective action indeed supports the idea that weaker identification with a disadvantaged group decreases individuals' support for collective action, their willingness to act, and their actual engagement in it (Van Zomeren et al., 2008a).

A key reason for this is that group identification facilitates adherence to the perceived group norms about collective action against collective disadvantage (e.g. Postmes & Spears, 1998; Reicher et al., 1995; van Zomeren et al., 2008a). This implies that lower identifiers are less likely to value and pursue collective action against collective disadvantage as a group goal than higher identifiers (Ellemers et al., 1997), especially when there is little hope and scope for achieving this goal (Doosje et al., 2002; Ellemers et al., 1999; Ouwerkerk et al., 2000; van Zomeren et al., 2008b). Lower identifiers with a disadvantaged group are thus portrayed as individuals who seek maximal subjective utility, defined in this case as narrow, individual self-interest (van Zomeren & Spears, 2009). As a consequence, they typically take a pragmatic and instrumental approach to their disadvantaged group membership; they resemble the classic free-riders described by Olson (1968), who prefer to do nothing while hoping to reap the collective benefits of collective action (Klandermans, 2002).

But this picture is incomplete. Another important difference between higher or lower identifiers is that higher identifiers typically view themselves as *interchangeable* group members, which allows the subjective inference that others will think, feel, and act just as they themselves do on identity-relevant dimensions. Lower identifiers, however, typically view themselves as *different* from their fellow group members, which effectively prevents such an inference. All else being equal, higher identifiers therefore tend to expect stronger in-group support than lower identifiers (or, put differently, they expect stronger consensus within the group). This is important because in-group support validates the group's norms about shared opinions and actions (i.e. about collective action against collective disadvantage), both of which make collective action more likely (van Zomeren et al., 2004). Indeed, van Zomeren et al. (2004) found across three experiments that both emotional in-group support (i.e. group norms about opposing their collective disadvantage), and instrumental in-group support (i.e. group norms about undertaking collective action against collective disadvantage) predicted individuals' willingness to participate in collective action.

However, these and other differences between higher and lower identifiers are not set in stone—it is possible that there are conditions under which lower identifiers can modify their assessment of in-group support. As we will outline below in more detail, one core feature of crowds should be very relevant for lower identifiers in particular, namely the *physical co-presence of in-group members*. Building on a rich tradition in social psychology to study the effects of mere co-presence (e.g. Steiner, 1972; Triplett, 1898; Zajonc, 1965; for a review, see Haslam, 2004), we propose that crowds convey a psychological cue to in-group support through the physical co-presence of its members. Importantly, this cue confirms higher identifiers' high expectations of in-group support, but disconfirms lower identifiers' low expectations of in-group support (Reicher *et al.*, 1995, 1998; Spears *et al.*, 2002). As a consequence, *higher identifiers* do not necessarily require this cue to infer the availability of in-group support because they already expect it to be available. However, the physical co-presence of in-group members should be an especially relevant cue to in-group support for *lower identifiers*. Thus, because the physical co-presence of group members is a key aspect of crowds, even lower identifiers with a disadvantaged group can become motivated to infer in-group support and to engage in collective action against collective disadvantage when they are in a crowd.

The crowd as a psychological cue to in-group support

Early theorising on crowds (e.g. LeBon, 1896) focused mainly on the dangers of being immersed in a group rather than on what they can (more positively) achieve. To use the language developed later individuals were believed, for example, to become *deindividuated* in the crowd (for a review, see Postmes & Spears, 1998). The claim was that individuals entered a regressive mode of primitive responding to the environment based on their animal instincts (Zimbardo, 1969). As a consequence, violence was never thought to be far away from crowds. However, many scholars have questioned this view of the crowd as a generically irrational entity that robbed individuals of what makes them supposedly human: their individuality and their reason (Drury & Reicher, 2009; Reicher, 2001). In fact, the social identity perspective has been quite clear and convincing in arguing that group behavior is *as rational and reasonable* as individual behavior. According to this approach, individuals do not lose themselves in a crowd, but shift their self-categorisation from the individual ('I') to the group level ('we'). Indeed, individuals who self-categorise as a group member (rather than as an individual) define and perceive themselves and their social world more in group (rather than individual) terms. As a consequence, their behavior is guided more by the group's norms (rather than one's personal norms), and one acts to achieve the group's goals (rather than individual goals). In this analysis, group behavior is as rational as individual behavior, but the particular self-underlying and motivating behavior is different (Postmes & Spears, 1998; Reicher, 2001; Spears, 2010).

With this recognition of the rationality of the group, it becomes possible to understand the crowd as a specific case of a psychological group in which in-group members are also *physically co-present*. Violence in crowds is therefore just one potential outcome of the collective action that individuals in crowds undertake, but solidarity and prosocial behavior are at least as likely (e.g. Drury *et al.*, 2009). Based on these insights into the crowd, theory and research has moved in different ways. For instance, the

ntity Model (ESIM) of Drury, Stott, Reicher, and colleagues ana-
ynamics that govern crowd behavior (e.g. Drury & Reicher, 2009;
iese depend on, for example, the group norms that develop over
how a crowd and the police (or more generally the out-group)
r. Rather than focusing on such intergroup dynamics, however,
group process of whether individuals in a crowd can use the phys-
-group members as a psychological cue to in-group support.

en focusing on intra-group processes, important aspects of the
remain important. For instance, we share the ESIM's assumption
ower differential (i.e. the collectively disadvantaged versus the
nsible for it) is an important factor in explaining how individuals
os become empowered through the process of undertaking collec-
Reicher (2005, 2009) suggest in this respect that self-categoris-
iber is an important basis for feelings of empowerment because
ions of (instrumental) in-group support. Complementing this
Social Identity model of Deindividuation Effects (SIDE) that
sical co-presence of in-group members stimulates individuals to
ive action because it provides them with emotional as well as
p support (Reicher *et al.*, 1995; Spears & Lea, 1994; Spears
cally, the physical co-presence of in-group members validates
dividuals that they are not alone. This leads to a perceptual *shift*
idual to the group level (e.g. Klein *et al.*, 2007; Reicher *et al.*,
ience, individuals adhere more strongly to group norms, and
lel predicts that the physical co-presence of in-group members
llective action that is *normative* from the perspective of the in-
, 1995; Spears *et al.*, 2002; for a meta-analysis, see Postmes &
stance, Reicher *et al.* (1998) found that the physical co-presence
or in-group members helped individuals in a disadvantaged group to resist powerful
out-group expectations of them (which can be interpreted as a form of collective resistance). However, no research of which we are aware has specifically tested whether the
physical co-presence of in-group members is a contextual cue to lower identifiers' in-
group support for and interest in undertaking collective action against collective
disadvantage.

We therefore designed a psychological experiment to test our two hypotheses. First,
we predicted that the physical co-presence of in-group members would increase lower
identifiers' expectations of emotional and instrumental in-group support. Second, we
predicted that as a consequence of this expectation, the physical co-presence of in-
group members would increase lower identifiers' interest in collective action against
collective disadvantage.

Empirical evidence

Fifty-four first-year students from the University of Amsterdam (mean age = 20.76
years, gender unrecorded) were randomly assigned to two experimental conditions:

physical co-presence versus physical absence of in-group members. Group identification was measured approximately 30 minutes before the experiment started (thus outside the context of collective disadvantage that we imposed at the start of the experiment). The experimental manipulation consisted simply of participants being seated in separate cubicles, or together in one room (per session three to eight people were present). The remainder of the experimental procedure was modelled after the procedure employed by van Zomeren *et al.* (2004). When the experiment started, all participants read that, ostensibly, an independent research body wanted to investigate first-year students' opinion on an issue by means of a survey study by an independent research body. This issue referred to a proposal of a University Committee to increase the amount of lab testing time, obliging first-year students of the University to fulfil 40 hours of testing in their first year, but now also 20 hours in their second year (i.e. a 50% increase). Participants were asked for their opinion about this proposal of the Committee before they were thanked and debriefed.

Before the experiment commenced, we measured group identification with three items (Cronbach's $a = 0.91$), tapping three important dimensions of the construct (self-categorisation, ties to the group and group evaluation; for a comprehensive review of more specific components of group identification, see Leach *et al.*, 2008). The items were: 'In general, I see myself as a first-year student/I feel a bond with other first-year students/I am glad to be a first-year student of the University of Amsterdam'. The response scales were seven-point scales (with anchors 1 = not at all, and 7 = very much). Conceptually, this measure reflects a general sense of identification with the group, but it should not be viewed as a personality-like measure because group identification is thought to vary by context, and over time (Turner *et al.*, 1987; also Leach *et al.*, 2008). In fact, this was the reason for taking this measure approximately 30 minutes before the start of this study and thus outside of the collective disadvantage context that we employed in the experiment. In the time between filling out this measure and starting the experiment, participants engaged in unrelated tasks. As intended through the procedure of random assignment, mean levels of group identification did not differ between the experimental and control condition, $t(52) = 0.64$, $p = 0.52$ (overall mean = 4.07, standard deviation (SD) = 1.75).

The bogus survey study included single-item measures of *emotional* in-group support (i.e. 'I think that other first-year students of the University of Amsterdam disagree with this proposal') and *instrumental* in-group support (i.e. 'I think that other first-year students of the University of Amsterdam are willing to do something against this proposal'). Both items were derived from van Zomeren *et al.* (2004) (with anchors 1 = not at all, and 7 = very much). As a proxy measure of participants' interest in collective action against collective disadvantage, we asked them to provide their personal email address that would be used to send them a digital petition against the proposed raise in required testing time. Participants who provided their email address were coded as 1 on collective action, whereas participants who refused were coded as 0 on this variable (Table 1 summarise relevant statistics).

We first tested the hypothesis that physical co-presence affected only lower identifiers' interest in collective action. We used two different statistical methods to test this hypothesis—the first examined frequencies (i.e. how many people provided their email address as a function of experimental condition and group identification), and the second used multiple regression analysis to regress interest in collective action onto experimental condition, group identification, and their two-way interaction (Aiken & West, 1991). The results of both analyses showed converging support for our hypothesis. First, results of a chi-square test with physical co-presence, group identification (which was, necessarily for this analysis, median split) and interest in collective action showed significant deviations for low identifiers from the expected frequencies in the physical co-presence versus control condition, $\chi^2(1) = 4.73$, $p = 0.03$. For high identifiers, frequencies were exactly the same in both conditions because all individuals provided their email address to receive the petition (26 out of 26 across the two conditions, i.e. 100%). In line with our first hypothesis, low identifiers in the physical co-presence condition were more likely to provide their email address (14 out of 16, equalling 87.5%) than low identifiers in the control (i.e. the no co-presence) condition (six out of 12, equalling 50%). Second, a multiple regression analysis confirmed this effect. For interest in collective action, we obtained the predicted two-way interaction between the experimental manipulation and group identification, $b = -0.05$, standard error (SE) = 0.02, $p < 0.04$. Simple slopes analysis (Aiken & West, 1991) revealed that for lower identifiers (tested at -1 SD from the mean of the group identification scale), physical co-presence significantly increased interest in collective action, $b = 0.16$, SE = 0.06, $p < 0.01$. However, this was not the case for higher identifiers (tested at $+1$ SD of the mean of the group identification scale), $b = -0.02$, SE = 0.06, $p > 0.79$. Thus, both statistical methods revealed support for our hypothesis that lower identifiers become more interested in collective action when in-group members are physically co-present.

We then tested whether we would find a similar pattern of results on our measures of emotional and instrumental in-group support. First, we indeed obtained the predicted two-way interaction for *emotional* in-group support, $b = -0.25$, SE = 0.08, $p < 0.01$. Simple slopes analysis revealed that for lower identifiers, physical co-presence significantly increased emotional in-group support, $b = 0.67$, SE = 0.20, $p < 0.01$. As expected, this was not the case for higher identifiers, $b = -0.19$, SE = 0.21, $p > 0.36$. Thus, the physical co-presence of in-group members indeed raised only lower identifiers' expectations of emotional in-group support (Figure 1). Second, we also obtained the predicted two-way interaction for *instrumental* in-group support, $b = -0.32$, SE = 0.12, $p < 0.01$. Simple slopes analysis revealed that for lower identifiers, physical co-presence significantly increased instrumental in-group support, $b = 0.73$, SE = 0.28, $p < 0.02$. Again, this was not the case for higher identifiers, $b = -0.40$, SE = 0.29, $p > 0.17$. Thus, the physical co-presence of in-group members also raised only lower identifiers' expectations of instrumental in-group support (Figure 2). These results confirm our hypothesis that lower identifiers perceive stronger emotional and instrumental in-group support when in-group members are physically co-present.

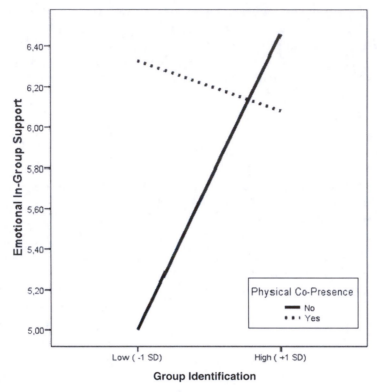

Figure 1. Two-way interaction effect between physical co-presence (manipulated) and group identification (measured) on emotional in-group support.

We proceeded with a test of the presumed mediation (i.e. explanation) of expectations of in-group support between the interaction between co-presence and group identification and interest in collective action (following the guidelines by Baron & Kenny, 1986). Initial tests suggested that emotional rather than instrumental in-group support was more relevant in predicting interest in collective action. We thus conducted another regression analysis in which we regressed behavior onto co-presence, group identification, their two-way interaction, and emotional in-group support. Statistical mediation is indicated by a reduced effect of the two-way interaction, and a positive effect of emotional support, on interest in collective action. Results confirmed the expected mediation in part: although the predictive effect of the two-way interaction was indeed reduced to non-significance (from $b = -0.25$, SE $= 0.08$, $p < 0.01$ to $b = -0.03$, SE $= 0.02$, $p > 0.17$), the predictive effect of emotional support was only marginally significant ($b = 0.06$, SE $= 0.04$, $p < 0.10$). Although the latter result is weaker than is ideally the case, the results as a whole nevertheless are consistent with our predictions.

In sum, the results of this experiment supported our two hypotheses about the potency of the crowd to cue in-group support for collective action against collective disadvantage. Specifically, the results show that lower identifiers with a disadvantaged

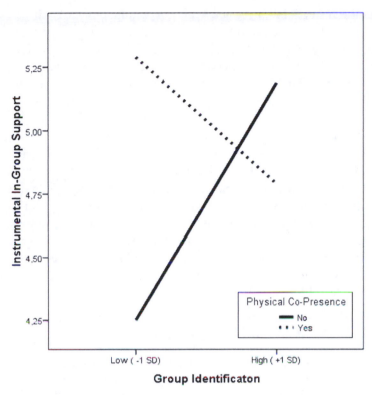

Figure 2. Two-way interaction effect between physical co-presence (manipulated) and group identification (measured) on instrumental in-group support.

group perceived more emotional and instrumental in-group support when in-group members were physically co-present (compared with the control condition). Moreover, lower identifiers became more interested in undertaking collective action against collective disadvantage in the presence of in-group members (compared with the control condition), and this was due in part to their expectations of emotional in-group support. Further, as expected, higher identifiers already expected in-group support and were already interested in undertaking collective action against collective disadvantage and thus the physical co-presence of in-group members did not affect them in this respect.

General discussion

The results of this psychological laboratory experiment supported our argument that the physical co-presence of in-group members is a relevant psychological cue for lower identifiers because it allows the subjective inference of the availability of emotional and instrumental in-group support (Reicher *et al.*, 1995, 1998; Spears *et al.*, 2002; also van Zomeren *et al.*, 2004). In further support of the social identity perspective in general and the SIDE model in particular, results showed that lower identifiers also became more interested in collective action against collective disadvantage in the same condition, and this appeared to be explained by their expectations of emotional in-group support. Further as expected, higher identifiers were unaffected by the physical co-presence of in-group members because they already unequivocally expected emotional and instrumental in-group support and were already interested in collective action against collective disadvantage. These findings illustrate that the physical co-presence of in-group members that the crowd presents is an important psychological cue to lower identifiers' expectations of emotional and instrumental in-group support. Hence, these findings offer an important pointer toward studying the psychological implications of the crowd in order to understand better whether and why individuals engage in collective action against collective disadvantage. Aside from the strong value of studying inter-group crowd *dynamics* with an eye to, for instance, crowd control (as in ESIM, e.g. Drury & Reicher, 2009; Stott *et al.*, 2001), studying key intra-group features of crowds such as the physical co-presence of in-group members in the laboratory may reveal important insights in the psychology of collective action against collective disadvantage. Below we discuss the theoretical, practical, and political implications of these findings.

Theoretical, practical and political implications

At a general level, our results tell us something new and important about a key feature of crowds—the physical co-presence of in-group members. In line with accounts of the crowd as an important case of inter-group dynamics and collective action (e.g. Drury & Reicher, 2009), one can view our experimental manipulation of putting individuals together in a room (versus in isolated cubicles) as a 'minimal crowd' (or at least as a rudimentary form of a crowd). The experimental method, as we used in the study we reported, has the strong advantage of isolating such subtle factors that are often interwoven with other factors in real life. Crowds, for example, are often also characterised by the possibility to communicate within the group (which is something that our participants could not do, verbally at least). Indeed, we do not believe that our groups reflect crowds in their fullest sense—crowds are obviously much more than group members being together in the same space. The SIDE model suggests in this respect that the possibility to *communicate* within the group or between groups (in the case of when the crowd meets the police) is an additional factor that is important in understanding intergroup dynamics. Most of the research on the SIDE model tended to focus on the availability of communication channels with the in-group (e.g. Spears *et al.*, 2002; also Scheepers *et al.*, 2006; van Zomeren *et al.*, 2010). The current experiment is therefore one of the first experimental studies to isolate the physical co-presence of in-group members as a key factor in the study of crowds and collective action. Future research should investigate the interplay between these two important aspects of crowds in motivating individuals for collective action against collective disadvantage.

Furthermore, our analysis builds on but also extends the social identity approach more generally (e.g. Drury & Reicher, 2009; Ellemers *et al.*, 1999; Klein *et al.*, 2007; Reicher *et al.*, 1995; Subasic *et al.*, 2008; Tajfel & Turner, 1979; Turner,

1991, 1999; Turner *et al.*, 1987; Van Zomeren *et al.*, 2008a) by showing that the physical co-presence of in-group members is an important cue to in-group support for lower (but not higher) identifiers (Spears & Lea, 1994). In crowds, the social identity approach predicts a perceptual shift from personal identity to social identity. As a consequence, people are more likely to adhere to group norms (Postmes & Spears, 1998), which can be negative or positive (e.g. rioting or cheering one's football team). Although this shift (called depersonalisation in self-categorisation theory) is generally more likely for higher identifiers, our analysis and findings suggest that the physical co-presence of in-group members might also (temporarily) depersonalise lower identifiers because it signals in-group support for collective action against collective disadvantage. Thus, the contextual cue to in-group support might be a cue to the salience of their social rather than their personal identity. This fits with the larger idea that, generally speaking, higher and lower identifiers psychologically live in very different social worlds (e.g. Van Zomeren *et al.*, 2008b); Veenstra & Haslam, 2000), but that situational cues can 'turn' lower identifiers into higher identifiers and vice versa (Drury & Reicher, 2009; Subasic *et al.*, 2008; Tajfel & Turner, 1979; Turner *et al.*, 1987). Future research can explore which other contextual cues are 'hidden' in the crowd.

Our experiment fits in a rich tradition in social psychology to study the effects of the physical co-presence of others on individuals' perception, experience, and behavior. For instance, Triplett (1898) found in a pioneering psychological experiment that racing cyclists performed better when another cyclist was co-present, even in the absence of explicit competition. Zajonc (1965) pinpointed this 'social facilitation' effect to a basic physiological process. According to him, the physical co-presence of others increases arousal, which makes individuals rely more on 'dominant responses' (i.e. responses already engrained in the organism). As a consequence, individuals' performance on tasks that require such a dominant response would be facilitated by the arousing presence of others (whereas tasks that require a non-dominant response would make individuals vulnerable to *social inhibition*—the opposite of social facilitation). The social identity explanation of social facilitation effects has focused more on the influence that the co-presence of *in-group members* have (Haslam, 2004), and, in line with our argument, on the importance of adherence of group norms as a function of viewing oneself as a group member rather than a unique individual. Nevertheless, it is important to recognise the rich tradition in social psychology to focus on how the mere presence of others can influence individuals.

We further note two alternative explanations of our findings. First, we have thus far conceptualised the effects of physical co-presence as providing a contextual cue to in-group support for lower identifiers. However, in line with the SIDE model the physical co-presence of in-group members might also provide a form of *surveillance* (Reicher *et al.*, 1995; Spears & Lea, 1994) such that lower identifiers conform more strongly to group norms, either because of group pressure (e.g. Deutsch & Gerard, 1955), or out of a sense of moral duty (e.g. 'to do the right thing'; McGarty *et al.*, 2000). This explanation is not a likely one for the current results because participants could not in any way be influenced by their in-group members (e.g. they could not communicate with each other, and their responses were anonymous and not visible to other group members). Theoretically, however, this effect of physical co-presence of in-group members is quite likely and thus important to research in the future.

Second, according to the ESIM the physical co-presence of in-group members might provide low identifiers with a stronger sense of social identity that *empowers* them because of the support they now expect from fellow group members. Although we believe there is generally strong merit in this explanation, results would have been more in line with it if we had found that *instrumental* in-group support explained the effects of co-presence among lower identifiers on their interest in collective action. Experimental research has shown that instrumental rather than emotional support is uniquely related to issues of subjective power, control, and efficacy (van Zomeren *et al.*, 2004). Therefore, this type of support should have been particularly important for disadvantaged group members to feel empowered in standing up against the powerful out-group. However, it was not. Admittedly, our results regarding mediation were not ideal, but they nevertheless seem to be more in line with SIDE's cue explanation than with ESIM's empowerment explanation. Future research can explore the empowering effects of the physical co-presence of in-group members.

We further note that subtle aspects of a situation such as the physical co-presence of in-group members are rarely acknowledged and examined in explanations of collective action against collective disadvantage (e.g. Klandermans, 1997; van Zomeren *et al.*, 2008). Yet, our results indicate that such subtle variables are consequential, at least in the current case for lower identifiers. Given that it is often hard to convert sympathisers of a group's cause into collective action participants (Klandermans & Oegema, 1987; Oegema & Klandermans, 1994; also Klandermans, 1997), the current results suggest a practical strategy for mobilising lower identifiers for collective action. Although we certainly do not claim that this is the 'magic bullet' for organisers of collective action, we do believe that organisations can become more effective in mobilising lower identifiers in the presence of in-group members (i.e. in teams). Indeed, according to our analysis and results, particularly the emotional in-group support provided by the physical co-presence of in-group members can motivate lower identifiers for collective action, or at least increase their interest in it. For instance, contacting individuals together with fellow group members (rather than one-on-one) might already lead to expectations of a sense of emotional and instrumental in-group support. Future research can test whether such a practical strategy is effective.

Finally, our findings can also have political implications. Indeed, the very same knowledge about which factors afford collective action among the disadvantaged also offer insights into how to *prevent* collective action from occurring. Our findings imply that the *possibility* for the physical co-presence of in-group members is very important for collective action to occur in the first place. However, this also means that prohibiting this possibility (e.g. by imposing sanctions on crowding) might be effective, according to our results, in preventing the psychological cues to in-group support that crowds can convey. As a consequence, lower identifiers would be likely to be confirmed in their expectation of low in-group support, and thus less interested in collective action. This reminds us that the psychological processes we examine operate independently of tyrannical or democratic ends.

Limitations and directions for future research

One limitation of the reported study is that it provides only a single source of empirical evidence and hence it would be good to replicate these results using a different population, group, and collective disadvantage. Nevertheless, a meta-analysis by van Zomeren *et al.* (2008) showed that key predictors of collective action against collective disadvantage such as group identification, perceptions and feelings of group-based injustice, and beliefs about the group's efficacy, are valid predictors of collective action across a wide range of populations, groups, and collective disadvantages. The literature therefore suggests that there is no *a priori* reason to assume that the current results would not generalise to other populations, groups, and collective disadvantages. Having said that, we do think it is possible that lower identifiers' interpretation of the cues conveyed by the crowd can differ as a function of different (cultural) contexts. For instance, in countries with a long history of surveillance, the physical co-presence of in-group members might be interpreted as 'being watched' by one's group rather than as being supported by them. Similarly, it is possible that (from the point of view from the in-group) crowds do not convey in-group support for non-normative collective action.

One further objection to the present research is that lower identifiers might not be expected to be in a crowd in the first place, and thus that it lacks ecological validity. While this observation may often be true, it is also true that there is always likely to be variation in the commitment of those present in the crowd (Van Zomeren *et al.*, 2008b) and a range of different initial motives for going on marches, rallies and demonstrations (including simply being coincidentally present). Moreover, as noted we believe that the key principles that we derive from our results move beyond the crowd itself. For instance, organisers of collective action can try to mobilise individuals in 'teams of organisers' that, through the co-presence of in-group members, convey high expectations of in-group support. Finally, our results suggest that the mere co-presence of others can be one factor in explaining a radicalising experience of being in the crowd (for further factors involved, see also Drury & Reicher, 2000). This points to the important transformational potential of the crowd to the extent that it can gear individuals up for collective action who, prior to the crowd context, were quite likely not to be interested in it.

Empirically, we note that we obtained the weakest support for the mediation hypothesis despite the significant predicted two-way interaction effects on in-group support and interest in collective action. Nevertheless, there are good theoretical and empirical reasons to interpret these findings as being in line with our analysis. Theoretically, alternative explanations seem either unlikely or less in line with the data than our theoretical account. Empirically, our measure of interest in collective action was a dichotomous measure that necessarily obscures more fine-grained patterns of variance

Table 1. Descriptive statistics and correlations

	2. Emotional in-group support	3. Instrumental in-group support
1. Interest in collective action	0.53*	0.46*
2. Emotional in-group support		0.30*
Mean	5.94	
SD	1.20	
3. Instrumental in-group support		
Mean	5.84	
SD	1.55	

Note: An asterisk (*) means that correlations differ significantly from zero at $p < 0.05$.

obtained with a continuous measure (e.g. seven-point scales), and thus also obscures the true relationship between the constructs involved. This is unavoidable, however, if psychologists want to predict action vs. inaction. Moreover, although we had a sufficient number of participants to test our hypotheses, it should be noted that our predicted interaction effects were based on a significant difference for half of the sample (i.e. for lower identifiers), and a lack of difference for the other half of the sample (i.e. for higher identifiers). This makes our statistical tests quite conservative tests of our hypothesis. Given the statistical significance of most of our findings we are therefore confident that our interpretation of the data is valid.

Our analysis and results offer important directions for future research in psychology and beyond. As noted, psychological research can test whether lower identifiers' sensitivity to contextual cues also occurs when the physical co-presence of in-group members reflects surveillance rather than in-group support. Moreover, it is important to study the potentially empowering consequences of the physical co-presence of in-group members. Applied research can also test whether a mobilisation campaign that targets individuals in the physical co-presence of in-group members may be more effective than campaigns that target individuals in isolation. Moreover, social scientists more generally can study whether the physical co-presence of in-group members and the possibility to communicate with in-group members (and perhaps out-group members) can be viewed as the essence of a crowd. Finally, it would be interesting to study whether the physical co-presence of in-group members cues in-group support for (from the point of view of the in-group) *anti-normative* action (e.g. extreme violent actions like terrorist acts). Thus, the current findings at the micro-level might inspire thinking about crowds at this level, but also at the meso- and macro-levels.

Conclusion

Collective action and crowds are important and partly overlapping social and psychological phenomena that offer a rich understanding of intra- and inter-group processes more generally. This is true in particular because theory and research on collective action and crowds bring together a plethora of socio-psychological factors that produce rational collective behavior by psychological group members. In this article we focused on one core feature of crowds, namely the physical co-presence of in-group members, to suggest that this feature of the crowd can be a psychological cue to in-group support for lower identifiers with the disadvantaged group. Indeed, the results of an experiment that carefully manipulated the physical co-presence of in-group members showed that lower identifiers perceived more in-group support and were more interested in collective action when in-group members were physically co-present than in a control condition. We therefore believe it is quite clear from our research that studying the crowd is essential in advancing our understanding of collective action against collective disadvantage, and beyond.

References

Aiken, L. S. & West, S. G. (1991) *Multiple regression: testing and interpreting interactions* (London, Sage).

Baron, R. M. & Kenny, D. A. (1986) The moderator–mediator variable distinction in social psychological research: conceptual, strategic, and statistical considerations, *Journal of Personality and Social Psychology*, 32, 519–530.

Deutsch, M. & Gerard, H. B. (1955) A study of normative and informational social influence upon individual judgment, *Journal of Abnormal and Social Psychology*, 51, 629–636.

Doosje, B., Spears, R. & Ellemers, N. (2002) Social identity as both cause and effect: the development of group identification in response to anticipated and actual changes in the intergroup status hierarchy, *British Journal of Social Psychology*, 41, 57–76.

Drury, J., Cocking, C. & Reicher, S. (2009) Everyone for themselves? A comparative study of crowd solidarity among emergency survivors, *British Journal of Social Psychology*, 48, 487–506.

Drury, J. & Reicher, S. D. (2000) Collective action and psychological change: the emergence of new social identities, *British Journal of Social Psychology*, 39, 579–604.

Drury, J. & Reicher, S. (2009) Collective psychological empowerment as a model of social change: researching crowds and power, *Journal of Social Issues*, 65, 707–725.

Ellemers, N. (1993) The influence of socio-structural variables on identity management strategies, in: W. Stroebe & M. Hewstone (Eds) *European review of social psychology* (Oxford, Blackwell), 22–57.

Ellemers, N., Spears, R. & Doosje, N. (1997) Sticking together of falling apart: in-group identification as a psychological determinant of group commitment versus individual mobility, *Journal of Personality and Social Psychology*, 72, 617–626.

Ellemers, N., Spears, R. & Doosje, B. (Eds) (1999) *Social identity: context, commitment, content* (Oxford, Blackwell).

Haslam, S. A. (2004) *Psychology of organizations: the social identity approach* (Thousand Oaks, CA, Sage).

Kelly, C. & Breinlinger, S. (1995) Identity and injustice: exploring women's participation in collective action, *Journal of Community and Applied Social Psychology*, 5, 41–57.

Klandermans, B. (1997) *The social psychology of protest* (Oxford, Basic Blackwell).

Klandermans, B. (2002) How group identification helps to overcome the dilemma of collective action, *American Behavioral Scientist*, 45, 887–900.

Klandermans, B. & Oegema, D. (1987) Potentials, networks, motivations, and barriers: steps toward participation in social movements, *American Sociological Review*, 52, 519–531.

Klein, O., Spears, R. & Reicher, S. (2007) Social identity performance: extending the strategic side of the SIDE model, *Personality and Social Psychology Review*, 11, 28–45.

Leach, C. W., van Zomeren, M., Zebel, S., Vliek, M., Pennekamp, S. F., Doosje, B., Ouwerkerk, J. P. & Spears, R. (2008) Group-level self-definition and self-investment: a hierarchical (multi-component) model of in-group Identification, *Journal of Personality and Social Psychology*, 95, 144–165.

LeBon, G. (1896) *The crowd: a study of the popular mind* (London, T.? Fisher Unwin).

McGarty, C., Taylor, N. & Douglas, K. (2000) Between commitment and compliance: obligation and the strategic dimension of SIDE, in: T. Postmes, R. Spears, M. Lea & S. D. Reicher (Eds) *SIDE issues centre stage: recent developments of de-individuation in groups*, Proceedings (Amsterdam, Dutch Royal Academy of Arts and Sciences), 143–150.

Oegema, D. & Klandermans, B. (1994) Why social movement sympathizers don't participate: erosion and non-conversion of support, *American Sociological Review*, 59, 703–722.

Olson, M. (1968) *The logic of collective action: Public goods and the theory of groups* (Cambridge, MA, Harvard University Press).

Ouwerkerk, J. W., de Gilder, D. & de Vries, N. K. (2000) When the going gets tough, the tough get going: social identification and individual effort in inter-group competition, *Personality and Social Psychology Bulletin*, 26, 1550–1559.

Postmes, T. & Spears, R. (1998) Deindividuation and anti-normative behavior: a meta-analysis, *Psychological Bulletin*, 123, 238–259.

Reicher, S. D. (1987) Crowd behaviour as social action, in: J. C. Turner, M. A. Hogg, P. J. Oakes, S. D. Reicher & M. S. Wetherell (Eds) *Rediscovering the social group: a self-categorization theory* (Oxford, Blackwell), 171–202.

Reicher, S. (2001) The psychology of crowd dynamics, in: M. A. Hogg & R. S. Tindale (Eds) *Blackwell handbook of social psychology: group processes* (Oxford, Blackwell), 182–208.

Reicher, S. D., Levine, M. & Gordijn, E. (1998) More on deindividuation, power relations between groups and the expression of social identity: three studies on the effects of visibility to the in-group, *British Journal of Social Psychology*, 37, 15–40.

Reicher, S. D., Spears, R. & Postmes, T. (1995) A social identity model of deindividuation phenomena, in: W. Stroebe & M. Hewstone (Eds) *European review of social psychology* (Oxford, Blackwell), 161–198.

Scheepers, D., Spears, R., Doosje, B. & Manstead, A. (2006) Diversity in in-group bias: structural factors, situational features, and social functions, *Journal of Personality and Social Psychology*, 90, 944–960.

Spears, R. (2010) Group rationale, collective sense: beyond intergroup bias, *British Journal of Social Psychology*, 49, 1–20.

Spears, R. & Lea, M. (1994) Panacea or panopticon? The hidden power in computer-mediated communication, *Communication Research*, 21, 427–459.

Spears, R., Lea, M., Corneliussen, R. A., Postmes, T. & Ter Haar, W. (2002) Computer mediated communication as a channel for social resistance: the strategic side of SIDE, *Small Group Research*, 33, 555–574.

Steiner, I. D. (1972) *Group processes and productivity* (New York, NY, Academic Press).

Stott, C. J., Hutchison, P. & Drury, J. (2001) 'Hooligans' abroad? Inter-group dynamics, social identity and participation in collective 'disorder' at the 1998 World Cup Finals, *British Journal of Social Psychology*, 40, 359–384.

Subasic, E., Reynolds, K. J. & Turner, J. C. (2008) The political solidarity model of social change: dynamics of self-categorization in intergroup power relations, *Personality and Social Psychology Review*, 12, 330–352.

Tajfel, H. (1978) The achievement of intergroup differentiation, in: H. Tajfel (Ed.) *Differentiation between social groups* (London, Academic Press), 77–100.

Tajfel, H. & Turner, J. C. (1979) An integrative theory of intergroup conflict, in: W. G. Austin & S. Worchel (Eds) *The social psychology of intergroup relations* (Monterey, CA, Brooks/Cole), 33–47.

Triplett, N. (1898) The dynamogenic factors in pacemaking and competition, *American Journal of Psychology*, 9, 507–533.

Turner, J. C. (1991) *Social influence*, (Milton Keynes, Open University Press and Pacific Grove, CA, Brooks/Cole).

Turner, J. C. (1999) Current issues in research on social identity and self-categorization theories, in: N. Ellemers, R. Spears & B. Doosje (Eds) *Social identity: context, commitment, content* (Oxford, Blackwell), 6–34.

Turner, J. C., Hogg, M. A., Oakes, P. J., Reicher, S. D. & Wetherell, M. S. (1987) *Rediscovering the social group: a self-categorization perspective* (Oxford, Basil Blackwell).

Van Zomeren, M. & Iyer, A. (2009) Toward integrative understanding of the social and psychological dynamics of collective action, *Journal of Social Issues*, 65, 645–660.

Van Zomeren, M., Postmes, T. & Spears, R. (2008a) Toward an integrative Social Identity Model of Collective Action: a quantitative research synthesis of three socio-psychological perspectives, *Psychological Bulletin*, 134, 504–535.

Van Zomeren, M., Spears, R. & Leach, C. W. (2008b) Exploring psychological mechanisms of collective action: does relevance of group identity influence how people cope with collective disadvantage?, *British Journal of Social Psychology*, 47, 353–372.

Van Zomeren, M., Postmes, T. & Spears, R. (2011) On convictions' collective consequences: integrating moral convictions with the Social Identity Model of Collective Action, *British Journal of Social Psychology*.

Van Zomeren, M. & Spears, R. (2009) Metaphors of protest: a classification of motivations of collective action, *Journal of Social Issues*, 65, 661–679.

Van Zomeren, M., Spears, R., Fischer, A. H. & Leach, C. W. (2004) Put your money where your mouth is!: explaining collective action tendencies through group-based anger and group efficacy, *Journal of Personality and Social Psychology*, 87, 649–664.

Van Zomeren, M., Spears, R. & Leach, C. W. (2010) Challenging the powerful: explaining the strategic expression of group-based anger, Unpublished manuscript, University of Groningen, Groningen.

Veenstra, K. & Haslam, S. A. (2000) Willingness to participate in industrial protest: exploring social identification in context, *British Journal of Social Psychology*, 39, 153–172.

Zajonc, R. B. (1965) Social facilitation, *Science*, 149, 269–274.

Zimbardo, P. (1969) The human choice: individuation, reason, and order versus deindidividuation, impulse and chaos, in: W. J. Arnold & D. Levine (Eds) *Nebraska symposium on motivation* Vol. 17 (Lincoln, NB, University of Nebraska Press).

Crowd disasters: a socio-technical systems perspective

Rose Challenger and Chris W. Clegg

Socio-Technical Centre, Leeds University Business School, University of Leeds, Leeds, UK

We present a socio-technical systems framework and underlying principles to help understand a sample of crowd-related disasters. Our approach is founded on the premise that disasters result from complex systems failures, wherein a series of interdependent factors combine in such a way as to cause problems. We explore the explanatory power of our approach by analysing three incidents; Hillsborough football stadium disaster (1989), King's Cross underground fire (1987), and Bradford City stadium fire (1985). We find a common set of fundamental, interrelated issues and consistent violations of our socio-technical design principles. We conclude by discussing how our framework, principles and socio-technical thinking more generally, may contribute to theory and practice.

Introduction

> Events of the magnitude of Hillsborough don't usually happen just for one single reason, nor is it usually possible to pin the blame on one single scapegoat... Disasters happen because a whole series of mistakes, misjudgments and mischances happen to come together in a deadly combination. (Dr John Habgood, Archbishop of York, speaking at the Hillsborough Memorial Service; cited in Taylor, 1989, p. 20)

Numerous disasters have occurred over the years across a range of domains, often resulting in injuries and lost lives. These include: air traffic control, e.g. the Tenerife airport disaster (1977); nuclear disasters, e.g. Three Mile Island (1979); gas explosions, e.g. Bhopal (1984); space exploration, e.g. the *Challenger* Space Shuttle disaster (1986); fires, e.g. Summerland leisure centre fire (1974); rail crashes, e.g. Ladbroke Grove (1999); and crowd crushes, e.g. Love Parade (2010). In the wake of such disasters, there is a tendency to search for 'simple technical solutions as a panacea' (Elliott & Smith, 1993, p. 226). Whole systems are rarely evaluated as organisations search for technical causes, seeking to assign responsibility and develop prevention techniques at the expense of addressing the underlying root causes (e.g. Canter *et al.*, 1989; Reason, 1990, 1991, 1995; Elliott *et al.*, 1997).

However, the literatures concerned with human factors, organisational safety and disaster/crisis management suggest disasters are rarely due to technical factors alone but result from complex systems failures (e.g. Shrivastava, 1987; Weick, 1990; Pidgeon, 1997; Toft & Reynolds, 2005; Elliott, 2006; Shrivastava *et al.*, 2006; Smith, 1990, 2006; Turner & Toft, 2006). We agree; 'it is better to think of the problem of understanding disasters as a "socio-technical" problem with social, organisational and technical processes interacting to produce the phenomenon to be studied' (Turner & Pidgeon, 1997, p. 3).

In accordance with this systems viewpoint, several theoretical models have emerged, most notably Turner's (1976, 1978, 1994) man-made disasters model, Reason's (1997, 1998) Swiss cheese model, and Perrow's (1981, 1984, 1994) normal accident theory. All share the basic premise that disasters/accidents result from a concatenation of unanticipated, seemingly insignificant, failures throughout the system, which, when triggered, interact to create a cascade of serious problems, ultimately resulting in system failure. Whilst we agree with this fundamental principle, we believe these theories are under-specified both theoretically and practically. Is it enough to argue simply that unanticipated events may come together to create disasters? Can we begin to specify the types of failures/factors typically involved? Can we use design principles to identify what violations may contribute to systems failure? Is there a way of providing greater specification of past and future issues for theoretical and practical purposes?

In this paper, we attempt to provide greater specificity by presenting a socio-technical systems framework and underpinning design principles for analysing disasters. If we can identify which socio-technical factors and/or design principles are involved in the occurrence of disasters, we have the opportunity to develop theory and guide and inform future practice, potentially reducing their occurrence. Although our approach should be applicable across different domains, we focus on crowd-related disasters, following our previous work for the Cabinet Office (Challenger *et al.*, 2010a, 2010b).

The objectives of this paper are as follows:

- To present our socio-technical systems framework and design principles for analysing disasters.
- To apply our ideas by analysing three crowd-related disasters; the Hillsborough football stadium disaster (1989), the King's Cross underground fire (1987), and the Bradford City stadium fire (1985).
- To make theoretical contributions to the academic literatures on disasters and socio-technical thinking by providing greater specification of the kinds of factors that come together to create major problems.
- To suggest ways forward for the practice of those involved in organising, planning and managing crowd events.

A socio-technical systems framework and design principles

Socio-technical systems theory advocates when designing and operating any new system it is critical to focus on and optimise both technical and social factors (e.g.

81

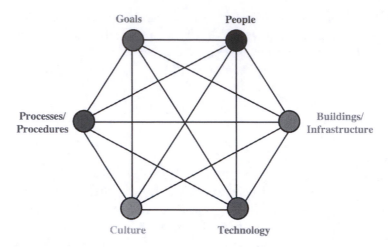

Figure 1. A socio-technical systems perspective (Challenger *et al.*, 2010a, p. 74)

Cherns, 1976, 1987). It is inevitable that changes to one part of a system will necessitate subsequent changes to other parts; thereby, to optimise success, the system should be considered holistically (e.g. Hendrick, 1997; Clegg & Shepherd, 2007). Thus, people, processes and procedures, goals, culture, technology, and buildings and infrastructure should all be viewed as interdependent and given joint consideration, as illustrated in our socio-technical systems framework (Figure 1). Furthermore, it is highly unlikely that any individual or group will understand all the component parts when considering the system overall. Therefore, new systems design should involve multiple stakeholders with a complementary range of knowledge and expertise, including end-users, managers, human resource experts, designers and clients (e.g. Clegg *et al.*, 2000). End-user participation in, and ownership of, systems design and implementation is critical (e.g. Clegg & Walsh, 2004; Mumford, 2006).

There are a number of interrelated principles for socio-technical systems design (Cherns, 1976, 1987; Clegg, 2000) that underpin our approach (Table 1). They have four primary functions: to highlight issues requiring particular attention in the design process; to stress the need for a series of interrelated perspectives on design; to provide a potential framework for systems analysis; and to enable predictions about future systems operation (Clegg, 2000).

Method

To assess the explanatory power of our socio-technical approach, we analysed retrospectively a number of crowd-related disasters. Our selection criteria were threefold. The disasters must: (1) involve crowds directly; (2) be independently and rigorously reviewed (by formal public inquiries and peer-reviewed publications); and (3) have similarities and differences (e.g. comparing event type and outcome) to explore the applicability and generalisability of our ideas.

Table 1. Principles of socio-technical systems design (adapted from Clegg, 2000)

Meta-principles (*capture an overall view of systems design*)

1 Design is systemic
   A system comprises a range of interrelated factors and should be designed to optimise social and technical concerns jointly

2 Values and mindsets are central to design
   Underlying values and mindsets strongly influence systems design and operation

3 Design involves making choices
   Design choices are interdependent and exist on many dimensions, e.g. how will the system be operated, managed and organised?

4 Design should reflect the needs of the business, its users and their managers
   Systems should be designed to meet the needs of all relevant stakeholders

5 Design is an extended social process
   Design continues throughout the life cycle of the system, as multiple stakeholders shape and reconfigure it over time

6 Design is socially shaped
   Design is a social phenomenon influenced by social norms, movements and trends

7 Design is contingent
   There is no 'one best way'; optimum design depends on a range of issues

Content principles (*concerned with the content of new systems design*)

8 Core processes should be integrated
   Design should avoid splitting core processes across artificial organisational boundaries; people should manage complete processes

9 Design entails multiple task allocations between and amongst humans and machines
   Tasks and roles should be allocated amongst humans or machines clearly, in an explicit, systematic way

10 System components should be congruent
   All system parts should be consistent with one another and fit with existing organisational systems and practices

11 Systems should be simple in design and make problems visible
   Design should maximise ease of use and understanding, learnability, and visibility of problems to allow quicker resolution

12 Problems should be controlled at source
   Design should enable system problems to be controlled directly on the ground by end-users, as local experts

13 The means of undertaking tasks should be flexibly specified
   Systems should not be over-specified; end-users should be able to adapt processes to suit their needs better

Process principles (*concerned with the process of systems design*)

14 Design practice is itself a socio-technical system
   Design processes are themselves complex systems involving an interdependent mix of social and technical subsystems

15 Systems and their design should be owned by their managers and users
   Ownership of a system should be afforded to those who will use, manage and support it, rather than being fragmented

16 Evaluation is an essential aspect of design
   System performance should be regularly evaluated against the goals of the organisation and its employees

17 Design involves multidisciplinary education
   Design should bring together knowledge, skills and expertise from multiple disciplines

18 Resources and support are required for design
   Design needs resource investment, e.g. time, effort and money; knowledge, skills and expertise; socio-technical methods, tools and techniques

19 System design involves political processes
   Complex systems design can be a political process; various stakeholders are affected by design, implementation, management and use

Based on these criteria, we selected the Hillsborough football stadium disaster (1989), the King's Cross underground fire (1987), and the Bradford City stadium fire (1985). All three involved crowds directly and were subject to independent public inquiries leading respectively to the Taylor Report (Taylor, 1989, 1990), the Fennell Report (Fennell, 1988), and the Popplewell Inquiry (Popplewell, 1985). Whilst these official reports were used as the primary data source, relevant academic papers were also examined. All three also share similarities and differences; Hillsborough and Bradford concerned football crowds, whereas King's Cross concerned commuter crowds; and King's Cross and Bradford were fires, whereas Hillsborough involved a crush.

Case studies

Hillsborough football stadium disaster (1989)

On 15 April 1989 the FA Cup semi-final was due to take place between Liverpool and Nottingham Forest at Hillsborough football stadium. Delayed journeys meant many of the 24,256 Liverpool supporters arrived late with only 30 minutes to enter the ground before the 3 p.m. kick-off (Taylor, 1989, 1990). To relieve the growing congestion at the Leppings Lane entrance, Chief Superintendent Duckenfield (the commanding officer) gave the order to open exit gate 'C'. This led to a rush of over 2000 supporters into the Leppings Lane terrace directly behind the goal, via a steep, narrow tunnel (Taylor, 1989). Several side pens remained half empty whilst the central two pens (3 and 4), with the easiest immediate access, became severely overcrowded. Mass crushing occurred and a barrier (124A) collapsed under immense crowd pressure (Scraton, 1999). Some fans started to climb the perimeter fence to escape the crush, whilst others forced open a small gate in the fencing and escaped onto the pitch. At 3.06 p.m., the police advised the referee to stop the match. Two perimeter gates were opened and fans evacuated onto the pitch. In total, 95 people died and over 400 were injured (Taylor, 1989, 1990).

Lord Justice Taylor's inquiries into the disaster (Taylor, 1989, 1990) concluded overcrowding and lack of police control were the primary causes. However, he also acknowledged the influence of issues such as complacency, poor facilities and ground conditions, concerns over hooliganism, and poor leadership (Taylor, 1990). It was apparent that multiple, interrelated factors contributed; 'the simultaneous occurrence of several minor factors, which in isolation might only have provoked minor inconveniences, resulted in a disaster of major proportions' (Lea *et al.*, 1998, p. 347). Indeed, mapping the findings of our analysis onto our systems framework it becomes clear that problems occurred across the six interrelated factors (Figure 2), underpinned by the design principles, as detailed below.

Primarily, we believe the mindsets and values at Hillsborough were incompatible with systems thinking (principle 2). The overall attitude was one of complacency. Those involved believed disaster would not occur and, therefore, thorough preparation and contingency planning were not necessary; 'it had never happened

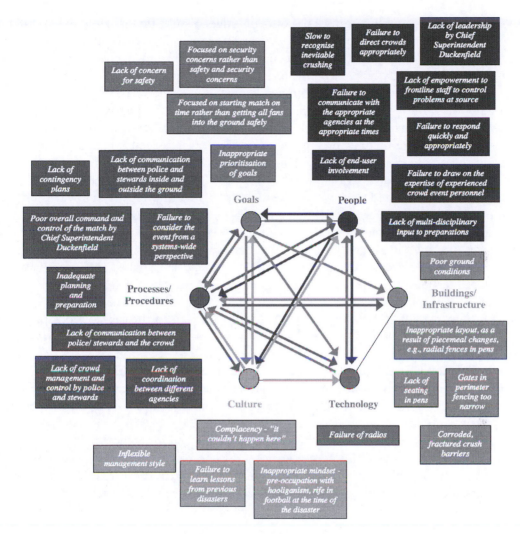

Figure 2. The Hillsborough football stadium disaster (1989) from a systems perspective.

before so there was no reason to foresee it' (Taylor, 1989, p. 36). In line with this attitude, there was a fundamental failure to learn lessons from previous incidents (principle 16). Taylor's Report (Taylor, 1990) was the ninth official report concerning crowd control and safety at football grounds. Indeed, crushing had been reported at Hillsborough during the 1988 FA Cup semi-final, when overcrowding in pens 3 and 4 was so severe that police blocked off the tunnel leading to them.

Moreover, widespread expectations about football crowds due to the prevalence of hooliganism at that time also influenced authorities' behaviours, particularly policing and crowd management strategies (e.g. Elliott & Smith, 1993, 1997, 2006; Smith & Elliott, 2007). Disorder and violence were the main preoccupation and the focus was on crowd control rather than safety (principles 1, 2 and 4). There was 'insufficient concern and vigilance for the safety and well-being of spectators ... compounded by a preoccupation with measures to control hooliganism' (Taylor, 1990, p. 4). Such were police expectations as a result of this mindset that alternative explanations for observed crowd behaviours were not considered. For instance, prior assumptions about antisocial behaviour led police to ignore fans' cries for help. Similarly, when fans were seen climbing the perimeter fences to escape the crushing, it was assumed they were invading the pitch and so perimeter gates were not opened (Taylor, 1989). Furthermore, given this mindset, the organisational resources in place to support the match were geared primarily towards security rather than supporting the whole system (i.e. safety and security); they were not compatible with a socio-technical approach (principle 18).

Problems also resulted from the failure to adopt a systemic approach towards preparations and management, with little consideration given to how actions would have knock-on effects for other components within the system (principles 1, 3, 4, 7 and 14). For example, there was a lack of crowd management and control by stewards and police, both inside and outside the ground. Whilst more fans arrived and crowd pressures mounted outside, the lack of management and direction inside resulted in an uneven distribution of people in the terraces (Scraton, 1999), leading to fatal overcrowding in pens 3 and 4 (Sime, 1995). Moreover, due to the lack of contingency plans, for instance outlining procedures should it be necessary to open an exit gate, neither police nor stewards knew how to act for the best (Scraton, 1999). This lack of contingency planning also meant there was little flexibility built into the system to accommodate changes in response to circumstances on the day (principles 5, 7 and 13). For example, delaying the start of the match to allow fans time to enter safely was not considered a viable option (Taylor, 1989).

Similarly, core processes were not congruent, integrated or transparent (principles 8–11). There was a lack of communication and coordination between the different parties involved, with each unsure about their roles and responsibilities in relation to others. For example, the police and stewards both inside and outside the ground failed to communicate effectively, particularly during the late rush of fans into the ground. Taylor (1989), in relation to Duckenfield's decision to open exit gate 'C', notes 'Neither the Club control room nor any police officers inside the turnstiles were told of this order before or after it was given or of any action it would require' (p. 12). Consequently, those inside the ground had no time to prepare for the influx of fans, whilst those outside were not aware of the mounting problems. Communication with the crowd was also ineffective, with fans trying to enter the ground not warned about the excessive congestion and overcrowding ahead.

There was also a lack of end-user ownership[1] at Hillsborough; it was very much a top-down approach, led by Chief Superintendent Duckenfield. Frontline, experienced officers were not given opportunities to offer insight into how best to manage the crowd or to control problems at source (principles 5, 6, 12, 13 and 15). They were under strict instructions not to open the perimeter gates leading onto the pitch unless specifically told to do so by Duckenfield. As such, individual police on the ground, who were the first to realise the nature of the crush and impending disaster, did not feel empowered to relieve the pressure by opening the perimeter gates (principle 12). Yet Duckenfield seemed unable to make appropriate and timely decisions, to take charge of his officers and, subsequently, to give consequential orders; 'he froze' (Taylor, 1989, p. 50). Moreover, event personnel were slow to recognise the incident unfolding before them; 'In the control room no-one noticed the overcrowding or anything amiss in pens 3 and 4 until the first fans spilt out onto the perimeter track just before kick-off' (Taylor, 1989, p. 13). Further problems were caused by the lack of input, in the form of wide-ranging knowledge and expertise, to the preparations and management of the match (principles 17 and 19).

Within the ground itself, the facilities were poor and the layout inappropriate, on account of piecemeal alterations (Taylor, 1989, 1990). The Leppings Lane terraces did not have individual seating but were divided into all-standing pens. The crush barriers, in particular barrier 124A, were corroded and fractured (Heyes & Tattersall, 1989). Many were inappropriately aligned or fell below the minimum height recommended by the Green Guide (Home Office, 1986) as a result of previous modifications to the height of the terrace steps (e.g. Collins & Waterhouse, 1990; Nicholson & Roebuck, 1995). Gates in the perimeter fencing round the pitch were also too narrow and too few (Taylor, 1990).

King's Cross underground fire (1987)

At around 7.30 p.m. on 18 November 1987, a fire broke out at King's Cross underground station on an escalator leading from the Piccadilly line into the ticket hall (Fennell, 1988). It is believed to have started when a lighted match was dropped between the moving stairway and the escalator side (Fennell, 1988). The alarm was raised independently by two passengers, who informed a member of staff and pressed the escalator's emergency stop button. Two British Transport Police present at the station went to investigate and, upon seeing a small fire, called the fire brigade at 7.34 p.m. (Fennell, 1988). The police began guiding passengers away from the Piccadilly line escalators towards those of the Victoria line. As trains continued to arrive, growing numbers of passengers were also evacuated from the underground platforms, via the Victoria line escalators and ticket hall (Donald & Canter, 1990, 1992). No water was applied to the fire during this time. The fire brigade arrived at approximately 7.43 p.m. but it was too late; 2 minutes later a flashover occurred in the ticket hall filling it with poisonous black smoke and balls of fire (Donald & Canter, 1990, 1992). The flashover spread into the passages leading to the ticket hall and into the Victoria line escalators, through which passengers were still being evacuated. In total, 31 people were killed and many more were injured (Fennell, 1988).

Fennell's inquiry (Fennell, 1988) acknowledged the influence of multiple issues, including poorly designed and maintained facilities, lack of staff training and poor communication. Once again, multiple, interrelated factors appear to have contributed; 'The King's Cross fire was a large, complex, interrelated set of incidents' (Donald & Canter, 1990, p. 19). Considering these in relation to our socio-technical framework, it again becomes clear that a complex web of problems and violated design principles led to the disaster.

Fundamentally, the mindsets and values at King's Cross were ones of inevitability and complacency (principle 2). Those involved believed fires were an inevitable occurrence, given the age and complexity of the underground system (Fennell, 1988). Indeed, the Chairman and Managing Director of London Underground Limited (operating company) deemed fires 'an occupational hazard', simply 'part of the nature' of the underground (Fennell, 1988, p. 31). Consequently, the importance of striving to prevent fires was overlooked in favour of simply trying to manage them (principle 6) and, accordingly, available organisational resources were not supportive of the whole system (principle 18). As Fennell observed, management were 'fundamentally in error' in their approach (p. 17).

Furthermore, despite the history of fires on underground station escalators (e.g. Oxford Circus, 1985; Green Park, 1985, 1987), lessons were not adequately learned (principle 16) (Toft & Reynolds, 2005). Since previous underground fires had not resulted in deaths, management were of the belief that when an inevitable fire occurred at King's Cross no deaths would result. However, such complacency resulted in what Fennell (1988) termed 'dangerous, blinkered self-sufficiency' (p. 31), with very little exchange of information or expertise, at either an intra- or inter-organisational level (principles 8, 10 and 17). In particular, management were unwilling to accept advice from external bodies; for instance, following the fire at Oxford Circus, London Fire Brigade repeatedly warned London Underground about the importance of calling the brigade at the first signs of every suspected fire (Toft & Reynolds, 2005). However, London Underground's disregard for this advice is evident in their rule book, stating that fire should be initially dealt with by staff and the fire brigade only called 'when the fire was beyond their control' (Fennell, 1988, p. 61).

This lack of safety culture was further compounded by a lack of role clarity, minimal cross-departmental working and poor industrial relations (principles 8, 10, 11, 17 and 19). The overall management of King's Cross was disjointed (Fennell, 1988). No individual or organisation was charged with overall responsibility for safety, nor were safety overlaps between departments and knock-on effects for other components within the system considered (principles 1, 3, 4, 9, 10 and 14). For example, London Regional Transport (responsible for providing public transport to the Greater London area) was of the opinion that safety, being an operational matter, was not their responsibility but that of the operating company, London Underground. Thus, whilst London Regional Transport strictly monitored issues related to productivity and costs, it did not regulate issues concerned with safety (Fennell, 1988). Similarly, the operations director (responsible for operational safety and staff training) did not concern himself with the safe working of escalators, deeming that to be the sole responsibility of the engineering director, and vice versa (Fennell, 1988).

Moreover, as a result of the complacent mindset and confused responsibilities at King's Cross, staff were 'woefully ill-equipped' (Fennell, 1988, p. 67) to deal with the situation themselves (principles 4, 12 and 15).[2] There was a lack of training in relation to fires and emergency evacuations, and no evacuation plan. Key individuals, including station staff and London Fire Brigade, were unfamiliar with King's Cross and its layout. Thus, their response was 'uncoordinated, haphazard and untrained' (Fennell, 1988, p. 19); there was no flexibility built into the system to deal with the unfolding situation (principles 5, 7 and 13). For instance, the relief station inspector did not inform the station manager or the line controller about the fire, nor did he use the water fog equipment; he was inadequately trained, unfamiliar with the station and inexperienced (Fennell, 1988).

In addition, there was no sense of urgency about responding immediately to the fire (e.g. Borodzicz, 2005) and little appreciation of the need for inter-agency coordination and communication, particularly between London Underground staff and London Fire Brigade (principles 17 and 19). However, as Fennell (1988) concludes, 'Good communications are at the heart of a modern system of mass transportation' (p. 19). Yet, no alarms sounded and warning messages were not coordinated. As a result, passengers were largely unaware of the situation unfolding and, consequently, of the most appropriate course of action to take (Donald & Canter, 1992).

The poorly maintained facilities within the underground also played a central role in the disaster. For instance, the escalators—already a fire hazard being constructed from wood—were not sufficiently cleaned and lubricated. Grease and detritus were allowed to accumulate in a 15 centimetre gap between two sets of wheels on running tracks beside the escalator (Fennell, 1988; Moodie, 1992). This created a seedbed for fire to develop and spread.

Bradford City stadium fire (1985)

On 11 May 1985, Bradford City played their last game of the football season against Lincoln City. At approximately 3.40 p.m. a fire broke out in Block G of the main stand (Popplewell, 1985). It is thought a discarded cigarette or match fell through a space beneath the seats in the stand, igniting a deep pile of rubbish (Popplewell, 1985). Problems became evident when fans near the back of Block G noticed flames beneath the stand. Whilst the majority remained seated watching the ongoing match, one fan went to the rear of the stand in search of a fire extinguisher; he found none, so informed a nearby police officer. After inspecting the problem himself, the officer shouted to a colleague on the pitch for an extinguisher. However, his message was misheard and the fire brigade were called instead, at approximately 3.43 p.m. (Popplewell, 1985). As the flames became more visible and the smoke denser, police began to evacuate the stand, and the referee stopped the match. The fire then rapidly took hold and a flashover engulfed Block G, with the entire main stand ablaze by approximately 3.46 p.m. (Popplewell, 1985). In total, 56 people died and hundreds were injured.

Whilst the poor condition of the stand can be seen as the primary cause, Popplewell (1985) acknowledged 'the overall mechanism is complex' (p. 60), involving multiple issues including the condition and design of the ground, evacuation practices and assumptions about human behaviours. When we map these issues onto our systems framework, we see problems across all six socio-technical factors and violations of the design principles, as discussed below.

Primarily, it is apparent that the overall attitude of those involved, and particularly those in leadership and management roles, was one of complacency with regard to safety. Thus, the mindsets and values underpinning actions at Bradford were inappropriate (principle 2). With the benefit of hindsight, the Director and Chairman of the club acknowledged 'there are a number of things we all wish had been done or had been thought of prior to this terrible tragedy' (Popplewell, 1985, p. 4). At the time of the fire, there was a fundamental failure to take safety seriously; compliance with the Green Guide (Home Office, 1976) was not considered a priority goal (principles 3, 4 and 6). Rather, management were chiefly concerned with maintaining the club's financial viability; safety was seen as an inconvenient expense (principles 18 and 19) (Popplewell, 1985).

Popplewell (1985) concluded 'Had the Green Guide been complied with, this tragedy would not have occurred' (p. 10). In our view, this non-compliance (which continued for almost ten more years; Elliott & Smith, 1997, 2006) played a key role in the disaster, in addition to having knock-on effects for the other interdependent components within the system, such as ground conditions and maintenance, inter-agency cooperation, and personnel training (principles 1, 3, 4, 9 and 14). For instance, the Green Guide clearly states that voids under the seating areas of stands are a fire hazard, as accumulating rubbish and combustible materials have the potential to be ignited unnoticed by a discarded heat source. Consequently, if such voids cannot be avoided in stadium design, they should be sealed off to reduce the risk of fire. Such voids at Bradford were not attended to and, as a result, provided the origin of the fire. Further non-compliance occurred in relation to evacuation requirements, namely the accessibility and quantity of emergency exits affecting evacuation times (Popplewell, 1985).

Related to this complacent attitude, there was a fundamental failure to learn lessons from previous incidents and to heed warnings from external bodies about potential risks (principle 16) (e.g. Popplewell, 1985; Elliott & Smith, 1993, 2006). Concerns about the condition of the ground, particularly the main stand, were expressed to Bradford City by the Health and Safety Executive, but no action was taken. For example, the inappropriate building materials, namely the timber framework and asphalt roof, and the void beneath the stand were considered hazardous by the authorities, but were not rectified by the club (Popplewell, 1985; Inglis, 1987; Elliott & Smith, 1993).

The lack of inter-agency communication and coordination, and associated lack of clarity about respective roles and responsibilities, further contributed to the neglect of safety (principles 8–11, 17 and 19). Ultimately, no party considered safety to be their responsibility and, therefore, despite being aware of the numerous risks, did not feel the need to act in advance (principles 11, 12 and 15). For example, having voiced their concerns to the club, the county council and fire brigade considered themselves 'under no obligation to take any further steps' (Popplewell, 1985, p. 21). Similarly, although fully aware of the recommendations in the Green Guide, the club secretary believed ensuring compliance was 'not really his responsibility' (Popplewell, 1985, pp. 22–23). Moreover, as the incident unfolded, communication both within and between the parties was hindered by inefficient communication systems and equipment. For instance, there were no loud hailers to inform fans of the escalating problem and the immediate need to evacuate. Likewise, problems were experienced with the police radios, with many messages to control being only partly relayed or not received at all (Popplewell, 1985).

The prevalence of football hooliganism in the 1980s also affected the actions and plans of those at Bradford (e.g. Elliott & Smith, 1993, 1997, 2006; Smith & Elliott, 2007). In order to prevent disorder and violence, crowd control took precedence over safety (principles 1, 2 and 4). Thus, entry turnstiles and exit gates leading off the corridor running along the rear of the main stand were locked during the match to prevent unauthorised access. However, this limited the number of escape routes available to fans. Similarly, fire extinguishers had been removed from the stand for fear of misuse by spectators, with staff largely unaware of their locations, and high-specification police radios were not utilised for fear of confrontation with hooligans (Popplewell, 1985). This not only impacted communications, but also reduced flexibility to deal with the unfolding situation and to tackle problems at source (principles 5, 7, 12 and 13).

Due to a lack of training and understanding about human behaviours in emergency situations, there was an underestimation of the seriousness of the situation by stadium officials, police officers and fans alike, considering it to be 'of no particular significance', merely a 'minor incident' (Popplewell, 1985, p. 7). They did not appreciate the speed at which the fire would escalate and, therefore, did not begin evacuating as soon as possible (e.g. Canter *et al.*, 1989; Donald & Canter, 1990, 1992).

Overall, therefore, our analyses across the three cases highlight how a number of socio-technical issues combined to contribute to the nature and scope of each of the disasters.

Discussion and conclusions

Summary

Our socio-technical systems approach, similar to well-established theorists in the area, is founded on the premise that disasters result from complex systems failures, wherein interdependent factors combine to cause problems. In this paper, we attempt to advance the field by being more specific about what those factors comprise. We offer a systems framework specifying people, processes and procedures, goals, culture, technology, and buildings and infrastructure (Figure 1) as the key interdependent factors typically involved. We also utilise existing socio-technical design principles (Clegg, 2000). We propose that crowd-related disasters, being systems failures, are underpinned by problems related to these factors and principles. Our analyses of Hillsborough, King's Cross and Bradford lend support to our proposition. Despite their differences, we see common socio-technical issues arising (Table 2) and consistent violations of our design principles.

What claims are we making?

We view our socio-technical framework and principles as an attempt to develop a more specific typology of the interdependent factors and design principles most likely to be

Table 2. Summary of the interrelated factors underpinning the Hillsborough, King's Cross and Bradford disasters

Key socio-technical factors	Hillsborough (1989)	King's Cross (1987)	Bradford (1985)
Culture	Complacency—'it couldn't happen here' Inappropriate mindset—a preoccupation with hooliganism A failure to learn lessons An inflexible management style	Complacency—'it couldn't happen here' Inappropriate mindset—'fire is inevitable' A failure to learn lessons A false sense of security given previous fires had not resulted in deaths Blinkered management—unwilling to listen to external advice	Complacency—'it couldn't happen here' Inappropriate mindset—a preoccupation with hooliganism A failure to learn lessons Blinkered management—unwilling to listen to external advice
Goals	Focused on security rather than on safety and security Lack of a concern for safety Focused on starting the match on time rather than getting all fans into the ground safely Inappropriate prioritisation of goals	Focused on fire precautions rather than fire prevention Lack of a concern for safety Concerned with keeping trains running as normal for as long as possible	Focused on security rather than on safety and security Lack of a concern for safety Lack of compliance with the Green Guide Ground improvements considered a low priority
Buildings/infrastructure	Poor ground conditions Corroded and fractured crush barriers Inappropriate layout as a result of piecemeal changes, e.g. radial fences in pens Gates in the perimeter fencing too narrow Lack of seating in pens	Poorly maintained facilities Escalators not cleaned and lubricated Inappropriate materials, e.g. escalators made of wood Inappropriate layout, e.g. Station Manager's office not in a central location	Poor ground conditions Void underneath the stand allowing rubbish to accumulate Inappropriate materials, e.g. the stand made of wood and asphalt Lack of emergency exits
Technology	A failure of radios	A failure of radios underground Lack of communications equipment	Problems with police radios Inefficient communications equipment, e.g. no loud hailers Lack of fire-fighting equipment in stands

(Continued)

Table 2 Continued

Key socio-technical factors	Hillsborough (1989)	King's Cross (1987)	Bradford (1985)
Processes/procedures	A failure to consider the event from a systems-wide perspective	A failure to consider the event from a systems-wide perspective	A failure to consider the event from a systems-wide perspective
	Poor overall command and control	Poor station management and leadership	Poor overall control and leadership
	Lack of coordination between agencies	Lack of coordination between leadership	Lack of coordination between agencies
	Lack of communication between police and stewards inside and outside the ground	Lack of communication and exchange of information between parties	Lack of communication and exchange of information between parties
	Lack of communication between police/ stewards and the crowd	Inadequate planning and preparation	Inadequate planning and preparation
	Inadequate planning and preparation	Confusion and uncertainty over roles and responsibilities	Confusion and uncertainty over roles and responsibilities
	Lack of contingency plans	Lack of evacuation plans	
	Lack of crowd management and control by police and stewards	Lack of contingency plans	
People	Lack of overall control, leadership and responsibility	Lack of overall control, leadership and responsibility	Lack of overall control, leadership and responsibility
	Slow to recognise crushing	Slow to recognise the seriousness of the situation	Slow to recognise the seriousness of the situation
	A failure to respond quickly and appropriately	A failure to respond quickly and appropriately	A failure to respond quickly and appropriately
	A failure to communicate with the appropriate agencies at the appropriate times	A failure to inform the correct people about the fire	Staff not trained for emergencies
	Lack of end-user involvement	Lack of training in fires, e.g. using water fog equipment	Lack of understanding about human behaviours
	Lack of multidisciplinary input	Lack of training in evacuation procedures	Ambiguity about roles and responsibilities
	A failure to draw on the expertise of experienced crowd event personnel	Lack of familiarity with the station's layout	No party willing to take responsibility for safety
	Lack of empowerment to frontline staff to control problems at source	A failure to use fire extinguishers or water fog equipment	
		Ambiguity about roles and responsibilities	
		Lack of empowerment to frontline staff to control problems at source	

significant in disaster causation. We believe specificity of the kind we are proposing is potentially much more useful in taking forward our understanding than simply saying major incidents occur when certain factors come together but without specifying in advance what those particular factors are likely to be. To the best of our knowledge, this approach is novel.

However, we need to be clear this systems view does not downplay the significance of important structural issues. Thus, we are not disputing fans died at Hillsborough because too many people rushed into a small space, or that the fires at King's Cross and Bradford occurred because discarded heat sources set light to combustible rubbish. Rather, what our approach does is to ask why such circumstances were allowed to occur and why particular events unfolded the way they did. Accordingly, we try to explain why these factors were in place and also to understand why the events had the scale of impact they did. We believe this gives a fuller understanding.

How can we take this area forward?

For research, we believe there are two immediate opportunities. First, we need to undertake similar analyses of both crowd-related and other disasters, to test the applicability and generalisability of our ideas across different domains. This should include more recent disasters, to address the potential criticism that our selection criteria resulted in analyses of incidents over 20 years old.

Second, continuing our drive for greater specificity, we need to develop more specific hypotheses about the roles of, and relationships between, our socio-technical factors and principles. Thus, for disasters to occur do there need to be problems in each of the six factors in our model and a spread of violations across the principles? Or are some more important than others? For example, does the combination of inappropriate mindsets, partial goals and a poor infrastructure lie at the heart of major disasters? To tease out these relationships, further empirical work is needed to explore which factors and/or principles may be necessary and which (if any) sufficient for disaster, and whether there are tipping points when disaster becomes inevitable. We need to examine existing literatures on crowd-related and other disasters and use the lessons learned to identify and study particular events and circumstances most likely to be at greatest risk in the future.

Based on our analyses thus far, we would hypothesise the following factors are necessary, but not alone sufficient, for crowd-related disasters:

- Singular dominant mindsets, that prove inappropriate for emerging circumstances (c.f. groupthink; Janis, 1972).
- Partial goals, reflected in a lack of attention to safety.
- Inappropriate or inadequate design of facilities and infrastructures.
- A failure to learn lessons from previous incidents, or to heed advice from external experts (c.f. 'failures of hindsight'; Turner, 1976).
- Poor or fragmented leadership.
- Poor coordination between key agencies and a lack of role clarity.

- Inadequate communication between parties and with the crowd.
- Failure to invest in appropriate safety training and education enabling people to cope with a range of contingencies.
- Failures in technology and inefficient communications equipment.
- A lack of engagement in design and planning by key actors.
- A lack of frontline empowerment to respond to arising problems.

We also believe our socio-technical ideas hold implications for practice. First, the framework and principles could be translated into 'good practice' guidelines for people planning and managing events, building on our previous research (Challenger *et al.*, 2010a, 2010b). Second, our ideas could inform various training and education opportunities for those involved in crowd events. Third, they could be used to develop a systems based risk assessment tool for those planning and managing events to assess and manage areas of risk. And fourth, there are opportunities to develop the scope and scale of simulation tools used to model crowd behaviours, to predict how different factors and violations in principles might lead to disasters.

Overall, we believe our socio-technical systems approach, framework and design principles have four potential functions. First, they emphasise the importance of adopting a systems perspective. Second, they can be used to analyse, understand and evaluate retrospectively crowd events, helping identify key lessons to learn. Third, they help identify what needs to be done for the development of both theory and practice. And fourth, they enable predictions about future crowd events, in particular pinpointing significant issues and risks requiring additional preparation and management. Ultimately, this approach should help reduce the chances of crowd-related disasters.

Acknowledgements

The authors would like to thank the Editors and anonymous reviewers for their feedback and assistance in improving the paper.

Notes

1. In this instance, end-users are the individuals delivering the systems (police, stewards) rather than the recipients (fans).
2. Whilst this idea about tackling problems at source may appear to contradict earlier suggestions for the need to call the fire brigade immediately, we are not advocating one course of action over the other, but rather the importance of doing both. This practice of requesting expert help and then attempting to address the issue at source is common in sailing, for example.

References

Borodzicz, E. P. (2005) *Risk, crisis and security management* (Chichester, Wiley).

Canter, D., Comber, M. & Uzzell, D. L. (1989) *Football in its place: an environmental psychology of football grounds* (London, Routledge).

Challenger, R., Clegg, C. W. & Robinson, M. A. (2010a) *Understanding crowd behaviours,* Vol. 1: *Practical guidance and lessons identified* (London, The Stationery Office (TSO)).

Challenger, R., Clegg, C. W. & Robinson, M. A. (2010b) *Understanding crowd behaviours,* Vol. 2: *Supporting theory and evidence* (London, The Stationery Office (TSO)).

Cherns, A. B. (1976) The principles of sociotechnical design, *Human Relations,* 29, 783–792.

Cherns, A. B. (1987) Principles of sociotechnical design revisited, *Human Relations,* 40, 153–162.

Clegg, C. W. (2000) Sociotechnical principles for system design, *Applied Ergonomics,* 31, 463–477.

Clegg, C. W. & Shepherd, C. (2007) The biggest computer programme in the world ever! Time for a change in mindset? *Journal of Information Technology,* 22, 212–221.

Clegg, C. W. & Walsh, S. (2004) Change management: time for a change!, *European Journal of Work and Organizational Psychology,* 13, 217–239.

Clegg, C. W., Older Gray, M. T. & Waterson, P. E. (2000) The charge of the 'Byte Brigade' and a sociotechnical response, *International Journal of Human Computer Studies,* 52, 235–251.

Collins, A. L. & Waterhouse, D. (1990) *An estimation of the maximum allowable capacities of pens 3 and 4* (Sheffield, Health and Safety Executive, Research and Laboratory Services Division).

Donald, I. & Canter, D. (1990) Behavioral aspects of the King's Cross underground fire, in: D. Canter (Ed.) *Fires and human behaviour* (2nd edn)(London, David Fulton), 15–30.

Donald, I. & Canter, D. (1992) Intentionality and fatality during the King's Cross underground fire, *European Journal of Social Psychology,* 22, 203–218.

Elliott, D. (2006) Crisis management into practice, in: D. Smith & D. Elliott (Eds) *Key readings in crisis management: systems and structures for prevention and recovery* (London, Routledge), 393–412.

Elliott, D., Frosdick, S. & Smith, D. (1997) The failure of 'legislation by crisis', in: S. Frosdick & L. Whalley (Eds) *Sport and safety management* (Oxford, Butterworth-Heinemann), 11–30.

Elliott, D. & Smith, D. (1993) Football stadia disasters in the United Kingdom: learning from tragedy? *Industrial and Environmental Crisis Quarterly,* 7, 205–229.

Elliott, D. & Smith, D. (1997) Waiting for the next one: management attitudes to safety in the UK football industry, in: S. Frosdick & L. Whalley (Eds) *Sport and safety management* (Oxford, Butterworth-Heinemann), 85–107.

Elliott, D. & Smith, D. (2006) Cultural readjustment after crisis: regulation and learning from crisis within the UK soccer industry, *Journal of Management Studies,* 43, 289–317.

Fennell, D. (1988) *Investigation into the King's Cross underground fire* (London, Department for Transport, HMSO).

Hendrick, H. (1997) Organizational design and macroergonomics, in: G. Salvendy (Ed.) *Handbook of human factors and ergonomics* (New York, NY, Wiley), 594–637.

Heyes, P. F. & Tattersall, J. G. (1989) *Examination of crush barriers from pens 3 and 4* (Sheffield, Health and Safety Executive, Research and Laboratory Services Division).

Home Office (1976) *Guide to safety at sports grounds* (London, HMSO).

Home Office (1986) *Guide to safety at sports grounds* (London, HMSO).

Inglis, S. (1987) *The football grounds of Great Britain* (London, Collins-Willow).

Janis, I. (1972) *Victims of groupthink* (Boston, MA, Houghton Mifflin).

Lea, W., Uttley, P. & Vasconcelos, A. C. (1998) Mistakes, misjudgements and mischances: using SSM to understand the Hillsborough disaster, *International Journal of Information Management,* 18, 345–357.

Moodie, K. (1992) The King's Cross fire: damage assessment and overview of the technical investigation, *Fire Safety Journal,* 18, 13–33.

Mumford, E. (2006) The story of socio-technical design: reflections on its successes, failures and potential, *Information Systems Journal,* 16, 317–342.

Nicholson, C. E. & Roebuck, B. (1995) The investigation of the Hillsborough disaster by the Health and Safety Executive, *Safety Science,* 18, 249–259.

Perrow, C. (1981) Normal accident at Three Mile Island, *Society,* 18, 17–26.

Perrow, C. (1984) *Normal accidents: living with high-risk technologies* (New York, NY, Basic).

Perrow, C. (1994) The limits of safety: the enhancements of a theory of accidents, *Journal of Contingencies and Crisis Management,* 2, 212–220.

Pidgeon, N. (1997) The limits to safety? Culture, politics, learning and man-made disasters, *Journal of Contingencies and Crisis Management*, 5, 1–14.

Popplewell, O. (1985) *Committee of inquiry in crowd safety and control at sports grounds: interim report* (London, HMSO).

Reason, J. (1990) *Human error* (Oxford, Oxford University Press).

Reason, J. (1991) Too little and too late: a commentary on accident and incident reporting systems, in: T. van der Schaaf, D. Lucas & A. Hale (Eds) *Near miss reporting as a safety tool* (Oxford, Butterworth-Heinemann), 9–26.

Reason, J. (1995) A systems approach to organizational error, *Ergonomics*, 38, 1708–1721.

Reason, J. (1997) *Managing the risks of organizational accidents* (Aldershot, Ashgate).

Reason, J. (1998) Achieving a safe culture: theory and practice, *Work and Stress*, 12, 293–306.

Scraton, P. (1999) Policing with contempt: the degrading truth and denial of justice in the aftermath of the Hillsborough disaster, *Journal of Law and Society*, 26, 273–297.

Shrivastava, P. (1987) *Bhopal: anatomy of a crisis* (Cambridge, MA, Ballinger).

Shrivastava, P., Mitroff, I. I., Miller, D. & Miglani, A. (2006) Understanding industrial crises, in: D. Smith & D. Elliott (Eds) *Key readings in crisis management: systems and structures for prevention and recovery* (London, Routledge), 29–46.

Sime, J. D. (1995) Crowd psychology and engineering, *Safety Science*, 21, 1–14.

Smith, D. (1990) Beyond contingency planning: towards a model of crisis management, *Industrial Crisis Quarterly*, 4, 263–275.

Smith, D. (2006) Crisis management: practice in search of a paradigm, in: D. Smith & D. Elliott (Eds) *Key readings in crisis management: systems and structures for prevention and recovery* (London, Routledge), 1–12.

Smith, D. & Elliott, D. (2007) Exploring the barriers to learning from crisis: organizational learning and crisis, *Management Learning*, 38, 519–538.

Taylor, P. (1989) *The Hillsborough Stadium disaster, 15 April 1989, interim report* (London, Home Office, HMSO).

Taylor, P. (1990) *The Hillsborough Stadium disaster, 15 April 1989, final report* (London, Home Office, HMSO).

Toft, B. & Reynolds, S. (2005) *Learning from disasters: a management approach* (3rd edn) (New York, NY, Palgrave Macmillan).

Turner, B. A. (1976) The organizational and interorganizational development of disasters, *Administrative Science Quarterly*, 21, 378–397.

Turner, B. A. (1978) *Manmade disasters* (London, Wykeham).

Turner, B. A. (1994) Causes of disaster: sloppy management, *British Journal of Management*, 5, 215–219.

Turner, B. A. & Pidgeon, N. F. (1997) *Man-made disasters* (2nd edn) (Oxford, Butterworth-Heinemann).

Turner, B. A. & Toft, B. (2006) Organizational learning from disasters, in: D. Smith & D. Elliott (Eds) *Key readings in crisis management: systems and structures for prevention and recovery* (London, Routledge), 191–204.

Weick, K. E. (1990) The vulnerable system: an analysis of the Tenerife air disaster, *Journal of Management*, 16, 571–593.

Part of the solution, not the problem: the crowd's role in emergency response

Jennifer Cole, Montine Walters and Mark Lynch
Royal United Services Institute, London, UK

This paper seeks to explore ways in which the response required to deal with terrorist threats of the 21st century differs from that required to respond to threats the UK has faced in the past, in particular the threat from the Irish Republican Army (IRA). It explores the resilience of crowds to suicide bomb attacks, including the ability of spontaneous, competent 'zero' responders to emerge from within the crowd before professional first responders arrive at the incident scene. The first part of the paper will cover the history of terrorist attacks on the UK and Europe that have resulted in large numbers of civilian casualties and will compare these with mass casualty incidents resulting from causes other than terrorism. The speed with which professional responders can reach the incident site will be considered and potential sources of immediate response, including that provided by members of the public who are themselves caught up in the event, will be discussed. The second part will consider scenarios in which the 'normal' response chain (in which professional first responders are summoned to the incident site and arrive promptly) is broken. Responders may be prohibited from reaching the casualties because the incident has taken place in a location that is difficult to access; because they cannot access the casualties without putting themselves in danger; and because of hostage situations in which terrorists actively deny access to the incident site. It will be argued that in such cases current thinking on the response to terrorism may need to be modified. At times the affected crowd may need to fend for itself, drawing on resources, knowledge and skills that exist within the crowd itself.

Introduction

The terrorist threat faced by the United Kingdom today has changed significantly from that previously experienced during the campaign waged by the Irish Republican Army (IRA) throughout the last quarter of the 20th century. Islamist-inspired suicide bombers, of the kind who attacked London's mass transport systems on '7/7' (i.e. 7 July 2005), are far more likely to target crowded public places and to inflict intentionally mass civilian casualties (Mowatt-Larsen, 2010). Understanding the complex challenges this presents to the UK security, resilience, and public safety sectors and emergency services is dependent on understanding how, and in precisely what ways, mass casualty terrorism differs from our current experience of terrorism on the one hand and mass casualty incidents on the other.

Terrorism per se is far from new to the UK: between 1970 and 2005, more than 19,000 IRA bombings took place on UK soil (Oppenheimer, 2008). In general, however, these attacks tended not to result in large numbers of civilian casualties (though it is acknowledged that there were some high-profile exceptions, such as the bombing of the Brighton hotel hosting the Conservative Party conference in October 1984; and the attack on a Remembrance Sunday ceremony in Enniskillen, Northern Ireland, in November 1987). Attacks on the innocent were seen to damage the IRA's cause (Coogan, 2002), and therefore the organisation often gave warnings of impending attacks so that targeted areas could be safely evacuated. The IRA aimed instead for material damage: the bomb that exploded in the City of London's Bishopsgate district on 24 April 1993, for example, caused damage estimated at between £1 billion and £2 billion, but claimed just one life, a pattern reflected in a number of other major IRA attacks throughout the 1980s and 1990s.

In contrast, the simultaneous suicide bombings carried out by Islamist terrorists on London's public transport systems on 7 July 2005 resulted in 52 deaths between the four incident scenes. More than 700 people were treated for injuries, of whom more than 400 required hospital treatment; in total, approximately 4000 people are thought to have been directly involved (London Assembly, 2006). A year prior to the London attacks, on 11 March 2004, approximately 1700 people were injured and 191 died when Islamist-inspired bombers placed a series of improvised explosive devices on 11 commuter trains en route to the Spanish capital, Madrid (Hinds, 2006). In both London and Spain, the transport networks were targeted at the busiest times of day with no warning given to enable evacuation, guaranteeing the maximum possible number of casualties. Worldwide between 1980 and 2001, suicide bombings accounted for only 3% of terrorist attacks but caused nearly 50% of casualties (Pape, 2003).

This focus on the crowd as a target, whether instead of or as well as buildings and infrastructure, should bring with it a corresponding focus on how resilience to such attacks is developed and maintained. In particular, we believe that valuable lessons can be learned, and a more productive future response to terrorist incidents planned, from considering the response of the crowd during mass casualty incidents resulting from any cause, such as the fire at King's Cross underground station on 18 November 1987, in which 31 people died; the crowd disaster at Hillsborough Football Stadium in Sheffield on 15 April 1989, which killed 96; the sinking of the pleasure boat *Marchioness* after a collision on the River Thames on 20 August 1989, in which 51 passengers were drowned; and the rail crash at Ladbroke Grove Junction in London on 5 October 1999, which resulted in 31 deaths. These show that the numbers of casualties encountered on 7 July 2005 are not remarkable in themselves. All mass casualty incidents require a multi-agency response and the majority will benefit, particularly in the immediate aftermath, on a response generated spontaneously from within the crowd itself to ensure that victims are helped and lives are saved.

Emergency managers and the planning policy they develop, however, often see the crowd as exacerbating the core problem—i.e. a train crash or a major fire—assuming that those involved will be prone, both individually and collectively, to panic and that external help will be needed to calm and control the situation (Furedi, 2008). This view is not upheld by the academic study of mass casualty incidents and other disasters; in contrast, such studies suggest that those caught up in the incident are more likely to remain calm and act rationally, helping and supporting one another as much as they can (Drury & Cocking, 2007). The existing academic literature widely suggests that the crowd should not be seen as part of the problem but as an additional source of assistance to professional responders and a valuable resource, able to provide additional manpower and to begin the recovery process spontaneously should there be a delay in the arrival of the professionals. This paper will argue that while a large crowd containing a high number of casualties may overwhelm the number of professional responders who are immediately available and the resources they carry, uninjured crowd members can act as a force multiplier, allowing the limited professional resources to be used where they will be most effective. As Furedi (2008, p. 658) states:

> [T]he tendency to professionalise disaster response may deprive a community of an opportunity to develop its resilience and inadvertently reinforce a sense of passivity and helplessness. ... [A] highly centralized professional response cannot deal with every contingency. In the end, encouraging people to take responsibility for their own well-being is essential for an effective response to an emergency situation.

Distinctions between 'the crowd' and 'the public'

Before we continue, it is important to highlight the difference between 'the crowd' and 'the public' and how each is identified in this paper. 'The public' refers to the UK population in general, and assumes that any crowd comprised largely of 'the public' will be typical of it; for example, if within the population as a whole, approximately 2% have received formal first aid training at some stage of their lives, it can be assumed that this figure will be mirrored within any crowd, unless there is reason to assume that the individuals comprising that crowd are unrepresentative of 'the public' as a whole.

'The crowd' on the other hand refers specifically to the mass of individuals caught up in the incident itself and exists as a coherent group only at that time and place. While it will largely comprise members of the public as defined above, there may also be some individuals who have skills and roles specific to the situation, such as on-duty stewards and first aiders at a sporting event, concert or festival or security staff at a large shopping centre. This 'crowd' correlates to the 'community of circumstance', identified within the current community resilience policy of the UK government's Civil Contingencies Secretariat, which shares a commonality only for the duration of the incident, in contrast to a 'community of interest' (such as worshippers at a local church or mosque, or members of an amateur dramatics group) or a community defined by geographic location, both of which share a common identity outside of the incident.

Addressing new threats to crowded places

Since the turn of the 21st century, the UK approach to combating the threat from suicide bombers has largely focused on strengthening physical security, by building barriers to entry and increasing the efficiency of screening technology, at airports in particular. The majority of this has been driven by the response to the failed suicide attacks of summer 2007, barely two years after the 7/7 bombings. Two car-bombs were placed outside the Tiger Tiger nightclub in London's Haymarket on 29 June, the second at the location where victims fleeing the first attack would be likely to congregate; fortunately, the devices failed to detonate. The following day, a suicide bomber with links to those who planted the devices in London attempted to drive a Jeep laden with propane gas canisters into a busy Glasgow Airport terminal; the vehicle was prevented from entering the terminal by security bollards and, once again, the canisters failed to ignite as intended. These attacks cemented understanding that crowded places are becoming increasingly popular targets for Islamist attackers (Bell, 2007) prompting the then Prime Minister Gordon Brown to commission Lord West of Spithead, then Home Office Parliamentary Under-Secretary of State for Security and Counter-Terrorism, to suggest methods and measures required for protecting crowded areas, including transport infrastructure and critical national infrastructure from terrorist attack (Ellis, 2007). This review resulted in two fundamental recommendations. Firstly, in the short-term, there was a need for increased physical security around crowded areas and that physical resilience against terrorism was dependent on engaging with a wide range of local partners, including local authorities and businesses (HM Government, 2010a). Secondly, a more long-term approach to protection has been provided by the Centre for the Protection of National Infrastructure (CPNI), an interdepartmental government agency that has developed and runs free briefings and training courses for architects, engineers, planners, designers and other built environment stakeholders to encourage the strengthening of existing hard security measures; the CPNI also provides more general security advice to businesses and the private sector.

In addition, considerable work has gone on within the emergency services to strengthen operational procedures and introduce specialist equipment that will improve the response to such attacks, some of which is discussed below. Neither these, nor the physical security measures discussed above, however, addresses how it might be possible to build resilience to an attack that has not been prevented by increasing the ability of the general public, and therefore the crowd present at such an incident when it occurs, to cope, though many previous studies (Jones et al.,

2004, 2006) show that doing so can help to minimise the psychological damage caused by the attack to both society as a whole and to the individuals directly involved.

In Israel, the ability to clear away the visible signs of damage caused by suicide bombings and to restore the area to normal as quickly as possible is a key part of the initial response, ensuring that the timeframe of the incident is kept as short as possible (Charlaff, 2008a). The operational procedures of the Israeli Emergency Medical Service, Magen David Adom, aim to have the first ambulances at a mass casualty event of up to 60 casualties within 5 minutes, and the scene cleared of all casualties within the first hour. This recognises the psychological importance of a fast and efficient response, as well as its importance to saving lives.

The speed of the professional response can be impaired in mass casualty terrorist attacks, however: professional responders may be unable to reach the casualties due to concerns over secondary devices, which may require them to hold back until the scene has been declared safe, or because the attackers are themselves preventing access to the scene. During the Islamist attacks on Mumbai in India in November 2008, which resulted in 175 deaths and more than 300 injuries, hostage situations at the Taj Mahal Palace and Tower Hotel and the Chabad Lubavitch Jewish centre (also known as Mumbai Chabad House) were sustained over 48 hours, with access denied to professional responders. Victims, including those who required urgent medical care, were left to fend for themselves and each other (Rabasa *et al.*, 2009).

If future attacks are likely to aim for mass casualties, more needs to be done to understand what happens to the victims of such incidents and to enable them to help themselves better. To what extent is it possible to embed resilience in the general population, enabling the crowd to respond to its own needs, at least in the initial phase? Emergency management circles have begun to adopt the term 'zero responder', coined by Professor Louise Lemyre of Ottawa University in Ontario, Canada, for such individuals, to distinguish spontaneous helpers from the professional first responders who are called to the scene (Lemyre, 2010); we shall adopt these terms—'zero responder' and 'professional first responder'—throughout to distinguish between the two. The ability of zero responders to emerge from the crowd is dependent on a number of interrelated factors, including an awareness of what is happening and how the situation is likely to develop, training in specific subjects such as first aid and safe evacuation procedures, combined with the availability at the incident site of self-help equipment such as first aid packs and fire extinguishers.

The immediate response: finding resources on the ground

Previous mass casualty incidents provide many lessons on the benefits of seeing the crowd as a potential solution rather than part of the problem. Firstly, it is important to remember than no matter how efficient and how well-managed is the response to any major incident—particularly one that is unexpected—professional responders cannot arrive at the scene instantaneously: they need to be called, dispatched, make their way to the incident site (possibly through congested traffic) and plan to enter potentially dangerous environments without putting their own lives in danger.

Their response may be dependent on equipment which, once at the scene, takes time to set up. The number of casualties requiring their attention may well overwhelm the personnel and resources available, at least until reinforcements and resupplies can be sourced.

The Madrid train bombings began at 07.38 hours on 11 March 2004, when four bombs exploded on a train just inside Atocha station, followed a minute later by three bombs on a train, 500 metres away. Two minutes later at 07.41 hours, a further two bombs exploded on a train at El Pozo del Tio Raimundo station and a minute after that, another on a train at Santa Eugenia station. It was not until 08.00 hours that emergency relief workers began arriving at the scenes. They were faced with 2062 casualties, of whom 83 were in critical condition (Bristow, 2004).

During the London bombings of 7 July 2005, the first 999 (emergency) call requesting assistance to Aldgate Street station was made at 08.51 hours, approximately a minute after the first device exploded, by a London Underground staff member. The first ambulance arrived at 09.14 hours, 23 minutes later.

The bomb in the tunnel between London's Russell Square and King's Cross underground stations exploded at around 08.53 hours; the last casualties were not transferred to hospital until 12.12 hours, more than 3 hours later.

The initial chaos following such attacks means that information flow in the immediate aftermath is difficult: in London, four simultaneous bombings combined with the fact that three had occurred deep underground meant that controllers were initially unsure how many incidents had occurred as injured passengers emerged from the underground tunnels at different stations. It took time to establish where exactly incidents had occurred, which incidents needed which emergency services, and in what quantities (London Assembly, 2006). Furthermore, when professional responders did arrive on the scene certain protocols resulted in some holding back when it would have been safe to go forward. Survivors giving evidence during the Coroner's Inquest into the bombings found both this, and the fact that most firefighters do not possess advanced first aid skills, difficult to understand (HM Coroner, 2011). Injured victims within the carriage, and during the initial stages of the evacuation, were dependent on one another until professional paramedics could arrive.

It is not unique to terrorism that the arrival of the professional responders—or of the appropriate professional responders—may in some situations be delayed. At the time of the Hillsborough Football Stadium disaster in 1989 it was not routine for emergency services, and in particular ambulance paramedics, to be present inside football stadia in significant numbers. Even when ambulances did arrive, they remained predominantly outside and casualties were ferried to them. The only emergency service typically represented in significant numbers at football matches of the time were police officers, whose primary task was to prevent pitch invasions by the hooligan element synonymous with the sport during the 1970s and 1980s. Like firefighters on 7/7, their first aid skills were limited and they were ill-equipped to assist or assess the casualties (Walsh, 1989).

Lessons taken from the Hillsborough disaster have resulted in a larger emergency services presence in today's sports stadia and at other large events such as music concerts and outdoor festivals, as well as an increase in the number of stadium staff who undergo first aid training and volunteer first aiders required to be present. There will be more than 3000 first aid volunteers at the London 2012 Olympic and Paralympics Games, for example, many of whom will be stationed at the events where the need for immediate medical assistance is likely to be greatest, such as at equestrian and cycling events (Budgett, 2010). Controlling the paramedic-to-spectator ratio at fixed venues, however, is very different from ensuring immediate cover on more fluid networks such as mass transport systems. Placing police and paramedics on every tube train would be impractical, not to mention prohibitively expensive. A more realistic proposition, and one this paper aims to put forward as a viable model, is to embed the skills needed to cope with the immediate aftermath of an attack within the population so that within any crowd, be it a static mass inside a football stadium, a fluid crowd at a major shopping centre, or commuters travelling on the mass transport system, there is always a critical mass of people who can respond immediately until the professional help arrives.

Don't panic: an understanding of crowd psychology in disasters

Historically, the ability to utilise the crowd as a zero responder in times of crisis was challenged by a prevailing view that mass hysteria encompasses groups in times of crisis, with people adopting Darwinian characteristics where individual survival would become the only priority at the expense of the crowd. Thus the crowd would not facilitate assistance in times of crisis but have the opposite effect, hindering access to the most at need and creating panic that would cause more harm. As Richard La Piere suggested, 'danger may turn a passive audience into a shrieking, milling mass which clogs the aisles and jams the exits' (La Piere, 1938, p. 437; cited in Chertkoff & Kushigian, 1999). Panic, which Mawson (2005, p. 96) defines as 'inappropriate or excessive fear', was often thought to prevail, leading to illogical and dangerous consequences. John Drury sums up the premise of mass panic theorists when he suggests that they conclude 'human reactions to emergencies ... lead to more problems (e.g. fatalities) than the danger that people are trying to escape from' (Drury, 2011, p. 198).

Later theories held that the commotion during a crisis does not reflect panic but a rational decision-making process seeking to garner the best possible outcome. For example, Mintz (1951) argued that individuals seek to be cooperative in a crowd as long as *the entire* crowd cooperates. Once someone seeks to act individually and gains a benefit from that action it makes no sense for the rest of the crowd to continue acting cooperatively, as they will be disadvantaged. Thus what appears to be mass panic may be a reflection of calculated risk; selfishness and individualism become the rational responses but make the concept of the crowd as zero responder difficult to comprehend.

More recent academic studies and other evidence suggest that solidarity and communal spirit appears to be far more prevalent than previously thought. During the Hillsborough disaster, for example, football fans trapped in the pens helped one another to 'unofficial emergency exits' over 2-metre fences. Despite the predominant image of football fans at the time as violent hooligans, the crowd's response was quiet and considered, with individuals assisting one another and calming the situation down (Drury *et al.*, 2009). Gary Burns, a survivor of the disaster, recalled a man helping him and encouraging him to, 'slow down lad, take your time' (Burns, 2011). The public assisted one another and carried the injured to the ambulances outside the stadium, preventing a potentially higher death toll.

At the evidence hearings for the Coroner's Inquests into the 7/7 London bombings in 2010, Davinia Douglass (née Turrell), whose face was severely injured by one of the explosions, gave evidence in a written statement (HM Coroner, 2011) that her fellow passengers gave immediate assistance for her injuries and led her from the bombed carriage. Several examples of heroic and selfless behaviour can be found in contemporary media reports of the Mumbai attacks of November 2008, ranging from hotel guests telephoning rooms to warn occupants to duck for cover, to guests hiding or dragging others to safety through the 'rabbit warren' of corridors (BBC News, 2008a, 2008b). All indications from past emergencies suggest that the crowd will help itself; therefore, the more ability it is given to do so, the better (Drury & Cocking, 2007).

Historical precedent: home defence and civil protection

The concept of training the population in the skills needed to substitute for professional responders until help arrives (and therefore to ensure that such skills will be present in the typical crowd) has both historical and international precedent. During the Second World War, an extensive self-help attitude was adopted in the UK, with individuals who had not joined the military effort (mostly because they were too old, too young or women) taking on public safety roles to respond to incidents caused by German bombing raids. This included fire wardens—who put out fires and pushed the burning bombs away from buildings—and air raid wardens, who would hurry civilians into designated shelters (Holgate, 2004). At the peak of activity, in March 1944, more than 1.5 million men and women were volunteering, unpaid, for Home Defence roles to work alongside 400,000 professional civil defence staff, which included police officers and firefighters. An additional 5 million citizens were legally required to serve 48 hours a month as fire wardens (Woolven, 2008).

The organisations raised for Home Defence continued after the Second World War as a resilience measure against nuclear attack throughout the Cold War. This included in particular the Civil Defence Corps, which had Head Quarters sections, Wardens, Welfare divisions, Ambulance and First Aid sections; an Auxiliary Fire Service; a National Health Service Reserve; and Scientific Intelligence Officers. At the height of Civil Defence activities, there were 320,000 civilian volunteers plus an additional 200,000 serving critical industries (Woolven, 2008). The training they received proved invaluable in a number of emergency situations including severe flooding at Linton and Lynmouth in 1952, the East Coast floods of 1953, train crashes at Sutton Coldfield in 1955 and Lewisham in 1957, and a serious mudslide at Aberfan, Wales, in 1966.

It is important to note, however, that an element of widely accepted and believed risk may be needed before the public will volunteer their services and take an active role in resilience. It was not until the Munich Pact of 1938, by which Nazi Germany annexed the Sudentenland areas of Czechoslovakia, that the UK's volunteer network began to swell, as people realised the imminent danger posed by Nazi Germany (Woolven, 1998). Following the end of the Second World War, when concern that the Cold War might lead to a nuclear strike on the UK was a less believable threat than German bombing raids, the Civil Defence Corps struggled to attract volunteers in the numbers hoped for (Grant, 2010), though cities that had been heavily bombed during the war years, such as Coventry, generally saw higher rates of recruitment than those that had not. It was not until more credible new threats emerged, such as the 1950–1953 Korean War and the 1962 Cuban missile crisis, that volunteer numbers increased. More recently, hurricane warnings issued to New Orleans in the wake of Hurricane Gustav in 2008 were heeded more widely than both those that had been issued prior to the devastating arrival of Hurricane Katrina three years previously and also those that were issued to residents in Texas at risk from Hurricane Ike (Cole, 2008b), as residents who had personal experience of the previous events were more willing to believe that action was necessary.

Interest in Civil Defence in the UK petered out during the 1950s and 1960s, but similar models still exist, and are still effective, around the world, most notably in regions where the regular threat of natural disasters such as earthquakes (in China) and hurricanes (in many US states) galvanises the public to take action against a real and present danger. Wherever such volunteering is found, first aid skills generally form a large part of the training those volunteers receive (Cole, 2008a) yet despite our long history of IRA terrorism, first aid training has never been given much priority in the UK, perhaps because the small number of casualties generally encountered during IRA attacks meant that there was little role for the public in responding to such incidents. Where the public were seen to have a role at all, it was generally in spotting and reporting suspicious activity and this is where efforts to involve and train the public in responding to Islamist terrorism have also been focused in recent years.

In relation to awareness of suspicious activity, the National Counter Terrorism Security Office (NaCTSO) has devised Project ARGUS (Area Reinforcement Gained Using Scenarios), an initiative that aims to increase awareness of counter-terrorism issues amongst businesses and make communities more resilient to attacks (City of London Police, 2011). The ARGUS training packages focus mainly on how to plan and assist safe evacuations of large venues, but do not contain training in first aid; neither does the training for Project Griffin, a linked initiative that trains security personnel and other professionals, such as traffic wardens, to help the police with evacuation procedures. Griffin in particular, which includes advice such as avoiding glass hazards during an attack, would seem a natural home for basic first aid training, or at the very least the promotion of its worth and relevance.

The UK is virtually the only country in the European Union where training in such skills is not a compulsory part of the school curriculum. Despite its fundamental usefulness, first aid has only recently been added to part of the school curriculum at all, as a result of lobbying by the British Red Cross's 'Life. Live It' campaign, and forms part of the optional subject Personal, Social and Health Education which does not lead to a qualification and is therefore not at the top of the agenda for most schools (British Red Cross, 2011).[1] Health & Safety guidelines require just one qualified first aider per 100 employees in low-risk environments, one in 50 for environments deemed to be moderate or high risk (Cole, 2009). Basic first aid is now included in driving lessons and theory tests, but there is no legal requirement for drivers in the UK to carry first aid kits, nor is there any requirement for drivers who qualified before it was introduced to take the additional lessons. At present, only around one in every 200 members of the UK population holds a currently valid first aid certificate and around 95% have never had any formal first aid training.

Yet the benefit of embedding first aid knowledge within the population is clear. Immediate treatment is vital in preventing death from traumatic injury, particularly the severe bleeding from traumatic amputations and penetration injuries that is a common effect of the type of explosive devices favoured by both the IRA and Islamist-inspired terrorists. Such catastrophic bleeding, as it is termed by the military, is a major cause of death on the battlefield, leading battlefield first aid training to focus strongly on stemming its flow (Dubick & Kheirabadi, 2010); however, despite the similar injuries likely to be caused by a suicide attack, and the increasing recognition within professional healthcare sector that the adoption of military practices has valuable application within civilian situations, few civilian first aid courses make catastrophic bleeding a priority, instead focusing on breathing difficulties and cardiac arrest. The use of tourniquets, for example, improvised examples of which saved several lives on 7/7, is not taught in civilian first aid. Immediate care is not only relevant to traumatic injury, either: following the 2002 Moscow siege, some of the victims choked to death on their own vomit and others choked after swallowing their tongues when gas was pumped into the theatre by the Russian authorities to disable the hostage-takers (Dolnik & Fitzgerald, 2008). Many of these victims may have survived had they been placed into the recovery position, a relatively simple first aid procedure that can be taught in minutes. More generally, initiatives to embed immediate care skills within the general population, such as the ability to recognise the symptoms of a stroke, have shown considerable improvements in the number of individuals recovering from such conditions (Wall et al., 2008).

The value of first aid skills is well understood in Israel, where suicide bombers have detonated numerous devices in crowded places such as markets and nightclubs. As a result, Israeli emergency response frameworks are heavily focused on casualty management and this has led to a number of particularly interesting approaches, from specialist chemical, biological, radiological and nuclear (CBRN) response exercises in which the entire population takes part, to formal first aid training provided to the general population by the military (Charlaff, 2008b). In particular, there is a strong focus on what is known in Israel as 'market forces'—the ability of the general public to provide help and assistance to those injured in the attack with whatever resources are to hand. The name comes from an incident in which professional first responders were unable to reach injured casualties in the narrow aisles of a market, and the market traders responded by using the tables from their stalls as makeshift stretchers to ferry the injured to the ambulances.

In recent years, this ability to harness a 'market forces' response has been formalised through the Multi-Casualty Response Vehicles (MCRV) owned by Magen David Adom (MDA), the Israeli Emergency Medical Service. When MDA is called to respond to a multi-casualty incident it sends not only ambulances and paramedics, but also an MCRV packed with additional resources that can be used by anyone present at the scene. This benefits in particular those casualties suffering from minor injuries who do not need to be evacuated to hospital immediately, if indeed at all.

This model works in Israel because the recognition of the importance of first aid and its utility during mass casualty incidents are high, as suicide bombings are common and therefore such a response is actioned frequently. Israel has been in continual conflict with its Palestinian and Arab neighbours since its formation, thus the Israeli public is acutely aware of danger and has vast experience dealing with mass casualty incidents (Halpern et al., 2003); Israel is also at risk from earthquakes and severe flooding, which further galvanises the population to take first aid seriously. The situations in the UK and Israel are very different, but nonetheless Israel does offer a useful a guide to the utility of widespread first aid training and the ability of the crowd to aid professional responders rather than drain their resources. The model shows that with the correct training the crowd at an incident site can be a very valuable resource, both before professional first responders arrive and in boosting their capacity once they do.

This ability to provide (and resupply) material resources at the incident site has been recognised and addressed in the UK in recent years. Following the issues encountered on 7/7 when, for example, ambulance crews at Liverpool Street station began reporting equipment shortages less than 20 minutes after arriving on the scene, the Department of Health has supplied more than 200 multi-casualty first aid kits to major transport hubs, with more being rolled out across England to additional transport hubs, shopping centres and other crowded places (Killens, 2010). They are designed to address the need for immediate first aid, providing supplies that can be used by station staff and the general public. In addition, National Capability Mass Casualty Equipment Vehicles have been introduced to Ambulance Services across England, equipped with resources to resupply professional responders at a mass casualty incident and specialist equipment needed to deal with traumatic amputations and other injuries likely to be encountered following a terrorist attack. Unlike the Israeli model, however, the UK vehicles and first aid kits generally aim to resupply the professional first responders, not to equip the public, who have little training or knowledge of how to use such equipment; if first aid training is not promoted as a life skill in general then it should at least be an important part of counter-terrorism awareness programmes, perhaps included as part of the previously mentioned Project ARGUS and Project Griffin packages.

If even a percentage of the crowd can act as zero responders, those requiring immediate medical assistance could be given an increased chance of survival. Survivors are more likely to remain at the scene and wait for professional first responders if they have an understanding of the advantages of doing so and are confident that those around them have the knowledge and skills necessary to give them the help and assistance they need until the professionals arrive. Leaving the incident site to make their own way to hospitals and healthcare facilities may delay their access to treatment and, in the case, of biological, chemical or radiological contamination, risk spreading the contamination further and affect people further away from the initial point of release. This was recognised following the Sarin gas attacks on the Tokyo Underground, a lesson from which was that all staff should receive training in life-saving skills in future (Funato, 2005).

Arming the public with skills and knowledge

The long-term impact of the Comprehensive Spending Review (HM Treasury, 2010) and the Strategic Defence and Security Review (HM Government, 2010b) may result in sufficient cuts to frontline emergency services that the voluntary sector such as St John Ambulance, non-governmental organizations (NGOs) and private operators, may be increasingly relied upon to deal with periods of high-volume call-outs. The role of existing Community First Responders—a Department of Health-run scheme in which local volunteers respond to 999 calls reporting heart attacks and treat patients until professional first responders arrive—may need to be expanded, with some local ambulance trusts needing to rely on them more heavily and for a wider range of assistance. First aid and casualty management training currently given to Special Constables could also be expanded to help them deal with mass casualty incidents.

Local authorities' emergency planning departments might also consider some kind of knowledge capture of local individuals who have gained medical experience through military service or overseas humanitarian aid, as well as former and recently retired emergency services personnel, for whom small amounts of regular re-training and practice could be enough to enable professional responders to draw them in to provide additional capacity at short notice—e.g., current and former military medics, particularly those from Territorial Army units, who have had experience in Iraq or Afghanistan. Such individuals will exist in most communities (with the possible exception of some ethnic and cultural minority communities, but these may have their own relevant experiences), but their whereabouts is currently invisible to any response plan.

During the London bombings, three of which took place in underground tunnels that were difficult to access immediately, help had to emerge from within the affected crowd itself, but in other incidents, such as the above-ground and more easily accessible incident sites in Madrid and Mumbai, a wider spread of emergency response capabilities amongst the general public and surrounding businesses could have enabled some of those who might otherwise die at the scene to be saved and provide effective and immediate basic emergency assistance to all victims prior to the arrival of the emergency services.

Conclusions

Response to terrorist threats in the 21st century requires a new approach. The assumption that an attack will comprise an explosion, followed by a 999 (emergency) call that summons professional responders to the scene, to which they arrive and treat casualties before dispatching them to hospital, fitted the old model of the IRA attack well, but when less conventional modes of attack are considered, such as mass casualty incidents, mass hostage situations and chemical, biological, radiological and nuclear (CBRN) dispersals, in which the normal response chain is broken or interrupted, the complexities increase.

If the UK is to be sufficiently resilient to the threat of suicide terrorism, current thinking needs to be extended beyond professional first responders to ensure that the resources needed to deal with a mass casualty incident, including knowledge as well as equipment, are easily and immediately available to those caught up in the incident itself. The evidence from past incidents explored in this paper shows that the affected crowd is frequently capable of taking a proactive role in the response, with individuals providing aid and reassurance to one another until the professionals arrive and can enter the incident scene. Providing the general public and therefore the crowd with the means to assist—in terms of accessible equipment and the knowledge to use it—may prove to be much more important in future terrorist attacks than it has been in the past.

The evidence given at the Coroner's Inquests into the 7 July London Bombings, and the media reactions to it, show that today's society expects professional first responders to be on the scene immediately and to multitask once they arrive; it expects police officers and firefighters to have similar skills to ambulance paramedics. While ensuring that they do has considerable value in itself, both professional emergency planning and community resilience initiatives need to move beyond dependence on professionals to more self-reliance. During a major incident, the affected crowd or community needs to come together to free up the emergency services to focus on the most severely in need. This form of self-reliance, drawing together for the protection of each other, is a model of unified assistance that proved effective during the Second World War, has shown value internationally in countries prone to earthquakes (China) and hurricanes (the United States), and with the right planning could prove equally effective in the UK today.

Note

1. PSHE is currently set to become a statutory subject from September 2011.

References

BBC News (2008a) Mumbai survivors talk of ordeal, *BBC News*, 29 November. Available online at: http://news.bbc.co.uk/1/hi/wales/south_east/7755962.stm/.

BBC News (2008b) Eyewitness: Mumbai survivors, *BBC News*, 29 November. Available online at: http://news.bbc.co.uk/1/hi/world/south_asia/7756616.stm/.

Bell, S. (2007) *Car bombs: inside vehicle borne improvised explosive devices (VBIEDs)*. RUSI Analysis Commentary. Available online at: http://www.rusi.org/analysis/commentary/ref:C468A125C1E6E1/%3E/.

Bristow, R. (2004) *Madrid bombings – March 11, 2004* (New York, NY, Great New York Hospital Association). Available online at: http://www.gnyha.org/8156/File.aspx/.

British Red Cross (2011) *Life. Live it*. First Aid Campaigns. Available online at: http://www.redcross.org.uk/What-we-do/First-aid/First-aid-campaigns/.

Budgett, R. (2010) Preparing for the Olympic Games. Paper presented at the *Inner Cordon 2010 HART Conference*, Liverpool, UK, June, 10, 2010.

Burns, G. (2011) *Hillsborough football disaster: Gary Burns survivor account*. Available online at: http://www.contrast.org/hillsborough/history/gary.shtm/.

Charlaff, J. (2008a) Maintaining resilience in the face of terror, *RUSI Monitor*, 7(2). Available online at: http://www.rusi.org/publications/monitor/ref:A4795E8EDAA8CD/.

Charlaff, J. (2008b) Chemical and biological attacks: medical preparedness, *RUSI Homeland Security and Resilience Monitor*, 7(9). Available online at: http://www.rusi.org/publications/monitor/ref:A48FC6B004A9C4/.

Chertkoff, J. & Kushigian, R. (1999) *Don't panic: the psychology of emergency egress and ingress*. (Abingdon, Praeger).

City of London Police (2011) *Project ARGUS—protecting against terrorist attacks*. Available online at: http://www.cityoflondon.police.uk/CityPolice/Departments/CT/ProjectArgus/.

Cole, J. (2008a) Exploring the emergency response, in: J. Cole (Ed.) *Civil defence and emergency response*. RUSI Workshop Report, London, 7–12.

Cole, J. (2008b) Hurricane Gustav—testing the lessons from Hurricane Katrina, *RUSI Monitor*, 7(10), 10–11.

Cole, J. (2009) Medical equipment available in the aftermath of terror attacks, *Emergency Services Times*, May, 26–67.

Coogan, T. P. (2002) *The Troubles: Ireland's ordeal, 1966–1996 and the search for peace* (New York, NY, Palgrave).

Dolnik, A. & Fitzgerald, K. M. (2008) *Negotiating hostage crises with the new terrorists* (London, Greenwood), 60–93.

Drury, J. (2011) Collective resilience in mass emergencies and disasters: a social identity model, in: J. Jetten, C. Haslam & S. A. Haslam (Eds) *The social cure: identity, health, and well-being* (Hove, Psychology Press), 195–215.

Drury, J. & Cocking, C. (2007) *The mass psychology of disasters and emergency evacuations: a research report and implications for practice* (Falmer, Brighton, University of Sussex). Available online at: http://www.liv.ac.uk/psychology/cpd/Drury_%26_Cocking_(2007).pdf/.

Drury, J., Cocking, C. & Reicher, S. C. (2009) Everyone for themselves? A comparative study of crowd solidarity among emergency survivors, *British Journal of Social Psychology*, 48, 487–506.

Dubick, M. & Kheirabadi, B. (2010) New technologies for treating severe bleeding in far-forward combat areas, Paper presented at the *RTO Human Factors and Medicine Panel (HFM) Symposium*, Essen, Germany, 19–21 April, 2010. Available online at: http://ftp.rta.nato.int/public/PubFullText/RTO/MP/RTO-MP-HFM-182/MP-HFM-182-21.doc/.

Ellis, N. (2007) *A 'simple sailor' in a crowded place: terrorism and society*, RUSI Analysis Commentary. Available online at: http://www.rusi.org/analysis/commentary/ref:C473DBBF531865/.

Funato, T. (2005) Lessons learned from 1995 Tokyo Subway sarin gas attack. Paper presented at the *European Conference of Ministers of Transport*, 2–3 March, 2005.

Furedi, F. (2008) Fear and security: a vulnerability-led policy response, *Social Policy and Administration*, 42(6), 645–661.

Grant, M. (2010) *After the bomb: civil defence and nuclear war in Britain, 1945–68* (Basingstoke, Palgrave Macmillan).

Coroner, HM (2011) *Coroner's inquest into the London bombings of 7 July 2005*. Available online at: http://7julyinquests.independent.gov.uk/.

Government, HM (2010a) *Crowded places: a response to the consultation*. Available online at: http://www.nactso.gov.uk/SiteCollectionDocuments/AreasOfRisk/crowded-places.pdf/.

Government, HM (2010b) *Securing Britain in an age of uncertainty: The Strategic Defence and Security Review*. Available online at: http://www.direct.gov.uk/prod_consum_dg/groups/dg_digitalassets/@dg/@en/documents/digitalasset/dg_191634.pdf/.

Halpern, P., Ming-Che, Tsai, Arnold, J. L., Stock, E. & Ersoy, G. (2003) Mass-casualty, terrorist bombings: implications for emergency department and hospital emergency response (Part II), *Prehospital and Disaster Medicine*, 18(3), 235–241.

Hinds, A. (2006) *JTIC Terrorism Case Study No. 1: The Madrid Rail Bombings*. Open Sources Information. Available online at: http://www.opensourcesinfo.org/journal/2006/1/29/jtic-terrorism-case-study-no1-the-madrid-rail-bombings.html/.

Holgate, J. (2004) The Night of the Baked Potatoes, *BBC WW2 People's War*. Available online at: http://www.bbc.co.uk/ww2peopleswar/stories/08/a2785908.shtml/.

Jones, E., Woolven, R., Durodie, B. & Wessely, S. (2004) Civilian morale during World War Two: responses to air raids re-examined, *Social History of Medicine*, 17, 463–479.

Jones, E., Woolven, R., Durodie, B. & Wessely, S. (2006) Public panic and morale: Second World War civilian responses re-examined in the light of the current anti-terrorist campaign, *Journal of Risk Research*, 9(1), 57–73.

Killens, J. (2010) HART and its effect on the National Ambulance Service. Paper presented at the *Inner Cordon 2010 HART Conference*, Liverpool, UK, 10 June, 2010.

Lemyre, L. (2010) Public communication of CBRN Risk in Canada: research, training and tools to enable. Paper presented at the *PIRATE Project Stakeholders Workshop*, HPA, London, UK.

London Assembly (2006) *Report of the 7 July Review Committee: Volume 2: Views and information from organisations*, June. Available online at: http://legacy.london.gov.uk/assembly/reports/7july/vol2-organisations.pdf/.

Mawson, A. (2005) Understanding mass panic and other collective responses to threat and disaster, *Psychiatry*, 68(2), 95–113.

Mintz, A. (1951) Non-adaptive group behaviour, *Journal of Abnormal and Social Psychology*, 46(2), 150–159.

Mowatt-Larsen, R. (2010) *Al Qaeda weapons of mass destruction threat: hype or reality?* (Belfer, Belfer Center for Science and International Affairs).

Oppenheimer, A. (2008) Improvised explosive devices: then and now, *RUSI Homeland Security and Resilience Monitor*, 7(3), 12–13.

Pape, R. A. (2003) *Dying to win: the strategic logic of suicide terrorism* (New York, NY, Random House).

Rabasa, A., Blackwill, R. D., Chalk, P., Cragin, P., Fair, C.C., Jackson, B. A., Jenkins, B. M., Jones, S. G., Shestak, N. & Tellis, A. (2009) *The lessons of Mumbai* (Santa Monica, CA, RAND Cooperation).

Treasury, HM (2010) *Spending Review*, 22 November. Available online at: http://www.hm-treasury.gov.uk/spend_index.htm/.

Wall, H. K., Beagan, B. M., O'Neill, J., Foell, K. & Boddie-Willis, R. (2008) Assessing stroke signs and symptoms through public education: the Stroke Heroes Act FAST campaign, *Preventing Chronic Disease: Public Health Research, Practice and Policy*, 5(2), 1–10.

Walsh, M. (1989) Taylor on Hillsborough: what can we learn? *Disasters*, 13(3), 274–277.

Woolven, R. (1998) London, Munich and ARP, *Journal of the Royal United Services Institute for Defence Studies*, 143(5), 54–58.

Woolven, R. (2008) Civil defence in historical perspective, in: J. Cole (Ed.) *Civil defence and emergency response*, RUSI Workshop Report, London, 15–20.

The experience of collective participation: shared identity, relatedness and emotionality

Fergus Neville and Stephen Reicher
School of Psychology, University of St Andrews, St Andrews, UK

This paper presents three studies that explore the experience of participating in crowd events. Analysis of semi-structured interviews with football supporters and student demonstrators is used to illustrate the role that shared identity plays in transforming within-crowd social relations (relatedness), and the positive impact this has upon emotionality of collective experience. Questionnaire data collected at a music festival are then used to confirm these claims. The paper argues for a conceptual distinction between shared identity and self-categorisation, and against the contention in classic crowd psychology that a loss of identity is at the root of collective emotion. It concludes by suggesting avenues for future research, including the potential role for collective experience in encouraging future co-action.

Introduction

Classic psychological theories of the crowd (e.g. Le Bon, 1895/2002; McDougal, 1920/1939) accounted for the passionate nature of collective behaviour by juxtaposing emotionality with a loss of identity and reason. A loss of personal identity was claimed to lead to a loss of behavioural constraint, and a consequent dominance of emotion over reason. By divorcing emotion and reason in this way, crowds came to symbolise irrationality. The characterisation of crowds as irrational was echoed in the work of subsequent theorists including Freud (1920/1922), Park (1904/1982) and Blumer (1939).

Reicher's social identity model (SIM; Reicher, 1984, 1987) and elaborated social identity model (ESIM; Drury & Reicher, 2000; Reicher, 1996; Stott & Reicher, 1998) of crowd behaviour have critiqued the irrationalist accounts of classic crowd psychology. Based upon the social identity approach to group behaviour (Tajfel & Turner, 1979; Turner *et al.*, 1987), this work has argued that identity is not lost within the crowd, but rather there is a *cognitive transformation* from personal to social level identification. In this way crowd members act meaningfully in terms of the norms of their salient social identity. By stressing the cognitive shift from personal to social identification, the social identity approach has therefore moved away from the classic portrayal of crowds as irrational explosions of emotion. However, there is a risk that the emotionality of crowd action has been consequently underemphasised, preserving the reason–emotion dichotomy but reversing its direction (Reicher, 2001, 2011).

In addition to the cognitive shift, recent work from within the social identity tradition has focused upon relational and emotional transformations within crowds. Firstly, there is evidence for a *relational transformation* (what we term 'relatedness') such that the quality of intragroup social relations improve as co-present others become part of the collective self, rather than 'other' at an individual level (Turner *et al.*, 1987; Tyler & Blader, 2001; Reicher, 2011). A number of experimental and interview studies have shown how shared ingroup membership can facilitate intragroup trust, cooperation, a decrease in stress, comfort in close physical proximity, and helping behaviours (Reicher & Haslam, 2006; Haslam & Reicher, 2006; Novelli *et al.*, 2010; Levine *et al.*, 2002; The Prayag Magh Mela Research Group (PMMRG), 2007; Drury *et al.*, 2009).

The basis of this relational transformation is not self-categorisation (as was the case for the cognitive shift), but the perception that co-present others *share* one's salient social identity (Reicher, 2011). If one identifies with a social category but does not perceive co-present others to share this membership, then one's relations with these others are unlikely to be transformed towards intimacy. The difference between shared identity ('*We* are members of this group') and self-categorisation ('*I* am a member of this group') has remained implicit within the social identity literature. A lack of explicit examination of shared identity has inevitably meant that how people come to appraise shared identity in others has likewise been overlooked.

Recent work within the social identity tradition has suggested that the relational shift within groups of shared identity may in turn lead to an *emotional transformation* (Reicher, 2011). Crowd members can feel empowered to shape their world when those around them successfully act in unison to realise shared goals (collective self-objectification, CSO), an experience characterised by intense positive affect (Drury & Reicher, 1999, 2005, 2009). This is in addition to the emotion generated as identity-relevant events are appraised on behalf of one's salient group membership (intergroup emotions theory, IET; Smith, 1993; Smith *et al.*, 2007).

This paper will explore the ways in which shared identity and relatedness can have affective consequences within crowds. In this sense we are examining the *experience* of collective participation. Our definition of 'experience' in this context includes the quality of social relations with co-present others, and how one feels about these relations. We use the term 'collective participation' broadly to refer to taking part in any form of crowd behaviour. This research is intended to complement IET—which is concerned with the appraisal of specific events giving rise to specific emotions—by exploring the appraisal of social relations, i.e. the emotionality of 'groupness'.

A limited number of studies have explored the emotional experience of collective participation. As noted previously, Drury and colleagues have examined the emotional consequences of CSO and empowerment (Drury & Reicher, 1999, 2005, 2009). Furthermore, the PMMRG have investigated the collective experiences of Hindu pilgrims at the Magh Mela festival in India (PMMRG, 2007). Their analysis suggests that crowd members can feel a sense of connectedness with others, recognition of their participation, and validation of group-relevant beliefs. The experience of these forms of relatedness is then seen to facilitate identity-enactment and group commitment.

The current paper differs from these projects in two ways. Firstly, we explicitly examine the impact of shared identity upon relatedness, and relatedness upon emotionality of experience. Secondly, whilst the PMMRG (2007) research explores a specific type of collective action in a particular setting, we present data collected at a series of diverse and mundane forms of crowd event. Studies 1 and 2 explore the collective experiences of student demonstrators and football supporters using participant interviews. Emergent hypotheses from this work are then examined quantitatively in Study 3 using questionnaire data collected at a music festival.

Studies 1 and 2

Studies 1 and 2 use qualitative methods to examine collective experience at two different types of crowd event. The methods and results from both studies are presented concurrently. In both studies the researcher was an 'ingroup member', such that he identified with the participating groups, and would have attended the events irrespective of the research. This functioned to facilitate trust and access to participants, and helped uncover dynamics that might have been hidden to an 'outsider' (Fontana & Frey, 2005; Drury & Stott, 2001; Hammersley, 2000).

Overview of events

Study 1 examines the collective experiences of football (soccer) fans. In 2007 the first author attended six Dundee United matches (three home and three away) with supporters' groups, and conducted interviews before, during and after games. Dundee United won two, drew three and lost one of the matches, and attendances ranged between approximately 4000 and 17,000.

Study 2 explores the experiences of University of St Andrews students who demonstrated against proposed changes to the university's student accommodation in May 2008. The university announced plans to demolish basic but cheap student flats and replace them with more luxurious and expensive apartments. Protestors assembled outside of the Student's Union before marching the short distance through town to St Mary's Quadrangle where they held a rally.[1] Participant turnout at the demonstration was estimated by the protest organisers to be 150, but only 70 by the police. Although the size of the demonstration was relatively small, it was the largest student protest in the town for over a decade, and was thus a unique experience for many of the participants.

Methods

Data-gathering.   A variety of data-gathering strategies were used to triangulate evidence (for triangulation, see Drury & Stott, 2001; Hammersley & Atkinson, 1995; Denzin, 1989). Ethnographic research in both studies included conducting 'onsite' semi-structured interviews, collecting audiovisual data (photographs and videos), and recording research field notes. These data were then used to inform themes for retrospective semi-structured interviews.

Semi-structured interview themes.   Interviews in both studies were concerned with (shared) social identity ('To what extent do you share an identity with other people in the crowd? What word or phrase would you use to describe this identity?'), relatedness ('How would you describe your relationship with other people in the crowd?' Can you describe any interactions that you have had with other people in the crowd?'), and collective experience ('Can you describe how it feels to be in the crowd today?'). Participant responses to these broad questions were then probed to yield more detailed answers. Although these themes were the primary focus of the interviews, participants were invited to raise additional topics of relevance. All interviews were recorded using a digital Dictaphone with participant consent.

Study 1.   Twenty-three Dundee United supporters (all male) were interviewed during match days. Participants were recruited by writing to supporters' clubs and requesting that the researcher spend a match day with them, and also by approaching additional fans at matches on an opportunistic basis. The interviews took place in pubs and supporters' buses before or after games, and inside the stadiums during matches. Interviews ranged in length from several hours (if the researcher spent the entire match day with one set of participants) to a few minutes. These data were supplemented by three retrospective semi-structured interviews conducted three months after the initial data collection. Four participants took part in these post-event interviews, three of whom had previously been interviewed, and one (the only female participant in the study) who had published accounts of her experiences attending Dundee United matches. The retrospective interviews lasted between 60 and 90 minutes. One participant was retrospectively interviewed on a supporters' bus, another in a bar and two in a flat that they shared together.

Study 2.   Onsite interviews during the protest were conducted with nine participants (four males and five females). This was done by approaching demonstrators on an opportunistic basis at appropriate moments of the protest (e.g. between speakers at the rally). All onsite interviews lasted less than ten minutes, and nobody who was approached refused to participate. Four retrospective semi-structured group interviews were conducted in which video footage of the protest was reviewed in order to facilitate recall and articulation of participant experience (cf. Reicher, 1996; Drury & Reicher, 1999). The discussion themes for the retrospective interviews were the same as for the ethnographic stage of research, but also included additional points that had arisen during previous discussions. In this sense data collection and analysis were not treated as independent moments, but rather were fed back into one another in a reflexive manner. The retrospective interviews took place within three weeks of the demonstration, and lasted between 60 and 90 minutes. A total of 14 participants (six males and eight females) were recruited during the protest to take part. One of the protestors interviewed post-event had also been interviewed during the demonstration. Participants in both type of interview were students at the University of St Andrews aged between 18 and 21. All participants were included in a prize draw to win a week's rent.

Data analysis. Participant accounts of collective experience were analysed using procedures based on Thematic Analysis (Braun & Clarke, 2006) in order to disentangle themes as they emerged from the data. The analysis was shaped by dual goals; the first was to represent accurately participant experiences without imposing a priori categories upon their responses, whilst the second was to approach the material in terms of specific research questions. The analysis therefore functioned as a compromise between the bottom-up approach of Grounded Theory and the top-down approach of Content Analysis. The following research questions led the analysis:

- To what extent did participants perceive other crowd members to share their salient social identity (*shared identity*)?
- How did participants characterise their social relations with other crowd members, and how/were these experiences shaped by shared identity (*relatedness*)?
- What were the antecedents, consequences and nature of participants' collective experiences (*collective experience*)?

These questions functioned as the basis for analytic decisions with regards the organisation or clustering of emergent themes (Drury & Reicher, 2005).

Analysis

Shared identity. Throughout the Study 1 interviews participants were clear that they self-categorised themselves as Dundee United supporters, and that co-present others shared this same identity. This was in part due to the segregation of Scottish football stadiums into 'home' and 'away' ends. In this sense, fans were aware that crowd members in their section were also supporters of their team:

> P27: You're there as a United fan [ ] You're part of what you believe in and everyone around you is.
>
> [Extract 1: Study 1, Interview conducted on a supporters' bus][2]

In Study 1 the display of ingroup symbols, particularly the wearing of team colours, could also be used as a sign of others' group membership, and thus participants' shared identity with them:

P49: I see somebody wearing tangerine—even if it's not anything to do with United—I think 'Oh that might be a United fan', you know?

[Extract 2: Study 1, Retrospective Interview]

Whilst participants in the football context universally defined themselves as Dundee United supporters, interviewees at the demonstration described their social identities in various ways. For some, political forms of social identity were most salient:

P20: for me it was more as a Socialist. [ ] And for me it was just that part of my identity that generally ... when I have a demonstration that is the main thing.

[Extract 3: Study 2, Retrospective Interview]

However, other participants felt that a student category best captured their social identity during the protest:

Int.: did you feel like you were there as a student?
P23: Yes, definitely.
P24: Yeah.
P23: I think it was very ... it was very much defined as kind of student identity.

[Extract 4: Study 2, Retrospective Interview]

Although some demonstrators were able to label their social identity in these ways, a number of participants found this task problematic. This was the case for P15, who recalled difficulty in defining his salient social identity despite reporting a strong identification with the group:

P15: I identify with the cause completely. I identify with the group a lot [...] Going back to the question about how you identified yourself, I struggled with that question because I didn't really see a word that, erm, fitted. I didn't really know how to describe 'identify' on my part.

[Extract 5: Study 2, Retrospective Interview]

Furthermore, other participants at the protest explained that whilst they had a strong sense of social identity, they did not feel that they shared this identity with others within the crowd. This was apparent in the following interview extract in which the difference between self-categorisation and shared identity was made explicit:

P10: I didn't quite fit in with that sort of crowd, I wasn't used to it so much. But I mean that doesn't mean I didn't feel strongly about it [ ]
Int.: Do you draw a distinction between your identification with the group and your identification with the cause?
P10: Yeah, yeah.
P11: Yeah I would, they're two different things certainly.

[Extract 6: Study 2, Retrospective Interview]

Retrospective interviews from Study 2 revealed that appraisals of shared identity were dynamic, and subject to change throughout the demonstration. During the rally protestors were invited to speak to the group about their personal experiences regarding university accommodation. At this point, some participants felt that the group's identity shifted to exclude those not personally vulnerable to the accommodation change. For these people, the change in category definition diminished their feeling of shared identity with others in the crowd:

P11: I think the crowd defined itself in a more specific way when they got to the Quad and everyone sat down and people began to speak. [ ]

P10: I think you're [Pt11] right in this subgroup type thing in that it was almost divided into people who were really directly affected and perhaps people who were more indirectly affected. [ ] Yeah, I would say I didn't quite feel like I fitted in with everybody else.

[Extract 7: Study 2, Retrospective Interview]

This shift in shared identity was made clear by Pt11. Whilst reviewing video footage of the demonstration he noted that he was at the physical centre of the crowd during the march ('I liked being in the middle, which is where I was'), but that he moved to the periphery of the group when he experienced doubts over his shared identity with others at the rally:

P11: I think I'm showing physically that I'm not as part of the group here because I'm not sitting down [with the other protestors], I'm standing right over there in the corner [points]. So it's actually a very different situation from when we were actually marching for me I think. And that's partly to do with people speaking about their own personal experiences and the fact that … it's not that I feel I can't be part of the group, it's just that I maybe ought not to pretend that I am.

[Extract 8: Study 2, Retrospective Interview]

Participants in Study 2 appraised their shared identity with others in a number of ways. As noted in the previous two extracts, the realisation that one was not vulnerable to the same fate as others could diminish one's sense of shared identity with them. In addition, P21 noted during a discussion of the chanting at the demonstration that this shared action functioned as an indicator of common group membership:

P21: If you're all saying the same thing then you're part of the same group.

[Extract 9: Study 2, Retrospective Interview]

Embodied emotion emerged as a further indicator of participants' shared identity. Protestors recalled how embodied expression of emotion could be used to appraise whether co-present others were members (or not) of one's social group:

P16: And just like you can see by their body language and by their facial expression that they are making themselves not part of it.

[Extract 10: Study 2, Retrospective Interview]

As noted previously in the analysis, participants' shared identity with other crowd members had a number of consequences. In physical terms, P11 explained how a shift in shared identity corresponded with a change in his desired physical proximity to other protestors (see Extract 8). In addition to this physical dimension, our data pointed to within-crowd relational changes.

Relatedness. Three forms of relatedness were identified in the data: connectedness, recognition and validation.

Connectedness. In both studies participants reported a positive transformation in social relations within the crowd. In the extract below a football fan in Study 1 explained how relationships with other supporters were characterised by intimacy. Her sense of familiarity with strangers was so pronounced that she likened her crowd experience to being surrounded by friends:

P49: Well you were amongst friends first off, even if you didn't know them, you were amongst friends. [ ] you could go and stand anywhere.

[Extract 11: Study 2, Retrospective Interview]

This theme was developed by P27 who noted that the connectedness he felt with other crowd members at the football would not exist in alternative social contexts:

P27: Okay you sit with your mates but you could be sitting with anybody. [ ] you make friendships and have conversations with people you'd probably never give a second glance to otherwise.

[Extract 12: Study 1, Interview conducted on a supporters' bus]

Recognition. In addition to connectedness, participants in both studies described a sense of recognition within the crowd. This operated on two levels. Firstly, some participants recalled being recognised personally within the crowd, for example P31 who unexpectedly met an old school friend at a Dundee United game:

P31: I can go to a match for the first time in ages, and certainly the first away match in ages, and like meet up with P32. It's like 'wow'. [ ] it's like almost going back into like a local bar or something and you're like 'Oh, everyone's around'.

[Extract 13: Study 1, Retrospective Interview]

Further to recognition at a personal level, participants in the demonstration described pleasure in others' recognition of them as valued members of the social group:

P13: even people who I didn't know very well, maybe acquaintances, maybe hadn't spoken to many times would come up to me and be like, 'Hey, yeah, good to see you. Meet my friend'.
Int.: Okay. So you were sort of noticed and acknowledged in the crowd?
P13: Yeah, it was good.
Int.: Why is that a positive thing do you think?
P12: It makes you . . . I don't know. It just made me feel more comfortable and I guess just accepted, yeah.
P13: You feel more part of the group as opposed to someone who's just tagging along.

[Extract 14: Study 2, Retrospective Interview]

Validation. A third form of relatedness experienced by participants was the validation of their identities, beliefs and emotional experiences within the crowd. At Dundee United matches P49 recalled a confirmation of her identity as a supporter when she was surrounded by fellow fans, in contrast to other contexts in which this identity was mocked:

P49: It's just everyone around you [in the crowd] is singing from the same hymn sheet. [ ] You know when people used to laugh at United and I would think 'Well it doesn't matter' because you know I'd people who'd feel the same as me. You didn't feel you were being stupid once you got onto the terracing, although you'd admit to feeling stupid when you were in work and things you know.

[Extract 15: Study 1, Retrospective Interview]

During the demonstration P1 made a similar comparison between the doubt and insecurity he experienced outside the crowd, with the validation of his beliefs within a group of like-minded others:

P1: [In the crowd] you're not alone in your struggle basically for what you believe in. And the fact that there are other people that believe in what you believe in and which clearly is always a reassuring thing. Because you're like, 'Am I doing something stupid here or am I not getting something?', and yet when you've got this number of people out there who also want exactly the same thing then you realise to yourself, 'Yes, I probably am actually right!'.

[Extract 16: Study 2, Onsite Interview]

Furthermore, as was implicit in the previous extract, P3 noted that the experience of collective participation could strengthen commitment to future group action:

P3: I think that is an effect that demonstrations have is that when you see other people who feel the same that it does like inspire you to, um, pursue it. Like I don't think I've been inspired enough to organise my own demonstration, but I would take part in anything they did in the future.

[Extract 17: Study 2, Retrospective Interview]

Interview data from both studies also suggested that one's emotional experience could be validated, and subsequently amplified, by co-present others. A reciprocal relationship where one's emotional excitation validated and augmented that of fellow group members, who in turn re-validated and amplified one's own emotional experience, was described by P13 when he recalled his experience at the protest:

P13: And the sort of enthusiasm caught on I guess.
Int.: How do you mean it 'caught on'?
P13: I mean it sort of like spread; once you saw other people being enthusiastic it made me want to be more enthusiastic, and then I'm sure every other person then became more enthusiastic. It just increased it I felt like.

[Extract 18: Study 2, Retrospective Interview]

Shared identity and relatedness. Analysis from both studies suggested that relatedness with other crowd members was a consequence of shared identity. For example, reflecting upon his experience at the demonstration, the following participant described the ease with which he talked to strangers within the crowd after categorising them as members of his social group:

P11: I found myself speaking naturally to people I had never met before in my life. [ ] So you did find that it was very easy because everybody was kind of connected by this group identity that you could suddenly speak to people quite easily [ ] It wasn't even as though it registered that I didn't know them at the time. It was just 'Oh, yeah, we're in the same group' kind of thing, so the unity kind of made it a lot easier actually for me.

[Extract 19: Study 2, Retrospective Interview]

The impact of shared identity upon relatedness was made particularly clear in Study 2 as participants compared their intragroup interactions at the demonstration, with experiences of anomie and isolation 'in the street':

Pt23: if you just walk up to someone in the street or something it wouldn't go the same way, but like everybody was there [at the demonstration] for the same reason. I think you could have just turned to someone. [ ] this seemed like something where you kind of broke down like social barriers that would ordinarily exist.

[Extract 20: Study 2, Retrospective Interview]

Importantly, when participants experienced a lack of shared identity with other crowd members, they felt unrelated and distant to them. For example, as noted previously in

Extract 8, during the rally P11 felt his sense of shared identity with other protestors diminish, leading him to sit alone on the periphery of the crowd. P10 likewise felt that she did not share a social identity with other protestors, resulting in an experience of detachment and isolation:

> P10: I would say I didn't quite feel like I fitted in with everybody else. [ ] I kind of felt like I didn't really know what was going on, that people … a lot of things had happened to people, and there was this group as you [P11] were saying who'd been in contact with the Union, who'd been doing stuff and I didn't really know about that so I felt a bit detached from that I suppose.
>
> [Extract 21: Study 2, Retrospective Interview]

Emotional experience. Throughout the interviews there were references to participants' emotionally intense and positive collective experiences. One demonstrator (P21) recalled that 'there was definitely some positive feeling from the protest itself', whilst a football supporter (Pt27) described the collective experience of watching his team score as 'better than an orgasm'. Extracts from other interviews suggested that the nature of participants' social relationships with other crowd members had a role to play in generating such collective passion. For example, P29 noted that her experience of the demonstration was emotionally intense in part due to the togetherness she felt with other protestors:

> P49: I think 'emotional' would be an appropriate word about it. Especially because of like the noise and the being together with other people.
>
> [Extract 23: Study 2, Retrospective Interview]

P11 was more explicit about his positive emotional experience of the protest. As noted in the following interview extract, he explained that this experience was in part a consequence of the relatedness he felt with fellow group members:

> P11: I wasn't just there for fun but the overriding emotion there was just having fun. I felt I was there for a good reason, I felt the group were really connected
>
> [Extract 24: Study 2, Retrospective Interview]

It is important to stress that not all participants experienced their time in the crowds as positive, but that collective experience appeared to operate as a function of intragroup relations. This was particularly clear for P10, who recalled how a lack of shared identity with other crowd members negatively impacted upon her experience of the protest:

> P10: I felt when I went there it just seemed to be a lot of extremists in some ways and I was just a bit disappointed [ ] I suppose in some ways I felt less good about it than I did to start with.
>
> [Extract 26: Study 2, Retrospective Interview]

Discussion

Studies 1 and 2 used qualitative methods to explore the nature of collective experience at two different forms of crowd event. For the football supporters in Study 1, self-categorisation and shared identity were empirically equivalent since all participants identified themselves as Dundee United fans, and felt that other crowd members shared this identity. This relationship was more complex for the student demonstrators in Study 2. The protestors could use different social identities to frame their participation, and some experienced difficulty in providing a label for their salient social identity. Nonetheless, participants were clearer about their sense of shared identity with others within the crowd, and it was this which appeared critical in shaping their collective experiences. This analysis suggests that self-categorisation and shared identity should be treated as conceptually distinct. Knowledge of one's shared identity (or lack thereof) with others was interpreted through embodied emotion (e.g. facial expressions), ingroup symbols (e.g. wearing team colours), shared action (e.g. chanting), and shared fate (e.g. vulnerability to rent increases). Furthermore, perception of shared identity was not static, but was subject to change with the dynamics of social context.

When participants did feel that co-present others shared their social identity, they described a breakdown of social barriers with strangers within the crowd; what we term relatedness. This allowed them to feel connected to, and recognised by, other group members. Participants also reported experiencing a validation of their beliefs, identities and emotions, a process which appeared to augment the strength of all three. Relatedness could be experienced with positive affect by participants, in part due to contrasting the experience with that of 'everyday' society. It is important to stress however that shared identity and relatedness were not experienced by all participants. Without shared identity, the experience of collective participation could instead be characterised by isolation and insecurity. Analyses from these studies therefore suggest a process in which relatedness was dependent upon shared identity. There was also preliminary evidence from Study 2 that the collective experience of participation could encourage future group commitment.

Limitations. Although the studies provide an incipient base from which to explore collective experience, they did have several weaknesses. The studies relied upon a limited number of respondents, running the risk that our samples were not representative of the populations who participated in the crowd events. However, a limited sample size was a necessary sacrifice in order to conduct the in-depth interviews that were required to generate hypotheses for the third study. The methodology could be also criticised for a lack of objectivity because of the dual role of the author as both researcher and actor in the crowd events. However, being an ingroup member has various advantages including gaining trust and access to participants (Fontana & Frey, 2005; Green, 1993). Furthermore, because the research did not focus upon the politics of the demonstration or the quality of the football, there was little opportunity for researcher bias along ideological grounds.

Hypotheses. The interview studies provide prima facie evidence for two hypotheses which were quantitatively tested in a third study. Our analysis suggests that shared identity—and not simply self-categorisation (to be operationalised in Study 3 as strength of social identity)—can transform intragroup social relations to produce a sense of relatedness. It is therefore hypothesised that shared identity will be a greater predictor of relatedness than strength of social identity (H1). Furthermore, data from Studies 1 and 2 indicated that relatedness could be experienced by participants with positivity and emotional intensity. Following from H1, our second hypothesis (H2) therefore predicts that relatedness will mediate the relationship between shared identity and emotionality (positivity and intensity) of experience. Study 3 shall test these hypotheses by examining questionnaire data collected at a third form of crowd event.

Study 3

Study 3 was a questionnaire study conducted at a music festival. The author and a research assistant attended the three-day Rock Ness festival in 2009, an annual event featuring a mixture of rock and dance acts which was attended by approximately 30,000 people. In total 98 participants completed questionnaires, 46 of whom were male and 48 female (four undisclosed), with a mean participant age of 26.6 (ranging from 16 to 47). All participants were included in a prize draw to win music vouchers.

Methods

Questionnaires were disseminated on an opportunistic basis throughout the event. This was primarily done in the campsite during the late mornings before festival-goers entered the main arena.

Questionnaire items and scale reliability. All questionnaire items used nine-point Likert scales. The questionnaires were kept as short as possible to encourage participation. At the start of the questionnaire participants were informed that 'The "crowd" in the following questions refers to the crowd watching the music, not the crowd at the campsite, queue for the bar etc.'.

Strength of social identity. In order to assess the strength of participants' salient social identity, they were invited to define what this identity was. This was done by firstly giving an example of what we meant by social identity. Participants were told that 'If I were to ask someone in a church to describe their identity they might give answers such as "a religious person" or "Christian" etc.'. They were then asked 'How would you describe your identity here at Rock Ness?' Participants were next informed that the questions that followed would refer to the social identity that they had provided. The strength of social identity scale contained the following two items adapted from (Cameron, 2004)[3] ($r = 0.61$); 'I often think of myself in terms of this identity' (Agree/Disagree), and 'I feel good when I think of myself in terms of this identity' (Agree/Disagree).

Shared identity. The shared identity scale had two items ($r = 0.52$). The first asked 'To what extent do you think that other people in the crowd at Rock Ness share this identity?' (Very Much So/Not At All). The second item presented participants with a series of two overlapping circles (adapted from Schubert & Otten, 2002) within which 'self' and 'others' were written, ranging from not overlapping at all (1) to entirely overlapping (9). Participants were then asked 'Which circles best represent the extent to which you share this identity with others in the Rock Ness crowd?'

Relatedness. The relatedness scale had the following three items ($\alpha = 0.81$): 'To what extent do you feel a sense of "connection" with other people in the crowd here at Rock Ness?' (Very Much So/Not At All), 'To what extent do you feel that the other people in the crowd are experiencing the festival in the same way as you?' (Very Much So/Not At All), and 'To what extent do you feel a sense of "oneness" with other people in the crowd here at Rock Ness?' (Very Much So/Not At All).

Positivity of experience. The positivity of experience scale had the following two items ($r = 0.57$); 'I enjoy being a part of the crowd at Rock Ness' (Totally Disagree/Totally Agree), and 'My experiences in the crowd at Rock Ness have been negative' (reverse coded) (Totally Disagree/Totally Agree).

Emotional intensity of experience. Emotional intensity of experience was measured using one item; 'My experiences in the crowd at Rock Ness have been emotionally intense' (Totally Disagree/Totally Agree).[4]

Analysis

Preliminary analysis. Skewness and kurtosis values for all variables were within recommended ranges (Kline, 2005). Two participants had missing data in their questionnaires. There were fewer than 5% missing data in each variable, and Little's Missing Completely At Random (MCAR) test (Little, 1988) was non-significant; $\chi^2(8) = 3.25$, $p = 0.92$, indicating that the missing data pattern was not dependent upon the observed data (Rubin, 1976).

Principal components analysis (PCA) was used to check that the shared identity and relatedness scales were tapping into separate concepts. PCA using varimax rotation extracted only one factor with an eigenvalue greater than 1, accounting for 58% of variance. Following examination of the scree plot, which indicated one further factor, a forced two-factor solution accounting for 75% of variance was extracted. The three relatedness items loaded onto the first factor, and the two shared identity items onto the second, allowing us to treat the two scales as distinct measures in accordance with our theoretical argument.

There were no significant effects of age or on which day of the festival the questionnaire was completed upon any of the variables. There was however a marginal effect of gender upon emotional intensity of experience, with males (mean = 6.29, standard deviation (SD) = 2.07) scoring significantly higher than females (mean = 5.38, SD = 2.27), $t(91) = 2.02$, p = 0.05. There were no other significant gender effects. Table 1 presents the descriptive statistics, scale reliabilities, and zero-order correlations for all of the variables.

Table 1. Zero-order correlations, means, standard deviations and reliability statistics

Variables	(a)	(b)	(c)	(d)	(e)
(a) *Strength of Social Identity*	1.00				
(b) *Shared Identity*	0.31**	1.00			
(c) *Relatedness*	0.28**	0.53**	1.00		
(d) *Positivity*	0.15	0.17	0.47**	1.00	
(e) *Emotional Intensity*	0.01	0.16	0.49**	0.24*	1.00
n	96	96	98	98	97
Mean	6.76	6.86	6.89	7.99	5.85
Standard deviation	1.83	1.42	1.46	1.37	2.25
Reliability	$r = 0.61$	$r = 0.52$	$\alpha = 0.81$	$r = 0.57$	–

Note: All p-values are two-tailed. $^*p < 0.05$, $^{**}p < 0.01$.

Hypothesis 1

H1 stated that shared identity would be a better predictor of relatedness than strength of social identity. Steiger's test confirmed that whilst relatedness correlated positively with both shared identity, $r(93) = 0.53$, $p < 0.01$, and strength of social identity, $r(93) = 0.28, p < 0.01$, the association with shared identity was significantly stronger, $Z = 2.34$, $p < 0.01$. Using linear regression, shared identity and strength of social identity were then simultaneously entered as predictors of relatedness. Shared identity significantly predicted relatedness, $\beta = 0.49$, standard error (SE) $= 0.09$, $t(94) = 5.34$, $p < 0.01$, but strength of social identity did not, $\beta = 0.10$, SE $= 0.07$, $t(94) = 1.38$, $p = 0.17$.

Hypothesis 2

H2 stated that relatedness would significantly mediate the relationships between shared identity and emotionality (positivity and intensity) of experience. Results based on 10,000 bootstrapped samples indicated that whilst the total effect (TE) of shared identity and relatedness upon positivity was non-significant (TE $= 0.16$, SE $= 0.10$, $p = 0.10$), and the direct effect (DE) of shared identity on positivity was also non-significant (DE $= -0.09$, SE $= 0.10$, $p = 0.38$), the indirect effect (IE) was significant (IE $= 0.25$, SE $= 0.07$, $p < 0.01$) (Figure 1).[5] Because zero is not

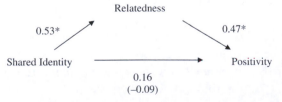

Figure 1. Relatedness as a mediator of the relationship between shared identity and positivity of experience. $n = 98$. Values represent unstandardized regression weights. $^*p < 0.01$.

in the 99% confidence interval (CI), (lower 99% CI = 0.11, upper 99% CI = 0.51) the IE is significantly different from zero at $p < 0.01$ (two tailed). Analysis using a Sobel Test yielded an equivalent result, $Z = 3.68, p < 0.01$.

Controlling for gender, results based on 10,000 bootstrapped samples likewise indicated that whilst the total effect of shared identity upon emotional intensity was non-significant (TE = 0.22, SE = 0.16, $p = 0.18$), and the direct effect of shared identity on emotional intensity was also non-significant (DE = −0.28, SE = 0.16, $p = 0.09$), the IE was significant (IE = 0.49, SE = 0.11, $p < 0.01$) (Figure 2). Because zero is not in the 99% CI, (lower 99% CI = 0.24, upper 99% CI = 0.82) the IE is significantly different from zero at $p < 0.01$ (two tailed). Analysis using a Sobel Test yielded an equivalent result, $Z = 4.16, p < 0.01$.

Discussion

The hypotheses generated from the first two qualitative studies were examined using a questionnaire study conducted at a music festival. H1 stated that shared identity, and not simply strength of social identity, would best predict participants' sense of relatedness with one another. Our analysis revealed that whilst relatedness correlated positively with both variables, the strength of association was significantly stronger with shared identity. Furthermore, using linear regression, only shared identity significantly predicted relatedness when both shared identity and strength of social identity were simultaneously entered as predictors. These results provided support for H1. H2 stated that the relationships between shared identity and emotional intensity, and shared identity and positivity of experience, would both be mediated by relatedness. This was confirmed using mediation analysis allowing us to accept the second hypothesis. Our results therefore provided support for the analysis from Studies 1 and 2 which suggested that shared identity can lead to a positive transformation of social relations, which in turn can be experienced with positivity and emotional intensity.

Limitations. The conclusions from Study 3 must be treated as tentative because our data were correlational and not causational. Furthermore, the scales used in the questionnaire were preliminary since they had not been used previously in the research literature (with the exception of social identity scale; Cameron, 2004). Despite this, all of the multi-item measures were reliable, and PCA confirmed that the shared identity

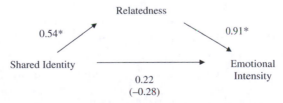

Figure 2. Relatedness as a mediator of the relationship between shared identity and emotional experience. $n = 98$. Values represent unstandardized regression weights. $^*p < 0.01$.

and relatedness items loaded onto different factors, providing prima facie evidence that the two measures were tapping into distinct concepts.

General discussion

The current paper has presented three studies exploring the under-researched topic of collective experience. The first two studies analysed interview data with student demonstrators and football fans, before hypotheses generated from these studies were subsequently confirmed using questionnaire data collected at a music festival.

The analysis revealed that when participants appraised co-present others as sharing their social identity (e.g. through shared ingroup symbols, action or embodied emotion), then social relations between crowd members could be positively trans-formed in a number of ways. This included a sense of connectedness or intimacy, and recognition such that one's presence in the crowd was noted and valued by others. Relatedness could further extend to the validation of one's beliefs, emotions and behaviours. In contrast to 'everyday' life which may be filled with doubt and inse-curity, within the crowd participants described an alleviation of personal uncertainty as their perspective on the world was reflected back at them by fellow group members. These findings were in line with Hindu pilgrims' accounts of collective relatedness at the Magh Mela festival (PMMRG, 2007).

Interview analysis from Studies 1 and 2 supported our claim that such a relational transformation was determined by participants' perception of shared identity with other crowd members, and not simply the self-categorisation required for the cogni-tive shift from personal to social identity (Turner et al., 1987). Whilst crowd members with shared identity could experience the crowds as supportive and nurturant, several participants without shared identity reported experiencing isolation and detachment. This claim received further support from Study 3 in which shared identity, and not strength of social identity, best predicted the experience of relatedness.

Analyses from the studies also provided support for the suggestion that such a rela-tional transformation could contribute to an emotional transformation towards inten-sity and positivity. The suggestion that collective emotionality could be determined by participants' salient social identities (via shared identity and relatedness) fits with IET (Smith, 1993; Smith et al., 1997), which contends that group-relevant events may be appraised on behalf of one's socially extended self, leading to specific emotions and action tendencies. Our findings also complement research conducted by Drury & Reicher (2005, 2009) which demonstrates that intragroup unity can facilitate CSO leading to empowerment and intense positive affect. However, whilst these two areas of work analyse the experience of specific types of group event, our analysis suggests that the quality of within-crowd social relations may themselves be appraised emotion-ally, leading to general emotional intensity and positivity of experience. For example, analysis of participant interviews at the student demonstration suggested that a recipro-cal validation of emotional experience by fellow ingroup members could lead to a mutual amplification of that experience. Our findings, in conjunction with IET and the empowerment literature, suggest that collective emotion is determined ultimately by the social identities of crowd members, contradicting the notion within classic crowd psychology that collective emotionality was rooted in a loss of identity.

Furthermore, in addition to our claim that collective experience was a consequence of crowd action, analysis from Study 2 suggested the intriguing possibility that this experience could in turn promote participation in future collective behaviour. This relates to work within the collective action literature which explores the roles of specific emotions including anger (van Zomeren *et al.*, 2004; Livingstone *et al.*, 2011) and contempt (Tausch *et al.*, 2011) in encouraging participation in collective action. Our analysis suggests that in addition to emotion generated through specific appraisal of events, there exists a dynamic process whereby experience of collective action may in turn give rise to future participation, i.e. collective experience should be considered as both an input and output of crowd action.

Future directions

It is acknowledged that the exploratory nature of the qualitative research and the limitations of the questionnaire study necessarily constrain the scope of their conclusions. The analysis presented in the current paper is not intended to provide a conclusive account of crowd experience, but should rather be treated as a starting point for future research. Firstly, the relationship between shared identity and relatedness should be examined experimentally. Whilst correlation and regression analyses from Study 3 provide support for the claim that relatedness operates as a function of shared identity, a study in which shared identity was manipulated and relatedness varied accordingly would significantly strengthen this argument. Such a study would require the further development of scales to interrogate these variables, moving beyond the modest collection of items used in Study 3.

Future work also needs to interrogate the relationship between relatedness and emotional experience, particularly the possibility of emotional amplification through reciprocal validation. The fieldwork methodologies utilised in the current paper could be supplemented with laboratory work. This would allow one to use a variety of methods (including psychophysiological measures) to examine changes in collective emotional experience over time as a function of relatedness. Finally, in order to develop a model that captures the dynamic nature crowd participation, longitudinal methods are required to explore the consequences as well as the antecedents of collective experience.

Conclusion

An analysis of three crowd events presented evidence that perception of shared identity, and not self-categorisation, determined the nature of participants' collective experiences. Within-crowd relatedness was transformed by shared identity to provide a sense of connectedness, recognition and validation. Preliminary evidence then suggested that relatedness contributed to the emotionality of participants' collective experiences. This analysis contradicts the contention from classic crowd psychology that crowd emotion emanates from a loss of identity, and further suggests that the experience of collective participation may have a role to play in encouraging group commitment.

Acknowledgements

This research was supported by an ESRC Postgraduate Studentship (PTA-030-2006-00100) awarded to the first author. The authors wish to thank the Editors and two anonymous reviewers for their constructive and valuable comments; as well as Oliver Lauenstein, Tom Clemens and Wendy van Rijswijk for help with data collection.

Notes

1. This venue was chosen because it was the meeting place for the University Court. Serendipitously, the adjacent building was the School of Psychology, allowing us to film the rally from an aerial vantage point.
2. Transcription conventions are based upon the suggestions given by Parker (1992, p. 124). Where text has been omitted from the transcript, it is signalled by a pair of empty brackets, thus '[ ]'. Pauses in speech lasting longer than three seconds are indicated with three full stops (an ellipsis), thus '...'. Information provided by the author for clarification, including a description of participant actions, is given within brackets, '[like this]'.
3. The questionnaire originally contained three social identity items, but the ingroup ties item ('I feel strong ties with others who share this identity') was removed prior to analysis due to its similarity to the relatedness measure.
4. A second emotional intensity of experience item, 'Being in the Rock Ness crowd is a dull experience' (reverse coded) (Totally Disagree/Totally Agree), was removed from the analysis because the term 'dull' may have led participants to answer the item in terms of the positivity of their experience.
5. The total effect of the independent variable and mediator upon the dependent variable does not need to be significant in order to demonstrate mediation (Hayes, 2009; Rucker et al., 2011).

References

Blumer, H. (1939) Collective behaviour, in: R. Park (Ed.) *Principles of sociology* (New York, NY, Barnes & Noble), 219–288.

Braun, V. & Clarke, V. (2006) Using thematic analysis in psychology, *Qualitative Research in Psychology*, 3, 77–101.

Cameron, J. (2004) A three-factor model of social identity, *Self and Identity*, 3, 239–262.

Denzin, N. (1989) *The research act: a theoretical introduction to sociological methods* (3rd edn) (Englewood Cliffs, NJ, Prentice-Hall).

Drury, J., Cocking, C. & Reicher, S. D. (2009) Everyone for themselves? A comparative study of crowd solidarity among emergency survivors, *British Journal of Social Psychology*, 48, 487–506.

Drury, J. & Reicher, S. D. (1999) The intergroup dynamics of collective empowerment: substantiating the social identity model of crowd behaviour, *Group Processes and Intergroup Relations*, 2, 1–22.

Drury, J. & Reicher, S. D. (2000) Collective action and psychological change: the emergence of new social identities, *British Journal of Social Psychology*, 39, 579–604.

Drury, J. & Reicher, S. D. (2005) Explaining enduring empowerment: a comparative study of collective action and psychological outcomes, *European Journal of Social Psychology*, 35, 35–58.

Drury, J. & Reicher, S. D. (2009) Collective psychological empowerment as a model of social change: researching crowds and power, *Journal of Social Issues*, 65, 707–725.

Drury, J. & Stott, C. (2001) Bias as a research strategy in participant observation: the case of intergroup conflict, *Field Methods*, 13, 47–67.

Fontana, A. & Frey, J. (2005) The interview: from neutral stance to political involvement, in: N. Denzin & Y. Lincoln (Eds) *The Sage handbook of qualitative research* (3rd edn)(Thousand Oaks, CA, Sage), 695–727.

Freud, S. (1920, Trans. 1922) *Group psychology and the analysis of the ego* (New York, NY, W. W. Morton).

Green, P. (1993) Taking sides: partisan research in the 1984–1985 miners' strike, in: D. Hobbs & T. May (Eds) *Interpreting the field: accounts of ethnography* (Oxford, Oxford University Press).

Hammersley, M. (2000) *Taking sides in social research: essays on partisanship and bias* (London, Routledge).

Hammersley, M. & Atkinson, P. (1995) *Ethnography: principles in practice* (2nd edn) (London, Routledge).

Haslam, S. A. & Reicher, S. D. (2006) Stressing the group: social identity and the unfolding dynamics of stress, *Journal of Applied Psychology*, 91, 1037–1052.

Hayes, A. F. (2009) Beyond Baron and Kenny: statistical mediation analysis in the new millennium, *Communication Monographs*, 76, 408–420.

Kline, R. B. (2005) *Principles and practice of structural equation modelling* (2nd edn) (New York, Guilford Press).

Le Bon, G. (1895 Trans. 2002) *The crowd: a study of the popular mind* (London, Ernest Benn).

Levine, M., Cassidy, C., Brazier, G. & Reicher, S. D. (2002) Self-categorisation and bystander intervention: two experimental studies, *Journal of Applied Social Psychology*, 7, 1452–1463.

Little, R. J. A. (1988) A test of missing completely at random for multivariate data with missing values, *Journal of the American Statistical Association*, 83, 1198–1202.

Livingstone, A., Spears, R., Manstead, A., Bruder, M. & Shepherd, L. (Forthcoming 2011) We feel, therefore we are: emotion as a basis for self-categorization and social action, *Emotion*.

McDougal, W. (1920/1939) *The group mind: the principles of collective psychology and their application to the interpretation of national life and character* (Cambridge, Cambridge University Press).

Novelli, D., Drury, J. & Reicher, S. (2010) Come together: two studies concerning the impact of group relations on 'personal space', *British Journal of Social Psychology*, 49, 223–236.

Park, R. (1904, Trans. 1982) *The crowd and the public* (Chicago, IL, University of Chicago Press).

Parker, I. (1992) *Discourse dynamics: critical analysis for social and individual psychology* (London, Routledge).

Reicher, S. D. (1984) The St Pauls' riot: an explanation of the limits of crowd action in terms of a social identity model, *European Journal of Social Psychology*, 14, 1–21.

Reicher, S. D. (1987) Crowd behaviour as social action, in: J. Turner, M. Hogg, P. Oakes, S. Reicher & M. Wetherell (Eds) *Rediscovering the social group: a self-categorization theory* (Oxford, Blackwell), 171–202.

Reicher, S. D. (1996) 'The Battle of Westminster': developing the social identity model of crowd behaviour in order to explain the initiation and development of collective conflict, *European Journal of Social Psychology*, 26, 115–134.

Reicher, S. D. (2001) The psychology of crowd dynamics, in: M. Hogg & R. Tindale (Eds) *Blackwell handbook of social psychology: group processes* (Oxford, Blackwell), 182–208.

Reicher, S. D. (Forthcoming 2011) Crowd psychology, in: V. S. Ramachandran (Ed.) *Encyclopedia of human behaviour* (2nd edn) (Oxford, Elsevier).

Reicher, S. D. & Haslam, S. A. (2006) Rethinking the psychology of tyranny: the BBC Prison Experiment, *British Journal of Social Psychology*, 45, 1–40.

Rubin, D. B. (1976) Inference and missing data, *Biometrika*, 63, 581–592.

Rucker, D. D., Preacher, K. J., Tormala, Z. L. & Petty, R. E. (2011) Mediation analysis in social psychology: current practices and new recommendations, *Social and Personality Psychology Compass*, 5/6, 359–371.

Schubert, T. & Otten, S. (2002) Overlap of self, ingroup and outgroup: pictorial measurement of self-categorization, *Self and Identity*, 4, 353–376.

Smith, E. (1993) Social identity and social emotions: toward new conceptualizations of prejudice, in: D. Mackie & D. Hamilton (Eds) *Affect, cognition, and stereotyping: interactive processes in group perception* (San Diego, CA, Academic Press), 297–315.

Smith, E., Seger, C. & Mackie, D. (2007) Can emotions be truly group level? Evidence regarding four conceptual criteria, *Journal of Personality and Social Psychology*, 93, 431–446.

Stott, C. & Reicher, S. D. (1998) Crowd action as intergroup process: introducing the police perspective, *European Journal of Social Psychology*, 28, 509–529.

Tajfel, H. & Turner, J. C. (1979) An integrative theory of intergroup conflict, in: W. Austin & S. Worchel S (Eds) *The social psychology of intergroup relations* (Monterey, CA, Brooks/Cole), 33–47.

Tausch, N., Becker, J., Spears, R., Christ, O., Saab, R., Singh, P. & Siddiqui, R. (2011) Explaining radical group behaviour: developing emotion and efficacy routes to normative and non-normative collective action, *Journal of Personality and Social Psychology*, 101, 129–148.

The Prayag Magh Mela Research Group (PMMRG) (2007) Experiencing the Magh Mela at Prayag: crowds, categories and social relations, *Psychological Studies*, 52, 293–301.

Turner, J., Hogg, M., Oakes, P., Reicher, S. D. & Wetherell, M. (1987) *Rediscovering the social group: a self-categorization theory* (Oxford, Blackwell).

Tyler, T. & Blader, S. (2001) Identity and prosocial behavior in groups, *Group Processes and Intergroup Relations*, 4, 207–226.

Van Zomeren, M., Spears, R., Leach, C. & Fischer, A. (2004) Put your money where your mouth is! Explaining collective action tendencies through group-based anger and group efficacy, *Journal of Personality and Social Psychology*, 87, 649–664.

On modelling the influence of group formations in a crowd

Gerta Köster[a], Michael Seitz[a], Franz Treml[a],
Dirk Hartmann[b] and Wolfram Klein[b]

[a]Department of Computer Science and Mathematics, University of Applied Sciences, Munich, Germany; [b]Siemens AG, Germany

Inspired by doubts from social scientists on the validity of computer models that see a crowd as a pure aggregation of individuals, we develop a mathematical model for group formation within crowds. It is based on a few simple characteristics. Most importantly, small groups stick together as they thread their way through a crowd. Additionally, groups have a tendency to walk abreast to ease communication. Through simulation, we establish that the occurrence of groups significantly impacts crowd movement, namely evacuation times. Further, we complement and validate the simulations by a small experiment: a classroom egress. The simulation results match the measurements qualitatively. We get a good quantitative match after calibrating the supposed desire to communicate while walking—and hence to walk abreast. We conclude that it is one of the crucial parameters to calibrate the group model against reality. While working on a mathematically complete model, a new gap between the mathematical modelling and the social sciences emerged: some model assumptions are based on the modeller's intuition rather than on sociological or psychological insight validated by the scientific community. We hope the findings—and resulting suggestions—will in return inspire new cooperation between the disciplines.

Introduction

'Families survive together or die together'—a fact that few in the community of crowd researchers and modellers seem to doubt. The authors of the present paper, all of them mathematicians or computer scientists, have been inspired by this critical comment from social scientist Annette Spellerberg (personal communication, 2009) on our previous work: the modelling of large crowds as an aggregation of individuals.

A crowd at a large event is often dominated by small groups (Aveni, 1977). Larger groups may again separate into smaller subgroups (James, 1951). In our specific case, we are interested in a crowd leaving a football stadium (Bogusch *et al.*, 2009). Groups stay together during an evacuation. In fact, there is empirical evidence that making contact with affiliated persons takes precedence over individual flight (Sime, 1983; Aguirre *et al.*, 1998). Even without prior close relationship, a shared identity may arise in an emergency situation and may make individuals stay closely together during the evacuation (Drury *et al.*, 2009). In view of this, how reliable are aggregate simulators when predicting crowd behaviour or planning, e.g. evacuations (Drury & Cocking, 2007; Novelli *et al.*, 2010; Spellerberg *et al.*, 2010)? And, how do we find a viable compromise between what social scientists and psychologist know about group behaviour and the restrictions that modellers have to comply with to create an efficient computer simulation?

Encouraged by these questions, we present an attempt to bridge this gap. We suggest a model for formations of small groups or subgroups in crowds that is based on very few and simple assumptions. Most importantly: small groups stick together as they thread their way through a crowd. They tend to walk in formations that facilitate communication (Moussaïd *et al.*, 2010). That is, they can chat with each other without having to turn their heads.

This simple model allows us to observe the effect of groups in a crowd on phenomena like congestion. We establish that the occurrence of groups significantly impacts crowd movement, at least in our model. The intuitive assumption, that the larger the average group size the slower the crowd moves as a whole, is confirmed by simulation. The effect becomes even more prominent at bottlenecks. A real-life experiment again confirms this hypothesis. However, it also shows that the effect may be reversed when the groups are coordinated with the intention to facilitate navigation.

While the outcome of our experiments makes intuitive sense, it also emphasises the need to incorporate groups in crowd simulators. And this creates a new dilemma. How do crowd modellers know what makes a group or even a crowd? And on which situational parameters might this depend? At many points, while creating our own mathematical model, we had to rely on intuition, a fact that we consider with a certain amount of unease. We feel that there is a very great need for cooperation between mathematical modellers, social scientists and psychologists. Thus, throughout the paper we indicate areas where we would like to trigger an in-depth interdisciplinary discussion.

The model

The cellular automaton model for pedestrian movement in relation to other microscopic mathematical models

Our mathematical model is a cellular automaton, where virtual persons move on a plane divided into cells and according to a set of rules that capture the principles of movement. Like many successful pedestrian movement models, among them Helbing & Molnar's (1995) social force model, the cellular automaton is inspired by a number of physical principles. These models assume that movement is governed by forces that act between pedestrians, pedestrians and obstacles, and pedestrians and targets. Most cellular automaton models stretch the analogy to electrodynamics, comparing persons to negatively charged particles that are repulsed by each other and attracted by targets.

In the case of social force models the forces are called 'social forces' emphasising that they should not be based on physics but on human interaction. They are, however, very much like the equations of Newtonian mechanics. As far as inspiration is concerned, the two model approaches are very similar in a modelling sense, both using forces to drive motion.

Social force models and other discrete element methods (DEM) rely on differential equations to express the interdependencies between the virtual persons, targets and obstacles (Langston *et al.*, 2006). Space is not discretised at all, which is often seen as the main advantage compared with computationally faster cellular automata. In a very recent work Moussaïd *et al.* (2011) restrict the social force approach to very crowded situations. Otherwise they use heuristic rules to, as they state themselves, clear the way for a more realistic modelling of collective social behaviour. At this point social groups are not included in the heuristic model.

Cellular automata are, compared with differential equations, a relatively novel mathematical modelling technique. Nagel & Schreckenberg (1992) introduced the concept to modelling highway traffic. Subsequently the idea was very successfully carried over to pedestrian traffic (Klüpfel, 2003). The obvious advantages are very fast simulation speed and intuitive rules that make the model easy to understand for researchers even without rigorous mathematical training. Also, while the rule-based update of the states in time may be inspired by physical analogies, it does not, unlike DEM models to a certain extent, employ Newton's laws of motion or any other physical law. In particular, it is convenient to introduce multi-agent modelling aspects through more refined rules to capture better individual or complex behaviour that cannot be matched by aggregated physical laws. For example, the authors have used multi-agent-type rules in a cellular automaton simulator to model temporary separation and reunion of groups that face an obstacle (Seitz *et al.*, 2011). In fact, one may see cellular automata-based pedestrian models as special cases of multi-agent systems (Dijkstra *et al.*, 2001). The main disadvantages of cellular automata are the artefacts introduced by the coarse discretisation of space into cells. Above all, the underlying cell grid only allows straight movement in directions where the grid points are arranged on a straight line. However, many of these disadvantages can be mitigated to an extent that we feel is acceptable in view of the accuracy that can reasonably be expected from any contemporary pedestrian stream model (Hartmann, 2010; Köster *et al.*, 2010). An alternative to physics-inspired models would be to build a true multi-agent model, where goals and sub-goals of agents are translated into actions triggered by sensory input. Multi-agent models can in principle capture very complex behaviour. However, complex decision rules introduce a multitude of decisional parameters that must be adjusted. This makes validation difficult. In addition, a complex agent structure increases computational effort, as soon as multiple agents are present, which may hamper practical application. Hence, our own solution strategy at this point is to introduce carefully selected agent aspects in the cellular automaton.

Methods of model validation

Parallel to the modelling attempts themselves, a lot of effort has gone into finding a way to measure crowd phenomena so that crowd models can be validated. The leading idea is to use the measured relationship between the density in a crowd and the velocity of the crowd or, equivalently, the flow, for validation. The denser the crowd, the more people get in each other's way: they slow down until all flow stops. In a dense crowd this is, to a certain extent, a physical effect. In a looser crowd we imagine socio-cultural aspects such as the need for personal space to have a great influence. Diagrams depicting this density–flow relationship are often called fundamental diagrams. Early examples are given by Predtechenskii & Milinskii (1969) and Weidmann (1992). More recent work provides experimental evidence that fundamental diagrams capture, at least to some degree, socio-cultural behaviour such as the need for personal space. For example, the speed of Indian participants is apparently less dependent on density than the speed of German participants who seem to have a more passive walking strategy allowing for more space between individuals (Chattaraj et al., 2009). By conducting a series of computer simulations inducing different crowd densities one can investigate whether a model reproduces the density–flow relationship at least roughly. In more advanced models it is possible to calibrate the parameters automatically, so that a given fundamental diagram is faithfully reproduced. This holds, in principle, for both social force models (Höcker & Milbradt, 2009) and cellular automata (Davidich & Köster, 2010). Our own model is capable of calibrating automatically and robustly to measured fundamental diagrams. For research purposes, as in this paper, we calibrate to the widely accepted benchmark fundamental diagram provided by Weidmann (1992) and use the distribution of free-flow velocities associated with it.

The cellular automaton model

We divide the area of observation in a lattice of hexagonal cells. Each cell at each time step has a status: empty or occupied by either a person, an obstacle or a target. Persons enter and leave through sources and targets, namely entrances and exits. The cells are updated by rules that together form the automaton. In principle, triangular, rectangular and hexagonal cells are possible (Schadschneider et al., 2008; Kinkeldey & Rose, 2003). Although square cells seem to be the most popular choice, we prefer a hexagonal grid for its two additional natural directions of movement compared with the square grid (Figure 1). The persons move in a single plane or several planes such as floors. Hence we may restrict ourselves to two spatial dimensions. Usually, the cell size is chosen to accommodate an average sized European male. The simulation dynamics themselves follow a specific kind of sequential update scheme: the cells containing persons are updated in the order the persons have entered the scenario from a source.

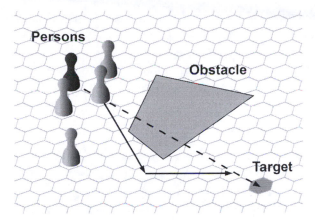

Figure 1. Pedestrians moving on a grid.

The core of the model is contained in the automaton, that is, the set of rules according to which the cell states are updated when the simulation steps forward in time. We borrow the fundamental idea from electrodynamics. In principle, pedestrians are treated as negatively charged particles, say electrons. Therefore pedestrians are attracted by positive charges, such as exits, and repelled by negative charges, such as other pedestrians or obstacles. We would like to emphasise that these repulsive forces can be interpreted as a human's need for personal space. In our model each individual adjusts his or her speed to the speed of the crowd ahead. A field of vision makes the model more realistic. The strength of the need for personal space expressed by the repulsive force and the tendency to reduce speed when nearing a crowd can be calibrated. Mathematically, the forces between pedestrians, targets and obstacles are expressed through a potential field, using the properties of conservative force fields from physics. That is, the forces are expressed as the gradient of a suitable scalar function: the potential. The pedestrians try to minimise the potential during the course of their movement by preferring the empty neighbour cell to which there is the steepest decline of the potential. In this, the model is very similar to many cellular automaton models based on potentials (Burstedde *et al.*, 2001; Hamacher & Tjandra, 2001; Klüpfel, 2003; Rogsch, 2005; Schadschneider *et al.*, 2008; TraffGo, 2010). Finding a smooth and realistic path towards an attracting goal is another challenge. We assume that as long as the path is free, the shortest path is preferred and that obstacles are efficiently skirted. We achieve this by computing the potential with a fast-marching algorithm that mimics the propagation of a wave front from the goal to the pedestrian's position (Hartmann, 2010). The pure electron-based approach clearly has its limitations when modelling human behaviour. The field of vision and the pathfinding strategy are examples of how our model enriches the basic ideas by a number of submodels to compensate for the most relevant shortcomings (Köster *et al.*, 2010). Using the terminology in Schadschneider *et al.* (2008), our model is microscopic, discrete and deterministic with stochastic aspects, rule based but potential driven.

This approach allows us to incorporate directly observable interaction in a very simple way. Once we have achieved an at least intuitive match with governing aspects of crowd motion while keeping the computational cost low, the question of more complete testing and validation remains. We believe that progressive work, such as introducing a group model, should be built on a thoroughly tested basic model. We make sure that when we enlarge the model, we do not lose desired properties by always going through a number of prescribed qualitative and quantitative test scenarios.

In this paper we do not strive to give a complete description of the, very successful, cellular automaton approach based on potential fields. Nor can we cover all of our particular choices of submodels or basic tests.[1] Our goal is to enhance any such model by a vital aspect for useful application suggested by social scientist research: group formation.

Group formation in the cellular automaton model

What is a group? In a first step we need to identify the relevant characteristics that must be captured by the mathematical model to reproduce correctly the geometric cohesion within the groups as well as further typical behaviour of groups. We consider each group as an accumulation of persons who stay together while moving. They move at approximately the same speed towards the same goal. Also, we assume that small groups display certain formations (Qiu & Hu, 2010; Singh et al., 2009). We think that one of the main challenges is to ensure the right type of cohesion: groups, as a whole, must remain very stable, while deformations of groups in time and space must be possible; even losing a group member must be feasible.

In the aggregate pedestrian stream simulator of our previous work, interaction between individuals among each other and with the surrounding world is handled through forces that can be described through potentials. To achieve an efficient implementation that maintains the fast simulation speed, we carry over the concept of potentials to group formation. But we also need to add or alter rules to make individuals recognise the group to which they belong and to treat fellow group members differently from strangers.

A simple group model using forces described by potentials and a basic communication scheme

Behavioural patterns

In this section we describe how we capture flexibility, and at the same time, stability, of group cohesion in one algorithm. We assume that the formation of groups is due to a set of behavioural patterns that must be reproduced by the algorithm. This leads to a list of requirements. With the diversity of group patterns in real life, the requirements are not necessarily fulfilled simultaneously by a real group. Nor is the list complete. However, we think, at least for small groups, that group behaviour may be determined by all the behavioural patterns described in detail below. To achieve these behavioural patterns, our model includes several concepts that we describe in the following sub-sections. Ideally, they are calibrated to measured data.

- All individuals in the group move towards the same goal.
- The members of a group stay together. Permanent separation of a member from the rest of the group may occur but only in extreme situations.
- All individuals in the group move with the same speed, except for temporal variations caused, for example, by avoiding obstacles and collisions with the rest of the crowd. The variations lead to changes in the spatial shape of the group.
- At each moment, there is an individual who gives orientation to the group. All members of the group follow this person at this particular moment. We call the person the group leader. However, this does not imply that the person has a superior social status or special influence in the group. In fact, the leader role, or rather orientation function, within a group is passed along between group individuals according to rules described below.
- The (cooperative) group slows down when a member stays behind.
- Groups have a basic spatial structure that stays relatively unchanged if walking across a free space, but can be deformed by external influences such as the presence of a crowd or obstacles. Moreover, the shape of a group, such as walking abreast, may be deformed, but will re-establish itself when the external force is removed. For example, a couple walks side by side and only shortly switches to a line formation to go through a small opening.
- We focus on small groups where all members wish to talk to each other with ease. We therefore assume that they favour walking abreast.

No repulsive potential among group members

The first and obvious step towards group formation is to switch off the repulsive forces between the members of a group. In addition, each group member is attracted by the potential of a specific group member, the 'leader'. Also, each group member is attracted by the same target, such as an exit, and assigned the same free-flow velocity.[2]

In a crowd of individuals the free-flow velocity is normally distributed, with for example a mean of 1.34 m/s and standard deviation of 0.26 m/s (Weidmann, 1992). It is not obvious how to assign free-flow velocities among groups. In certain situations, for example, the velocity of the slowest may dominate the group speed. In our research work we are interested in regional evacuation (REPKA, 2010). An experiment was conducted within the REPKA research project suggesting that group speed was not dominated by the slowest member (Gerhardt *et al.*, 2011). Instead, we will assume that the free-flow velocity of groups is normally distributed. However, we would very much welcome the suggestions from the social sciences to improve and ground our modelling work.

As in the model for individuals, group members slow down when they are in a dense crowd. The deceleration depends on the density of the surrounding crowd. Since individuals who are close together experience the same crowd density their tendency to walk at the same speed is enforced. All this allows group members to stay together. With a careful choice of the leader potential—with respect to form and parameters—it is even possible to generate certain group formations, such as walking abreast.

The leader and follower concept

The method is based on an asymmetric group, in which one person is temporarily distinguished from all other members of the same group. This distinguished member takes over the leadership of the group in a certain sense and will be referred to as the leader. The basic idea of a leader has been used in several models for social groups within crowd simulation (Moussaïd *et al.* 2010; Singh *et al.*, 2009). In our model the leader is the member most advanced towards the target. When the leader falls behind he or she can no longer serve as a point of orientation and passes the role on to the new leader. The leader has an attractive potential that affects group members but not strangers. Each follower adds the influence of the leader potential to the sum of all the other potentials that govern his or her decision where to make the next step: the attracting potential of the target, repulsive potentials of obstacles and of strange individuals.

We experimented with several ideas on how to assign the orientation function. At first we used a centre of mass instead of a group member, but without a decision-making entity the group could not decide which way to proceed and sometimes got stuck. Choosing a group member as leader solved this problem. We picked the person ahead of the group, because pedestrians usually look in the walking direction and we presume that, when choosing their path, they orientate themselves towards the fellow group members ahead. In other scenarios, for example, when only one person is well informed about the best path, other assignations of the leader role may be better or necessary. Also, a real group may not always have a leader even in the loose sense used here. However, the model yields very natural visual results (Figure 2).

Communication within the group and the group centre of gravity

Group members are also individuals. They obey the usual rules of motion for individuals unless a group rule overwrites a rule for individuals or completes a rule. So far, we

Figure 2. Formation of groups in a computer simulation.

Figure 3. Classroom egress in an experiment.

have not introduced any communication within the group. Left at this stage groups will have a tendency to stay together, but members who had to slow down temporarily, for example to avoid an obstacle or an individual from outside the group, will be lost far too often. Hence we make group members wait for their last fellow. Each group member, including the leader, slows down with growing distance to the last member. This ensures that groups do not gradually drift apart.

In a next step we wish to achieve a certain group formation. The idea is that group members want to talk with each other. Group formations are empirically observed and modelled with fixed attractor points around the leader by Singh *et al.* (2009). Another concept, where a system of differential equations is used to model the communication, was developed by Moussaïd *et al.* (2010). Their model is based on empirical research on group formations and the assumption that people want to communicate within a group. People can talk comfortably only if they do not have to turn their heads backwards or shout to somebody in front. Group members ahead of the group would have to turn their head backwards by a certain angle. They are then told to slow down. Members who trail behind accelerate by a similar mechanism. This means they tend to walk abreast. We wish to adopt these ideas. However, in the cellular automaton, to maintain the automaton's efficiency, one tries to avoid the computationally costly step of solving differential equations. Thus, we look at the behaviour that must be captured and translate it straight into an update rule. In our model, the amount by which they slow down directly depends on the angle. However, the two approaches to express acceleration can be shown to be close in their first-order approximations.

Persons walking abreast and at the same speed are well aligned for communication. Hence they do not adapt their velocity and continue to walk companionably in a way that allows them to talk to each other with maximum ease. Obviously this is a model apt to capture the behaviour of small groups of, say, friends, and not so much large groups or groups with an enforced formation, such as a school class walking in pairs. The authors would like to learn more about which parameters affect the formation of larger groups and how these might split up in subgroups. Also, the authors suspect that the desire to communicate—expressed in the tendency to walk abreast—might be deliberately suppressed by the group members when they face a bottleneck. As a consequence, the communication model can be switched on and off in the computer implementation.

Altogether, in the model presented here, the behaviour of each group member is governed by a balance of mathematically expressed influences:

- Influences that affect each individual: being attracted by a target, being repulsed by obstacles and strangers, and being slowed down by a dense crowd. This leads to a reasonable representation of an aggregated crowd.
- Influences that are caused by being a follower or leader in a group. This entails not being repulsed by fellow group members but being attracted by the leader and, as a consequence, ensures that groups stay together.
- Influences that are caused by an awareness of the other group members. In our model all persons in a group wait for the last member. This part of the model further helps to keep the group together.
- Influences that are caused by communication between group members, that is, by a desire to chat while walking and hence to walk abreast. This means that the group members have to adjust to the rest of the group. The rest of the group is represented by the group's centre of gravity.

Generation of pedestrian groups

In our simulations pedestrians enter a scene coming from a source. At this source the size of a new group about to emerge must be fixed. James (1951) suggests that the members of a group bigger than four are not able to maintain continuous relationships and thus are unstable und divided into subgroups. This might also apply to pedestrian groups. In a later work, James (1953) analyses prior observations of pedestrian group sizes at various places and times. In the data presented 66% of the pedestrians were alone, 34% came in pairs, 7% belonged to a group of three and only 2% belonged to groups of sizes bigger than three. As a concrete distribution of group sizes a zero-truncated Poisson distribution has been suggested (James, 1953; Coleman & James, 1961). The distribution certainly depends on the scenario that is considered. We use a zero-truncated Poisson distribution as default, but the concrete percentage of groups of a particular size can be adjusted according to the scenario.

Visual validation of the simulation

A first step towards validation of a computer model is to compare visually the outcome with expected results. The authors have conducted a series of computer simulations and produced short videos of the resulting pedestrian streams. The snapshot below shows a simulation where groups are generated at one end of a wide corridor (on the left in Figure 2) and walk to the other end of the corridor. Group members show a clear tendency to walk abreast when the path is clear. They temporarily give up that preferred formation when they need to negotiate their path between other groups. This is exactly what the authors want to achieve.

A small experiment: groups matter—but do not necessarily slow down egress

The authors conducted a small experiment with a class of 30 computer science students in their first semester: a very homogenous group of 27 males and three females, all about 20 years old and fit. The objective of the experiment is to provide a test for the validity of our group model. Quantitative tests are difficult to design, because one needs a parameter that can be measured not only in the simulation, but also in reality. We choose the egress time at a bottleneck as experimental parameter, because it is at the same time of vital important for practice. We asked the students to stand at their desks and, at a signal, to leave the classroom. They were not given any instructions on how to communicate—in the hope that they would behave naturally. Outside the classroom, in the hallway, they were asked to turn left and walk across a line between the hallway and the larger entrance hall. The time was measured from the signal to the moment when the last student crossed the line. On the way out there was essentially only one bottleneck: the door.

Then, again at a signal, the students returned from their mostly unchanged positions in the hallway to their assigned seats (without sitting down in order to keep paths relatively free). The time between the signal and the arrival of the last student at his or her place was measured. Here the students encountered three types of bottleneck: the narrowing from hall to hallway, the door, and finally the narrow aisles between the rows of desks in the classroom.

In a second round, the students were paired with their desk neighbours and told to stay together. In a third round triplets were formed. The classroom has rows of desks with eight seats per row, so that some of the triplets were split across rows. The final round was conducted with groups of four. In order to quantify the influence of group size on the egress time, a linear regression was carried out. As expected, there was a positive relationship between group size and egress time, $\beta = 1.16$, $(t(5) = 2.52, p = 0.05)$ (Figures 4 and 5).[3] The same model is analysed for the ingress scenario. This time the relation was significant but negative, $\beta = -1.59$ $(t(4) = -3.63, p = 0.02)$.[4]

In both cases we see an impact of groups. The egress result seems intuitively clear from comparison with physical effects: The coarser the grain the more difficult it is to feed it through a funnel. Larger groups correspond to a coarser grain in that picture. With increasing group size, it becomes more difficult to stay together at the door and the overall evacuation time increases. This explanation also agrees well with the personal experience of the authors and, maybe, of some of the readers.

The ingress case is more complicated. Why are the students faster when they form groups? This is not what we expected when we set up the experiment. Let us therefore

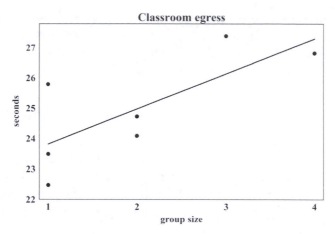

Figure 4. Experiment: dependency of classroom egress time on group size.

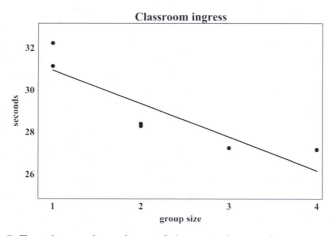

Figure 5. Experiment: dependency of classroom ingress time on group size.

have a closer look at the situation. We believe that the reason for the discrepancy lies in the fact that the students must navigate their way back to their seats. As soon as the students form groups as prescribed in the experiment's choreography, they are already positioned and ordered in the hallway according to the location of their seats in the classroom. This greatly facilitates navigation in the crowd. They no longer impede each other. The organisation is optimal with groups of four, the maximum group size in the experiment.

By these results we are encouraged in our hypothesis, that the occurrence of groups aggravates congestion at isolated bottlenecks and that the impact increases with average group size. But we also learn that against our first intuition groups are not necessarily worse in an evacuation scenario. On the contrary, groups might help. Yang *et al.* (2005) simulated evacuation processes with a different model of inter-action. They also found that cooperative interactions of persons among a crowd can result in faster evacuation. Qiu & Hu (2010) simulated crowds with an agent-based model and obtained results that show an increase of flow along with increasing group size in certain situations. Although the mentioned authors present no empirical data to confirm their findings, it shows that these interactions can have a positive impact on the macroscopic outcome of a simulation. We would like to discuss this with fellow scientists from the social sciences, especially since mathematical modellers need not only a collection and classification of possible scenarios, but also must reduce the variety of scenarios to a number that can be handled by computer models.

Simulations experiments and validation against measurements

Pedestrians walking along a corridor

In this simulation a crowd moves along corridors with varying width. The number of persons entering the corridor per time unit is always the same. Thus, the smaller the corridor, the denser the crowd. For each corridor width, the parameter *average group size* is gradually increased from 1, corresponding to an aggregate crowd of individuals, to 4. The simulations results are shown in Figures 6 and 7. We see a strong decrease of the mean velocity with the mean group size. It is evident even in the quasi-free-flow case, suggesting that groups may impede each other, even in the absence of restricting walls, as long as they wish to walk along the same (shortest) path. This is certainly the case in this simulation. The mean crowd density in the corridor (Figure 7) increases with the group size although the same numbers of persons are inserted in the corridor. This is another way to look at the same effect: Groups impair each other's progress, which results in slower progress, and hence congestion. The results of the simulation correspond to our intuition and thus complement the qualitative visual validation of group formation in Figure 2.

Reconstruction of the experiment in a simulation

For every experiment in this section, we ran 1000 simulations where the free-flow velocity is randomly assigned to the groups using a normal distribution as described in the model section.

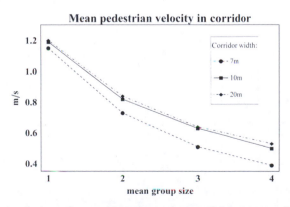

Figure 6. Computer simulation of a corridor: dependency of the mean walking velocity on mean group size.

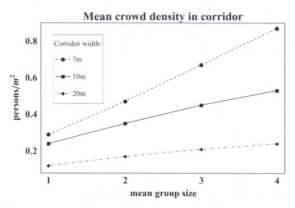

Figure 7. Computer simulation of a corridor: dependency of crowd density on mean group size.

Computer simulation of egress—communication model without calibration. First we present a simulation without attempting quantitatively to match the results. We want to see whether the egress time increases with the group size. For this we generate individuals, pairs and groups of sizes three and four behind the desks, as in the experiment (Figure 8). The egress simulation qualitatively matches the experiment: the bigger the group size, the slower the egress. For individuals the simulated egress time is actually already close to the experiment, indicating that the order of magnitude of the simulation results for individuals is already quite good. This is not surprising since the model has been carefully calibrated for the case of individuals (Davidich & Köster, 2010).

However, the impact of groups is largely overestimated (Figure 9, dashed line). Why is that? We had a closer look at the videos: the students do not appear to talk to each other much while they are queuing—one behind the other—for the door. Since the class is usually a rather lively one, we suspect that the students deliberately suppress their natural penchant for chatting to get through the bottleneck better. The virtual students in the simulation, on the other hand, try to walk abreast (Figure 8). We conclude that our uncalibrated model overemphasises communication.

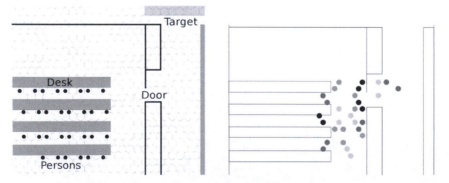

Figures 8. (left) Geometry of the computer simulation; and (right) snapshot of the computer simulation without calibration.

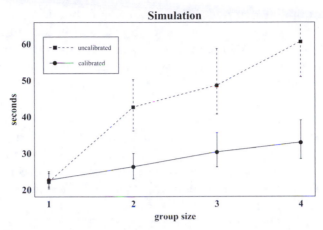

Figure 9. Computer simulation of classroom egress with an uncalibrated (dashed line) and a calibrated (solid line) communication model.

Computer simulation of egress—communication model with calibration. In our uncalibrated model the spatial formation of the group is mainly enforced by group members slowing down to wait and less by group members accelerating to catch up. Hence, in our final simulation we adjust these model parameters with the goal still to make the groups stay together but with a weaker tendency to walk abreast at bottlenecks. For this, we make our virtual leaders wait less and our virtual followers catch up faster. In the visualisations of the simulations we finally observe the desired behaviour: the virtual students stay together—with a tendency to walk one behind the other through the bottleneck and to walk abreast once they reach the hallway. The quantitative results also mirror the experiments.

This is exactly what we hoped for. However, in view of the size of the sample in the experiment one should not over-interpret the results. In particular, one should not fine-tune the simulation parameters against the measurements. Nonetheless the very good reproduction of the experiment strongly encourages us in our belief that our computer model indeed captures the governing characteristics of group behaviour in small groups. To a certain extent it does it even quantitatively. We also conclude that the strength of the desire for intensive communication (chatting) may be the crucial calibration parameter when investigating bottleneck scenarios.

This poses a true challenge to the mathematical modeller and software architect because in a real scenario different types of bottlenecks are common so that it may not be possible to adjust the parameter once and for all. But what is the worth of a calibration that can be used for one scenario only? Obviously, to make the task manageable the number of scenarios must be limited and a common denominator must be found. Insight from the social sciences would be an immense help.

Conclusion

In this article we presented a mathematical model of group formation in a moving crowd based on a cellular automaton. The model incorporates a mechanism that is based on the assumption that pedestrians wish to communicate while walking and therefore prefer walking abreast when the path is free. We demonstrated how far it reproduces reality by validating the model against intuition as well as measurements. We conducted an experiment for classroom egress and compared it with simulation results where we varied the desire for communication. Close inspection of the egress video footage from the experiment showed that the students did not talk much during the egress but tended to walk one behind the other through the classroom door. We concluded that people who navigate a bottleneck as a group temporarily suppress their wish to communicate. We calibrated our model parameters so that the behaviour at the door was reproduced without losing the correct group formation in the free flow. The resulting simulations matched the experiment not only qualitatively, but also quantitatively.

The future challenge lies in better quantifying this effect. When, to which degree and for how long do people give up their desire to communicate in favour of easier navigation? And how do we incorporate the dependency on the 'when', 'where', 'how much' and 'how long' efficiently into a computer model? We will continue our work in this area—and will seek assistance from the social sciences in this endeavour.

This brings us to our second goal: we did not present our work for the sake of the model and simulation results only. We also used it to demonstrate the process of mathematical modelling of crowds to our colleagues from sociology and psychology. One of the major difficulties we faced is that we can only incorporate a very limited number of influences while maintaining computational efficiency. Hence it is crucial to select the governing influences correctly. However, so far this selection has often been based on the intuition of the mathematical modeller, not on accepted sociological or psychological facts. Thus, we also tried to point out where our mathematical formulations lack a scientific foundation from the partner sciences.

Our hope is to trigger more interdisciplinary cooperation in the field of crowd modelling. We believe that the work has just begun. At the same time, the results enjoy considerable public attention making it perhaps even more attractive to join efforts across the usual scientific boundaries.

Acknowledgement

This work was partially funded by the German Federal Ministry of Education and Research through the priority programme Schutz und Rettung von Menschen within the project REPKA—Regional Evacuation: Planning, Control and Adaptation.

Notes

1. For a more detailed description, see Davidich & Köster (2010), Hartmann (2010), Köster *et al.* (2010) and Kneidl *et al.* (2010).
2. Free-flow velocity is the technical term used to describe the speed at which a person likes to walk when their path is free. It is the desired speed of an individual.
3. There is a small-order effect. We introduce *round number* as an additional explanatory variable in the regression model, $\beta_2 = 0.19$, $t(4) = 3.18$, $p = 0.03$.

4. Again the order effect is small. With *round number* as an additional explanatory variable, $\beta_2 = 0.27$, $t(3) = -7.42$, $p = 0.005$.

References

Aguirre, B. E., Wenger, D. & Vigo, G. (1998) A test of the emergent norm theory of collective behaviour, *Sociological Forum*, 13(2), 301–320.

Aveni, A. F. (1977) The not-so-lonely crowd: friendship groups in collective behavior, *Sociometry*, 40(1), 96–99.

Bogusch, S., Spellerberg, A., Topp, H. & West, C. (Eds) (2009) *Organisation und Folgewirkung von Großveranstaltungen—Interdisziplinäre Studien zur FIFA Fussball-WM 2006* (Wiesbaden, VS Verlag für Sozialwissenschaften).

Burstedde, C., Klauck, K., Schadschneider, A. & Zittartz, J. (2001) Simulation of pedestrian dynamics using a two-dimensional cellular automaton, *Physica A*, 295, 507–525.

Chattaraj, U., Seyfried, A. & Chakroborty, P. (2009) Comparison of pedestrian fundamental diagram across cultures, *Advances in Complex Systems*, 393–405.

Coleman, J. S. & James, J. (1961) The equilibrium size distribution of freely-forming groups, *Sociometry*, 24(1), 36–45.

Davidich, M. & Köster, G. (2010) Towards automatic and robust adjustment of human behavioral parameters in a pedestrian stream model to measured data, in: Proceedings of the 5th International Conference on Pedestrian and Evacuation Dynamics, Gaithersburg, MD, USA, 8–10 March, 2010.

Dijkstra, J., Jessurun, J. & Timmermans, H. (2001) A multi-agent cellular automata model of pedestrian movement, in: M. Schreckenberg & S. D. Sharma (Eds) *Pedestrian and evacuation dynamics* (Berlin, Springer), 173–181.

Drury, J. & Cocking, C. (2007) *The mass psychology of disasters and emergency evacuations: a research report and implications for practice* (Brighton, Department of Psychology, University of Sussex).

Drury, J., Cocking, C. & Reicher, S. (2009) Everyone for themselves? A comparative study of crowd solidarity among emergency survivors, *British Journal of Social Psychology*, 48, 487–506.

Gerhardt, K., Köster, K., Seitz, M., Treml, F. & Klein, W. (2011) On free-flow velocities for groups, in: Proceedings of the International Conference on Emergency Evacuation of People from Buildings, Warsaw, Poland, 31 March–1 April 2011.

Hamacher, H. W. & Tjandra, S. A. (2001) *Mathematical modelling of evacuation problems: a state of art*. Report No. 24 (Kaiserslautern, Fraunhofer-Institut für Techno- und Wirtschaftsmathematik (ITWM)).

Hartmann, D. (2010) Adaptive pedestrian dynamics based on geodesics, *New Journal of Physics*, 12(4), available online at: http://www.njp.org/ (doi:10.1088/1367-2630/12/4/043032).

Helbing, D. & Molnar, P. (1995) Social force model for pedestrian dynamics, *Physical Review E*, 51(5), 4282–4286.

Höcker, M. & Milbradt, P. (2009) Genetic algorithms as a means of adjusting pedestrian dynamics models, in: Proceedings of the 1st International Conference on Soft Computing Technology in Civil, Structural and Environmental Engineering, Funchal, Madeira, Spain, 2009.

James, J. (1951) A preliminary study of the size determinant in small group interaction, *American Sociological Review*, 16(4), 474–477.

James, J. (1953) The distribution of free-forming small group size, *American Sociological Review*, 18(5), 569–570.

Kinkeldey, C. & Rose, M. (2003) Fußgängersimulation auf der Basis sechseckiger zellularer Automaten, in: K. Kaapke & A. Wulf (Eds) *Forum Bauinformatik 2003—Junge Wissenschaftler forschen* (Aachen, Shaker).

Klüpfel, H. L. (2003) *A cellular automaton model for crowd movement and egress simulation.* Dissertation, Universität Duisburg-Essen.

Kneidl, A., Thiemann, M., Borrmann, A., Ruzika, S., Hamacher, H. W., Köster, G. & Rank, E. (2010) Bidirectional coupling of macroscopic and microscopic approaches for pedestrian behaviour prediction, in: Proceedings of the 5th International Conference on Pedestrian and Evacuation Dynamics, Gaithersburg, MD, USA, 8–10 March 2010.

Köster, G., Hartmann, D. & Klein, W. (2010) Microscopic pedestrian simulations: From passenger exchange times to regional evacuation, Proceedings of the International Conference on Operations Research: Mastering Complexity, Munich, Germany, 1–3 September 2010.

Langston, P. A., Masling, R. & Asmar, B. N. (2006) Crowd dynamics discrete element multi-circle model, *Safety Science*, 44(5), 395–417.

Moussaïd, M., Helbing, D. & Theraulaz, G. (2011) How simple rules determine pedestrian behaviour and crowd disasters, *Proceedings of the National Academy of Sciences, USA*, 108(17), 6884–6888.

Moussaïd, M., Perozo, N., Garnier, S., Helbing, D. & Theraulaz, G. (2010) The walking behaviour of pedestrian social groups and its impact on crowd dynamics, *PloS ONE*, 5(4).

Nagel, K. & Schreckenberg, M. (1992) A cellular automaton model for freeway traffic, *Journal de Physique I*, 2(12), 2221–2229.

Novelli, D., Drury, J. & Reicher, S. (2010) Come together: two studies concerning the impact of group relations on personal space, *British Journal of Social Psychology*, 49(2), 223–236.

Predtechenskii, V. M. & Milinskii, A. I. (1969) Planning for foot traffic flow in buildings (Moscow, Stroizdat; repr. National Bureau of Standards/Amerind, 1978).

Qiu, F. & Hu, X. (2010) Modeling group structures in pedestrian crowd simulation, *Simulation Modelling Practice and Theory*, 18, 190–205.

REPKA (2010) *Regionale Evakuierung: Planung, Kontrolle und Anpassung.* Available online at: http://www.repka-evakuierung.de/.

Rogsch, C. (2005) *Vergleichende Untersuchungen zur dynamischen Simulation von Personenströmen.* Report No. 4185 (Jülich, Forschungszentrum Jülich).

Schadschneider, A., Klingsch, W., Klüpfel, H., Kretz, T., Rogsch, C. & Seyfried, A. (2008) Evacuation dynamics: empirical results, modeling and applications, arXiv:0802.1620.

Seitz, M., Köster, G. & Hartmann, D. (2011) On modeling the separation and reunion of social groups, in: Proceedings of the International Conference on Emergency Evacuation of People from Buildings, Warsaw, Poland, 31 March–1 April 2011.

Sime, J. D. (1983) Affiliative behaviour during escape to building exits, *Journal of Environmental Psychology*, 3(1), 21–41.

Singh, H., Arter, R., Dodd, L., Langston, P., Lester, E. & Drury, J. (2009) Modelling subgroup behaviour in crowd dynamics DEM simulation, *Applied Mathematical Modelling*, 33, 4408–4423.

Spellerberg, A., Reuter, V. & Würbach, A. (2010) *Meilensteinbericht über soziologische Aspekte des REPKA Forschungsprojekts zu regionaler Evakuierung* [Milestone report on sociological aspects in the REPKA research project] (Nürnberg).

TraffGo (2010) *Handbuch*, Available online at: http://www.traffgo-ht.com/de/pedestrians/downloads/index.html/.

Weidmann, U. (1992) *Transporttechnik für Fussgänger*, Schriftenreihe des IVT, 90.

Yang, L. Z., Zhao, D. L., Li, J. & Fang, T. Y. (2005) Simulation of the kin behavior in building occupant evacuation based on cellular automaton, *Building and Environment*, 40, 411–415.

Contributions of social science to agent-based models of building evacuation

B. E. Aguirre[a,b], Sherif El-Tawil[c], Eric Best[b],
Kimberly B. Gill[a,b] and Vladimir Fedorov[d]

[a]Department of Sociology and Criminal Justice; [b]Core Faculty, Disaster Research Center, University of Delaware, Newark, DE, USA; [c]Department of Civil and Environmental Engineering, University of Michigan, Ann Arbor, MI, USA; [d]Stanford University, Stanford, CA, USA

This paper describes the general characteristics of the agent-based models (ABM) approach to the simulation of building evacuations, and offers details of some popular computer codes for building evacuation. Contemporary ABM computer programming emphasising the characteristics of individuals and their propensities to act should be supplemented with codes informed by group-level dimensions such as norms, values, commitments to lines of action, leadership, and a sense of identification and membership in meaningful groups. The paper discusses social science considerations that need to be borne in mind when developing an ABM simulation of building evacuation in a disaster. It includes information on an ABM simulation of a disastrous incident: the fire in a US nightclub in Rhode Island in 2003. The model incorporates aspects of the physical environment in which the evacuation took place, the nature and spread of the fire and the smoke, information on individual and groups in the fire, and the impact of the density of human collectivities on the ability of individual and groups to evacuate. It concludes with seven suggestions for computer programmers developing ABM of human behaviour in building evacuation.

Introduction

Improvements in contemporary computerised simulations of evacuations in buildings on fire require incorporating detailed social scientific research findings that identify social mechanisms explaining the behaviour of people during building evacuations. It is in the hope of trying to draw attention to this methodology among social scientists

151

as well as to improve its use that this paper presents a parallel yet opposite development, offering suggestions from social science into computer simulation modelling. Computer modellers are extremely influential in the design of public space and emergency planning, and it is an opportune time for this applied field to be more informed by current thinking in psychology and sociology.

Agent-based models (ABM)

Agent-based modelling is a computational simulation methodology used to build an artificial society. The simulation is populated with computer-driven agents that have their own characteristics, are different from others, and are adaptive and capable of interacting with each other and with their environment. The interactions of interdependent agents generate complex systems, usually understood as emergence, that otherwise could not be obtained through the addition of the parts. ABM represents a real-world social system as a collection of dynamically interacting rule-based entities called agents (Epstein & Axtell, 1996). Each agent learns behavioural options that evolve during the simulation. The agents are heterogeneous and adaptive. Instead of determining the optimal course of action based on complete information of all alternatives, adaptive agents rely on heuristics or rules of thumb that are learned over time through experience. The main advantages of ABM are that it is flexible and captures emergent phenomena, providing a natural and real-world description of the system. ABM provides information relevant to the conduct of experiments for which real-world data collection would be unethical, impractical or prohibitively expensive (Macal & North, 2010). It is also a natural framework for examining the determinants of collective behaviour in evacuations in building fires.

Developing ABM for building evacuation

Kuligowski & Peacock (2005) trace the development of computational models for building evacuation simulations. Of the 30 models discussed, only ten were termed 'behavioural' models. Of these ten models, only a few were in the public domain at the time of publication. The following discussion provides a brief description of what we deem to be the most technically sophisticated ABM evacuation codes publicly available for which there are enough details to allow other code writers to build their own models. The list encompasses only one of the codes discussed by Kuligowski & Peacock (2005) and is augmented by three of the most recently published codes.

MASSEgress is an ABM developed by Pan (2006) and Pan *et al.* (2006) for modelling emergency evacuation. Each agent in a MASSEgress simulation observes the surrounding environment and makes independent decisions based on these observations. Incorporating the human cognitive process into the individual behaviour model in this intuitive manner allows the program to simulate real-life phenomena such as bidirectional flow. Agents employ instinct rules, past experiences, social rules and rational inference to choose a behaviour type (Pan *et al.*, 2006). This complexity allows agents to choose independently an escape route at the micro level. It results in complex behaviour like cooperative queuing and competitive herding near exits. A limitation of MASSEgress is its reliance on visual sensory input for controlling agent response, as well as its inability to model extreme crowding when agent responses occur in high-density situations, such as when throngs of people are attempting to escape. In addition, while it does account for some limited group effects, such as negotiation within a group to determine priority at an exit point, MASSEgress does not explicitly account for group effects that reflect the social ties among agents.

Two other programs that have similarities to MASSEgress are AutoEscape developed at Tsinghua University, China (Tang & Ren, 2008), and AIEva, also developed in China (Shi *et al.*, 2009). Key limitations of these two programs are that they can not model the effects of extreme crowding or take into account group effects. The last model we wish to mention is buildingEXODUS (Gwynne *et al.*, 2000, 2006), which is one of the most successful commercially available evacuation simulation models. As with the other codes, buildingEXODUS does not take into account the effects on evacuation of extreme crowd densities, and its treatment of group effects is limited, such as agents being able to form groups based on pre-existing or new social ties, communicate and socially adapt to the information they learn (Gwynne *et al.*, 2006).

Despite the potential value of ABM simulation methodology for improving building safety—and more generally for developing of knowledge in the sciences—there has been a general lack of validation of ABM models of building evacuations as well as a tendency to adopt irrational, panic explanations of human behaviour.

Lack of validation

Sime (1995) pointed out almost two decades ago, when writing about computer modelling and simulation of fire evacuation, what is still true today (see the acknowledgment by Shi *et al.*, 2009, pp. 346–347; Galea, 2004): human cognition, decision-making and behaviour have not been fully integrated into ABM. This lack of validation has allowed the results of simulations to stray from the social world they are intended to help explain. The decision rules used to guide the action of avatars in ABM simulations are usually not grounded in validated assumptions about the social behaviour of people and their collectivities, their decision to evacuate, and their evacuation behaviours in buildings on fire.

One of the most commonly used validation strategies is to compare the response of a code with previous codes that have been 'validated' against experimental data (Olsson & Regan, 2001). A pervasive approach is to study the effect of exit width on the flow rate of a crowd. An experiment of this type was conducted to assess the validity of the Simulex model (Thompson & Marchant, 1995). Because the flow rates predicted by Simulex closely matched the prescribed flow rates of a UK building code, the creators of Simulex concluded that their model had the propensity to produce realistic results. Another example of this practice is the validation of AutoEscape by Tang & Ren (2008); they used buildingEXODUS (Gwynne *et al.*, 2000) validation data. These 'chain' approaches to validation have limited value since the collectivity flows in the original tests may not be representative of a real response during actual emergencies, compromising the validity of subsequent studies. Since the validation is usually based on one or two global characteristics, e.g. egress time or flow rate, favourable comparisons between new ABM and existing 'validated' codes are not irrefutable proof of the accuracy of the new codes.

Limited understanding of social and cultural emergence

The promise of ABM is its ability to allow for emergent organisation that results from the interaction of agents (Gilbert, 2008). In real social life, however, emergence is never disassociated from the socio-cultural milieu or the context in which it occurs. This is the principle of continuity advocated by E. L. Quarantelli years ago (Quarantelli, 1996). It is not possible to understand the emerging social organisation in the aftermath of disasters without recognising that to a varying extent it is determined by what existed before the incident. Nor is it possible to understand the future, the period of reconstruction and recovery from whatever crisis is at hand, without understanding what happened during the crisis. It is necessary to abandon the common practice of assuming a tabula rasa, or the idea that computer programmers can create cyber agents without worrying about the past of the cyber agent such as familiarity with the building in which the evacuation takes place, experience with other fire evacuations and other similar crises, leadership capacity, and level of intimacy with others in their groups when the fire occurs; more broadly, without considering the impact of socialisation on the person who is being simulated and the history of the collectivity that in important ways shape the individual and collective behaviour that is being simulated. The simulation must be true to the reality it wishes to examine.

The practice of giving cybernetic agents a limited set of specific propensities to act on the basis of individual characteristics assigned to them, and then allow them to interact presumably to develop emergent social organisational patterns representing aspects of the social world, is not realistic since social actors do not simply act; rather their acts are enmeshed in lines of actions that connect their past, present, and future and shape their social identities.

Group-level processes in collective behaviour during building evacuations have a number of significant effects that are insufficiently recognised at present, to wit:

- A significant number of ABM models of evacuations in buildings on fire conceptualise the cyber actor as an unattached individual. Despite the popularity of such an approach, it contradicts what is known about social behaviours in these situations, and cannot be valid if the object is to create facsimile models of social life. The sole actor is rare in collective behaviour incidents, for groups are the fundamental unit inside these precipitated gatherings of people (Aguirre, 2006). Emergent social organisation that is created by the interaction of the individual cybernetic actors during the simulation is to a large extent a product of group interaction and inter-group dynamics. These are key omissions in many present-day computational models.

Quarantelli's (1981; also Quarantelli, 2008) exhaustive summary of the extensive literature on social and cultural emergence in disasters, and his typology of complex organisational emergence co-authored with R.R. Dynes (Dynes, 1970; Dynes & Quarantelli, 1968), show that people do not usually act alone when faced with great dangers. New groups that did not exist prior to the crisis come into being to respond to the demands created by the disaster; existing organisations and groups adapt in different ways to the emergency, either keeping their structures while adopting new patterns of social action or changing their structures and carrying out new tasks, or both. Relevant group-level variables include: the size of the group; whether group members are physically near each other when the danger materialises; members' knowledge of the environment through which they must evacuate; possible physical liabilities of members that make it difficult for the group to evacuate quickly; the presence of trusted leaders in the group; and the types of social ties among group members, such as family members, dating partners, business associates, work groups and groups newly formed in the context of the evacuation.

The prevailing understanding of emergence is a form of individualist emergentism (Sawyer, 2001, p. 560), or the emergence of new, complex, large-scale socio-cultural organisation resulting from the interaction of cybernetic agents with no central authority helping organise the avatars. An alternative assumption would also consider other types of emergence involving not only individuals but also groups and complex organisations. Emergence would vary in the extent to which: (1) specific entities organise the operation of coordination and leadership; (2) the degree and scope of the process of newness in the emergence, from completely new ways of collective behaviour of a collectivity, to the continuation of existing customs and forms of social organisation; and (3) the extent to which social or cultural aspects of the emergence predominate (Weller & Quarantelli, 1973). It is unsurprising that some current ABM simulation models such as the ones previously reviewed, which treat evacuation from buildings on fire as the result of the interaction of cyber agents without a 'past', show agents following other agents and developing types of collective behaviour referred to as panic. These results are the logical outcomes of the use of inappropriate social psychological assumptions and a lack of familiarity with group behaviour during evacuation.

- Often current models create cyber agents using variables tapping personality structure, emotions, attitudes, perceptions, identifications, and psychological stress and anxiety. The emphasis is on the aggregated patterns that emerge from the interactions of individual agents. However, such assumptions are based on an under-theorised sociological understanding of interaction, which very often reverts to the use of ad-hoc concepts such as hysteria, panic, herd, mob, crowd and cascade (for criticisms of these practices, see Aguirre & Quarantelli, 1983; McPhail, 1991). Mechanisms of contagion and convergence are often combined with irrationality to explain collective behaviour. The alternative view, assuming the presence of maximising individuals (Simon, 1957) and the importance of group-level dimensions such as norms, values, the intimacy of human relations, commitments to lines of action, leadership, and a sense of identification and membership in meaningful groups is seldom incorporated into existing models.

- Paired with the absence of groups in evacuation is the frequent assumption that cyber emergence can be created through the use of simple rules. Examples abound such as the celebrated simulations of urban racial segregation and the flight of flocks of geese (Shelling, 1978, ch. 4). The principle is valid if it includes mechanisms that explain the evacuation behaviour, for a goal of science is to maximise simplicity in explanations of systems. Still, models of reality such as those created through the use of simple rules often do not include plausible explanations of social practices. The principle of simple rules is useful if the object is to control and monitor a mechanical or electronic process, say an inventory of parts, or if the intent is one of prediction, in which through trial and error a formula or algorithm is found that predicts outcomes in social life, for example identifying the correlates that maximised the risk of cancer before the causal mechanism associated with tobacco was known. The creation of facsimile models of cultural and social organisation through simple rules is much more complex when the goal is developing explanations of actual social mechanisms, for the correspondence between the cyber representation and the dynamics of social life is anything but straightforward.

- Evacuation from a building fire is a form of collective behaviour. It is an example of an unexpected and extreme case of a coordination and cooperation for mutual advantage involving throngs of people (Hardin, 2003, p. 47). They coordinate their behaviour and cooperate with each other to get the task of evacuating the building done in as timely and safe a fashion as they can, for the benefit of everyone involved. As emergent norm theory posits (Turner & Killian, 1987), their pre-existing social organisation is challenged by the threatening hazard, and they interact to develop new, shared understandings of the situation that will allow them to respond to it. It can be hypothesised that what makes this possible are the very often taken-for-granted assumptions of everyday life: the established habits of coordinating and working together with others to solve shared problems, which suddenly become a real asset for responding to the crisis; their sense of community and responsibility for the welfare of others provides justification for their actions; their trust of members of their groups, and their friendships or acquaintances with others nearby outside their groups create commitment to lines of action; as well as the knowledge about what to do at times of danger acquired from participating in fire alarm exercises, or during previous real-life incidents. These become activated during crises, in which a sizeable per cent of social behaviour is guided by personal habit and group custom rather than consciously decided and pre-planned social action. Very often the new set of norms surprises the survivors of the fire, who report on the calm and order of the evacuation and the mutual assistance of people evacuating with them (e.g., Rauner, 2007; cf. Fahy & Proulx, 2008). It also shows that emotion does not always precede collective behaviour nor is a precondition for it (Turner & Killian, 1987). The coordination that we often observe in evacuations, in which people use their past, as it were, to orient their collective action to respond to the crisis they face, solves the current difficulties in writing computer code about how to move the avatar from a normal to a crisis mode.

- Many modellers adopt a panic perspective on people's behaviour during fire instead of a social and affiliate group-level perspective more in keeping with present day social science understanding of collective behaviour (Aguirre, 2006; Drury *et al.*, 2009). The panic-based view was replaced in the 1980s and 1990s by, among others, the research of Norris Johnson (1988), William Feinberg (Feinberg and Johnson, 2001; Keating, 1982; for a review of the panic perspective, see Quarantelli, 1999). They pointed out that in crises and major emergencies people did not panic and did not abandon their ties to others. Instead, they continued to be social actors embedded in social organisations and deeply concerned for the fate of others. They often imperilled their own lives on behalf of others (cf. Helbing *et al.*, 2000, 2007; for an excellent review of theories of panic, see Chertkoff & Kushigian, 1999). Social and fire science has documented that panic is a rare occurrence (e.g. Chertkoff & Kushigian, 1999; Keating, 1982; Pauls, 1978). Tubbs & Meacham (2007, pp. 229–252) summarise this consensus, which presumes the presence of socialised individuals responding to crisis rationally but not ideally in many cases, bounded by their culture, social relations, and the limitations imposed on them by the man-made environment in which they find themselves, the nature of the hazard they confront, and the ineffective communication and understandings that often frustrate their goals.

Rather than accepting the view that all members of a collectivity panic, it would be more useful to think of a collectivity's response to hazards such as a building fire as having a space and time context and different levels of lethality distributed in these dimensions. In most of this affected space what is observed during situations of imminent danger is socially appropriate, norm-guided behaviour, in which people help each other out sometimes at great risk to themselves. However, there may be moments in particular subspaces when the imminent danger to life is so severe that some, but not all, people in these coordinates act as individual agents (Aguirre *et al.*, 2011). Even then, their individual-centred behaviour is social, for many of them continue to be tied to their significant others if only in their imagination (Torres, 2010). Such patterns of actions are part of a normal range of socially appropriate behaviour patterns.

In contrast to panic explanations of collective behaviour in crises, normative, affiliation and social identity approaches to building evacuations assume that antisocial and selfish behaviours among members of evacuating gatherings are rare and tend to be isolated incidents, and evacuations are generally orderly. Furthermore, among members of evacuating gatherings helping behaviour and cooperation are common; pre-existing social affiliations have an important effect on the collective behaviour of people. Participants with meaningful social relations at the site of the incident tend to stay together, often increasing the dangers they face (Drury *et al.*, 2009). The view of heterogeneous actors acting rationally and normatively has a number of important implications for the modelling of the direction of movement during emergency evacuation; movement cannot be assumed to be unidirectional, since it is rational and normative, and the product of symbolic interaction. It is multidirectional, with some people returning to the place they evacuated to help others, try to rescue friends and salvage important belongings (Johnson, 1987; Johnson *et al.*, 1994).

The next section describes the ongoing effort made by the authors to take some of these ideas into consideration in the design of an ABM evacuation simulation of The Station nightclub fire.

Validating an ABM of building evacuation

This final section presents an example of an ongoing effort to develop a validation of an ABM using detailed information collected from the crisis evacuation at The Station nightclub during the fire in 2003.

This simulation was made easier by the availability of information on the 465 persons who were at The Station nightclub at the time of the fire collected by the Rhode Island Police Department, the Rhode Island Office of the Attorney General, and *The Providence Journal* (for details of this fire and a timeline, see Tubbs & Meacham, 2007, pp. 83–86). Aguirre *et al.* (2011) analysed it, using regression analysis to test hypotheses about the effects of group-level predictors of the counts of dead and injured in the 179 groups at the nightclub. The results indicated that group-level factors such as the distance of group members from each other at the start of the fire, the number of intimate relations among them, the extent to which they had visited the nightclub prior to the incident, and the average length of the evacuation route they used predicted counts of injured and dead. The research also looked at what behavioural differences existed between survivors and those who perished, ascertained the existence of role extension mostly among male employees of the nightclub, and provided marginal support for the affirmation that dangerous contexts at times negated the protective influence of intimate relations in groups. Figure 1 shows the number of people who evacuated the building through each of the doors and windows in the building and the death rates of the locations in the building expressed as the number of dead found in a given location divided by the total population inside The Station nightclub at the start of the fire.

This information about what people did to escape the fire, and the results of the previous social science study in which some key processes related to the evacuation were unearthed, made it easier to validate the simulation we are developing. Such information helped us make choices in the writing of computer code when multiple options existed. The wealth of background material, however, makes it necessary to clarify our approach, for it is possible to develop a code that is over-specified, so that the avatars do not have the freedom of interaction necessary for the emergence of social organisation, or show attributes that could only be known after the experiments. The ABM we are developing is specific to the evacuation during the fire at The Station nightclub, a one-story building with a relatively open-floor plan that made it easy for patrons to have visual access of the interior space, particularly of

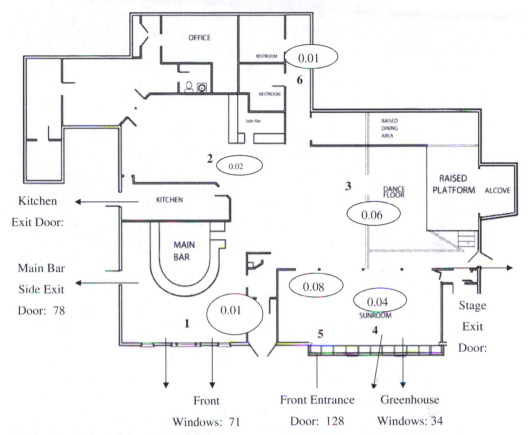

Figure 1. Number of evacuees using exits, and death rates by location: 1, Horseshoe Bar; 2, Back Bar; 3, soundboard/dance floor; 4, greenhouse/pool tables; 5, ticket booth; and 6, bathrooms/hallway. Source of floor plan: see http://www.nist.gov/public_affairs/factsheet/mar_3_rfindings.htm/

the dance area, bandstand and bar areas. To summarise, the most important limitations of this phase of the ABM are that, first, the people in The Station, and the avatars constructed to represent them, had a near unobstructed view of the developing hazard; awareness of the hazard was almost instantaneous (Aguirre et al., 2011). Second, the evacuation occurred in a one-story building. It did not involve the use of stairways, a very challenging setting for building evacuation (Pauls, 2006). Finally, the characteristics of the building, and the spread of the fire and smoke did not change from experiment to experiment.

Our strategy was to develop an ABM using the information we had on The Station nightclub to validate it. The intent was to obtain results that approximated the historical patterns observed in The Station nightclub fire. These patterns are the number of people who died (100), and the number of people who used each of the doors and windows to exit the building (Figure 1). Once these results were obtained, we intended to retest the code in another fire-related evacuation occurring in a different building environment to increase the generalisability of the model. It can be anticipated that some aspects of the code will have to be rewritten to approximate what actually happens in this new environment. The end result will be a generalised and validated package of social behaviour elements that can be added to a variety of modelling scenarios.

So far, the model has five dimensions tapping aspects of the physical environment, hazards, individual and group behavioural configurations, and the effects of high human density (Grosshandler et al., 2005).

For the physical environment, the first part of the model has three main areas: structure, hazards and agents used to represent people. The structure is by far the simplest category to discuss. The physical environment of the nightclub is a passive element in the model. The study attempts to replicate a historical event, in which the walls did not move and there were no earthquakes during the evacuation. Creating the environment required finding a floor plan of The Station, reconciling that with the video footage of the nightclub at the time of the fire, and positioning all of the furniture and other incidentals as well as each agent in the locations at the inception of the fire. Upon completion, we had an approximation of The Station as it existed at the start of the fire.

The next dimension in the model is the hazards. Findings from public health and fire science studies of this incident showed that different locations in the building experienced different levels of the hazards that contributed to injury and death of the patrons at the nightclub. These factors are fire, the decreased visibility from smoke, temperature, and per cent of oxygen depletion and carbon monoxide (for details, see Gill et al., 2011). The characteristics of the layout of The Station and the propagation of the hazard in these locations were hard-coded to remain the same in all simulation runs. This was done since we are not modelling the hazard itself, but the human behaviour in reaction to it. Every hazard factor with the exception of visibility from smoke has a point reduction value in each location and time (for example, -1/second for carbon monoxide). Each avatar has a resistance value from which these points are subtracted, which is calculated based on the demographic characteristics attributed to the avatars; for example, it is safe to assume based on previous findings that a 30-year-old will have a higher resistance than a baby. Based on the data gathered about The Station, it is possible to estimate where each patron was at the start of the fire, which way they exited, the place where some of them perished, and the relative presence of the evolving hazards in the ecologies that caused injury and death (Gill et al., 2011). This information has the potential to create an enormously complicated set of weightings, which we continue to explore.

In the specific model being developed the attempt is to recreate an event in which there is detailed demographic and some activity information about each person involved in the incident. The starting points were individual behaviour traits: age, gender, physical impairment and familiarity with the environment. Traits like physical impairment, age and gender are important to consider because they can impact how quickly avatars can move, how much space they might take up, and indicate preferences to lead or follow. A trait like familiarity with the environment can be important because avatars with these characteristics should be more likely to be aware of egress options that are outside the line of sight, or be aware that certain rooms or hallways do not lead to any exits. It is also important to include information on their relations with others they were with at the time of the fire incident, and the nature of their groups.

It was necessary to create a large number of preferences and rules to model avatar behaviour. It involved deciding how to code individual, social and crowd behaviour attributes into the avatars, which in this case is based on the information on this incident and the findings from social science research on fire evacuations. A single avatar initialises in an environment and evaluates available potential target points. Target points are simply defined as the best exits available to the avatars. Target points, therefore, possess a value in which a 'destination' has a higher potential than a 'checkpoint'. A checkpoint is a structural feature through which an avatar must pass in order to reach their destination. At any given time the target point potentials are arranged in descending order so that the lower a value, the better or more attractive it is to the avatar. When a point is selected based on availability and distance (with the lowest potential value), the avatar will attempt to move towards it, using lateral movement and forward movement, avoiding fire and smoke, trending towards walls if applicable, and re-evaluating their movement at every step. When a target point is reached and the avatar is still active in the simulation, they will re-evaluate and find a new target point with a lower potential value than the point reached previously. If one is not available, the agent will return to the previous point and re-evaluate. These calculations are made 20 times a second. The likelihood of choosing new goals depends on individual attributes. For instance, according to social science information (Aguirre *et al.*, 2011) male avatars should have more risk-tolerant profiles and should be more willing to help others than female avatars, and thus might be more likely to change course during the evacuation.

Adding even a second avatar creates a great deal of complexity. Based on each avatar's behaviour model, there are traits in the model that account for comfortable space between avatars, the willingness to bypass other avatars, the willingness to change goals, speed and the willingness to bump into other avatars. Many of these traits are not called upon unless avatars are crowded in with others. Again, these preferences are different for different agent profiles. A unique aspect of the model is the ability for individual behaviour models to change based on changes in the environment. It assumes that as hazards become more dangerous, or when current parameters are not working, avatars should be willing to change their behaviour to include traits that would not exist in a normal situation. At this time avatars only communicate visually, so decreased visibility from smoke has a major impact on their ability to engage in group behaviour. Adding other parameters, such as auditory identification, is the next step pursued. It is likely that several of the weightings related to the other hazards and also several avatar behavioural traits will have to be modified when this factor is added.

The key dimensions that guided coding at this level of analysis are whether persons were alone or with others at the start of the incident, the sizes of their groups, the presence of kin, close relatives and friends in these groups, and whether group members were in close proximity at the start of the incident and thus did not have to spend time looking for each other. Rules of timing, space and movement are layered upon communication protocols and translators required for group networking.

Our model classifies group members as leaders and followers. In the current model, a leader is chosen based on demographic traits such as age, gender and familiarity with the environment. After a leader is selected, the members in the group follow the leader if they are in the leader's line of sight, or follow the leader's target point if other group members are in their line of sight. If followers lose line of sight of all group members they will revert back to individual behaviour after a stated time period. If a leader chooses to revert back to individual behaviour, or leaves the group through external factors (death, getting out of the building), then a new leader will assume responsibility for selecting target points for the group. If all members of a group but one becomes inactive in the group, the remaining member will automatically return to individual behaviour.

Crowding, or high human density in a constrained space are important to the simulation, for it impacts the behaviour profiles. The 'supra force' is an interaction effect of a set of conditions external to the avatar and the location of the avatar in the gathering of avatars. In historical incidents (e.g., Rauner, 2007) the probability for the supra force to occur increases with human density, rigid physical boundaries that can only be breached with difficulty if at all, and location of persons away from the outward borders of the evacuating collectivity. In such contexts people and groups have enormous difficulty in exercising individual volition; they and their groups are overwhelmed by the movements of others and are carried away by the force and aggregate movement of the collectivity. In our model, if an avatar is surrounded on all sides by inanimate physical barriers or by more than two layers of other avatars for more than a quarter of a second, they are subjected to supra force until these conditions change.

The goal for the ABM is to reproduce the already documented pattern of egress, injuries and deaths caused by this fire, as well as to replicate some key findings about group effects mentioned previously, such as that people in groups with intimate relations and separated from each other at the start of the fire delayed their evacuation as they searched for each other, which in turn increased their likelihood of injury and death. Once this validation is done it will be possible to research 'what if' questions for which there is very scant information, if any, such as the effects of different arrangements of internal space on the recognition of the developing danger.

Preliminary results

A number of differences can be observed when we compare versions of our model with and without social behaviour elements such as group membership and the effects of the supra force. In our group models, agents have individual goals, group goals and the presence of supra force, creating a larger set of evacuation possibilities. As shown in Table 1, when group behaviour is enabled, avatars are not as likely to take the exit closest to them, and instead look for members of their social group. Avatars that are in high-density situations surrounded for an extended period of time abandon their individual and group goals until they can move again freely. In the

Table 1. Simulated[a] and the actual number of persons using exits and dying in the station fire, by exits and three versions of the model

	Individuals	Intermediate groups	Full groups	Actual
Bar exit	37.35	34.04	112.75	78
Kitchen exit	164.09	177.00	7.01	17
Main exit	119.28	105.16	126.45	128
Stage exit	29.12	28.97	24.45	24
Bar window	2.11	10.34	56.25	71
Greenhouse window	5.71	5.92	1.86	34
Deceased	108.21	103.71	136.84	100
Total	465.87	465.14	465.62	452

Note: [a]Means generated by 75 simulations of the model.

individual model, avatars mostly attempt to exit via the closest exit, creating jams at major doorways.

The preliminary results are from three versions of our model. These versions contain the same hazard propagation and severity profile, the same starting position of each avatar, and the same type of social groups. Comparing 75 simulations each of (a) individual behaviour, (b) intermediate group behaviour (where avatars are likely to revert to individual behaviour while in duress), and (c) full group behaviour, we find large differences in specific exit choices. In the individual behaviour model, which excludes social groups, each avatar, as they attempt to exit the building, evaluates its own most efficient potential exit based on their position and the position of other avatars. The avatars search for the best exit for themselves, unaffected by social bonds. Our intermediate group behaviour model accounts for social bonds, but avatars are quick to revert to individual behaviour if barriers or distance exist between them and other group members. Our group behaviour model gives most importance to social bonds. In this model, agents will prioritise group goals above individual goals even after their health begins to decline and the dangers near them become severe; avatars in intimate social groups will not revert to individual behaviour unless failing to do so means death. The results are highlighted in Table 1.

Based on validation of evacuation models that only considers the number of deceased, the intermediate group behaviour model appears to be the best fit for our study, followed by the individual model with 108 simulated deaths. The intermediate group behaviour model averages 103.71 deceased avatars, compared with the 100 deaths in the fire. However, when examining the results for exit choices, the full-group behaviour model is a much better fit compared with what happened in the fire (Figure 1). Errors in exit choice are much lower for the full group behaviour model even though the death count is significantly higher for it than for other versions of the model. This is probably because avatars in the full groups are less likely to abandon their groups and instead spend more time trying to find group members, which means in effect moving away from available exits and then arriving at exits when there are many avatars in front of them.

The two biggest discrepancies between the findings for the full group behaviour model and the actual event are the higher average number of avatars exiting via the bar side door and the lower number of avatars exiting via the greenhouse windows. In the simulation, the main room windows are almost impassable by fire and smoke by the time windows become an attractive exit, which takes place late in the simulation, and they are used by the avatars on average much less than during the actual fire. The bar exit is used more often by the avatars than they were used in the actual fire because it is an optimal second choice for avatars that cannot exit via the front door. The biggest discrepancy for the intermediate group and individual models are the number of avatars that use the kitchen exit. Our simulations show a much greater average use of the kitchen exit than the actual occurrence because the kitchen door becomes a viable option to many avatars crowded out of the main exit. Since the full-group behaviour model spreads out the avatars much more, there is less crowding at the front door, so the kitchen exit does not become as desirable. In the actual event, many patrons were not aware of the kitchen exit because it was not open to the public.

Epistemologically, the incident at The Station is only one of a large number of incidents of its type; the true scores from this population of incidents is not known. We thus wish to avoid claiming that the historical results from The Station fire documented by Aguirre *et al.* (2011) are the 'true' representations of human behaviours in building evacuations. It is also important to emphasise that these results come from a preliminary model. Nevertheless, our hope is that they will encourage other modellers to consider including the social behaviour of avatars when modelling building evacuations, particularly their membership in groups. Social behaviour elements have a place in computer simulation models of building evacuation, and there is a need to begin a conversation about how to create generalised social behaviour modelling traits that are not limited to one building design or to an instance of building evacuation.

Conclusion

Many ABM models lack understanding of the social science processes that are inherent in the dynamics they wish to represent. This is particularly the case of the process of social and cultural emergence that is central to the effective use of ABM. The majority of social scientists have not recognised the value of ABM as a novel methodology that could revolutionise their disciplines. Because of this and other reasons, very often ABMs lack validation, are based on false panic explanations of social behaviour, and do not include group and inter-group dynamics. It is infrequent to read research papers that recognise that membership in groups often influence or even determine individual actions. Scholars who assume that people are flooded with emotion at times of crisis and become incapacitated so that they can only imitate others need to become familiar with a number of contrary findings from sociology, disaster studies, social psychology and other disciplines that show the importance, on the development of human personality, of the effects of socialisation and internalisation of culture, and the ability of people to act very effectively in the midst of unimaginable collective suffering and personal dangers. Many present-day practices often rob ABMs of building evacuations of its most promising feature, namely the potential it has of creating ontologically appropriate emergent cyber social organisations in which it will be possible to perform experiments that cannot be done using standard methods available at present (Zacharias *et al.*, 2008). ABM could help to develop answers to questions that cannot be explored at present due in large part to the limitations imposed by ethical standards generated by the probability of harm to human subjects (Gilbert, 2008; Zacharias *et al.*, 2008, pp. 237–260).

Computer programmers creating ABM simulations of collectivities of people evacuating from buildings on fire should do the following:

- Ground their model on what people do in the situations that are being simulated, so as to increase the validity of the simulation.
- Conceptualise the cyber actor both as an unattached individual and as groups, so as to examine group interaction and inter-group dynamics.
- Create facsimile models of cultural and social organisation not through the use of simple rules but rather, as we are currently doing with The Station nightclub incident, using rules that correspond to what is known in the social and fire sciences about the way people behave in structural fire and in crisis situations more generally.
- Abandon the common practice of assuming a tabula rasa, or the idea that the computer programmers can create cyber agents without worrying about the 'past' of the cyber agent; without considering the impact of socialisation on the person who is being simulated, or the history of the collectivity, which in important ways shape the individual and collective behaviour that is being simulated.
- Do not continue to use primarily variables tapping personality structure, emotions, attitudes, perceptions, psychological stress, anxiety and fear, but should also include social relations and group affiliations.
- Abandon a panic perspective on people's behaviour during fire, and instead adopt a social and affiliate perspective more in keeping with present-day social scientific understanding of what happens during these crises.
- Find means to validate developed codes rigorously. The pervasive use of cameras and other recording devices in many public locations means that that many disasters are captured as they occur. The presence of such recordings provides unique, authentic data that can and should be exploited for validating ABM building evacuation codes. Another source of information readily available, if its quality could be improved through training and better survey instruments, is the National Fire Incident Reporting System (NFIRS) (US Fire Administration, 2004; Hall & Harwood, 1989).

Acknowledgements

This research was supported in part by the Disaster Research Center, University of Delaware; the Department of Civil and Environmental Engineering, University of

Michigan; and the National Science Foundation through Grant Numbers SES-0824737 and 0825182. The authors are solely responsible for the contents of the paper.

References

Aguirre, B. E. (2006) The sociology of collective behavior, in: C. D. Bryant & D. L. Peck (Eds) *The handbook of 21st century sociology* (Berkeley, CA, Sage).

Aguirre, B. E. & Quarantelli, E. L. (1983) Methodological, ideological, and conceptual–theoretical criticisms of the field of collective behavior: a critical evaluation and implications for future studies, *Sociological Focus*, 16(3), 195–216.

Aguirre, B. E., Torres, M. R., Gill, K. B. & Hotchkiss, H. L. (2011) Normative collective behavior in the station building fire, *Social Science Quarterly*, 92(1), 100–118.

Chertkoff, J. M. & Kushigian, R. H. (1999) *Don't panic. The psychology of emergency egress and ingress* (Westport, CT, Praeger).

Drury, J., Cocking, C. & Reicher, S. (2009) Everyone for themselves? A comparative study of crowd solidarity among emergency survivors, *British Journal of Social Psychology*, 48, 487–506.

Dynes, R. R. (1970) *Organized behavior in disaster* (Lexington, MA, D. C. Heath).

Dynes, R. R. & Quarantelli, E. L. (1968) *Organizational communications and decision making in crisis* (Newark, DE, University of Delaware Disaster Research Center).

Epstein, J. M. & Axtell, R. L. (1996) *Growing artificial societies: social science from the bottom up* (Cambridge, MA, MIT Press).

Fahy, R. N. & Proulx, G. (2008) *Panic and human behavior in fire*, No. NRCC-51384 (Ottawa, Institute for Research in Construction).

Feinberg, W. E. & Johnson, N. R. (2001) Primary group size and fatality risk in a fire disaster, *in: Human behavior in fire. Understanding human behavior for better fire safety design*. 2nd International Symposium, London, UK (Interscience).

Galea, E. R. (2004) Computational fire engineering—do we have what we need? *Proceedings of the 3rd International Symposium on Human Behaviour in Fire* Belfast, UK, 21–22.

Gilbert, N. (2008) *Agent based models* (Los Angeles, CA, Sage).

Gill, K. B., Laposata, E. A., Dalton, C. F. & Aguirre, B. E. (2011) *Analysis of severe injury and fatality in The Station Nightclub Fire* (Newark, DE, University of Delaware Disaster Research Center).

Grosshandler, W., Bryner, N., Madrizykowski, D. & Kuntz, K. (2005) *A report of the technical investigation of The Station Nightclub Fire*, No. NIST, NCSTAR2 (1).

Gwynne, S., Galea, E. R. & Lawrence, P. J. (2006) The introduction of social adaptation within evacuation modeling, *Fire and Materials*, 30, 285–309.

Gwynne, S., Galea, E. R., Lawrence, P. & Filippidis, L. (2000) *Modeling occupant interaction with fire conditions using the building EXODUS evacuation model (Rep. No. 00/IM/54)* (London, University of Greenwich).

Hall Jr, J. R. & Harwood, B. (1989) The national estimates approach to U.S. fire statistics, *Fire Technology*, 25(2), 99–113.

Hardin, R. (2003) *Indeterminacy and society* (Princeton, NJ, Princeton University Press).

Helbing, D., Farkas, I. & Vicsek, T. (2000) Simulating dynamical features of escape panic, *Nature*, 487, 487–490.

Helbing, D., Johansson, A. & Al-Abideen, H. Z. (2007) Dynamics of crowd disasters: an empirical study, *Physical Review*, E 75, 046109.

Johnson, N. R. (1987) Panic and the breakdown of social order: popular myth, social theory, empirical evidence, *Sociological Focus*, 20, 171–183.

Johnson, N. R. (1988) Fire in a crowded theater: a descriptive investigation of the emergence of panic, *International Journal of Mass Emergencies and Disasters*, 6(1), 7–26.

Johnson, N. R., Feinberg, W. E. & Johnston, D. M. (1994) Microstructure and panic: the impact of social bonds on individual action in collective flight from the Beverly Hills Supper Club Fire, in: R. R. Dynes & K. Tierney (Eds) *Disasters. Collective behavior and social organization* (Newark, DE, University of Delaware Press), 168–189.

Keating, J. P. (1982) The myth of panic, *Fire Journal*, 56(May), 56–61, 147.

Kuligowski, E. D. & Peacock, R. D. (2005) *A review of building evacuation models* (Washington, DC, Fire Research Division, National Institute of Standards and Technology).

Macal, C. M. & North, M. J. (2010) Tutorial on agent-based modelling and simulation, *Journal of Simulation*, 4, 151–162.

McPhail, C. (1991) *The myth of the madding crowd* (New York, NY, Aldine de Gruyter).

Olsson, P. A. & Regan, M. A. (2001) A comparison between actual and predicted evacuation times, *Safety Science*, 38, 139–145.

Pan, X. (2006) *Computational modeling of human and social behaviors for emergency egress analysis*. PhD thesis, Stanford University, Stanford, CA.

Pan, X., Han, C. S., Dauber, K. & Law, K. H. (2006) Human and social behavior in computational modeling and analysis of egress, *Automation in Construction*, 15, 448–461.

Pan, X. (2006) *Computational modeling of human and social behaviors for emergency egress analysis*. PhD thesis, Civil and Environmental Engineering Department, Stanford University, Stanford, CA, June.

Pauls, J. L. (1978) *Management and movements of building occupants in emergencies* (Ottawa, ON, National Research Council Division of Building).

Pauls, J. L. (2006) *Stairways and ergonomics* (Seattle, WA, American Society of Safety Engineers).

Quarantelli, E. L. (1981) Panic behavior in fire situations: findings and a model from the English language research literature, *in: Proceedings of the 4th Joint Panel Meeting of the U.J.N.R. Panel on Fire Research and Safety* (Tokyo, Building Research Institute), 405–428.

Quarantelli, E. L. (1996) Emergent behaviors and groups in the crisis time of disasters, in: K. Kwan (Ed.) *Individuality and social control: essays in honor of Tamotsu Shibutani* (Greenwich, CT, JAI Press), 46–68.

Quarantelli, E. L. (1999) *The sociology of panic* (Newark, DE, University of Delaware Disaster Research Center).

Quarantelli, E. L. (2008) *Conventional beliefs and counterintuitive realities* (Newark, DE, University of Delaware Disaster Research Center).

Rauner, M. (2007) *Panic specialists bring order to the Hajj*. Available online at: http://www.spiegel.de/international/world/0,1518,512858,00.html (accessed 25 October 2007).

Sawyer, R. K. (2001) Emergence in sociology: contemporary philosophy of mind and some implications for sociological theory, *American Journal of Sociology*, 107, 551–585.

Shelling, T. C. (1978) *Micromotives and macrobehavior* (New York, NY, W. W. Norton).

Shi, J., Ren, A. & Chen, C. (2009) Agent-based evacuation model of large public buildings under fire conditions, *Automation in Construction*, 18, 338–347.

Sime, J. D. (1995) Crowd psychology and engineering, *Safety Science*, 21, 1–14.

Simon, H. A. (1957) *Models of man, social and rational: mathematical essays on rational human behavior* (New York, NY, Wiley).

Tang, F. & Ren, A. (2008) Agent-based evacuation model incorporating fire scene and building geometry, *Tsinghua Science and Technology Journal*, 13(5), 708–714.

Thompson, P. A. & Marchant, E. W. (1995) A computer model for the evacuation of large building populations, *Fire Safety Journal*, 24, 131–148.

Torres, M. R. (2010) *Every man for himself? Testing multiple conceptual approaches of emergency egress on building evacuation during a fire*. PhD thesis, University of Delaware, Newark, DE.

Tubbs, J. & Meacham, B. J. (2007) *Egress design solutions: a guide to evacuation and crowd management planning* (New York, NY, Wiley).

Turner, R. & Killian, L. M. (1987) *Collective behavior* (Englewood Cliffs, NJ, Prentice-Hall).

US Fire Administration (2004) *Fire in the United States 1992–2001*, (13th edn) (Washington, DC, Federal Emergency Management Agency, National Fire Data Center).

Weller, J. & Quarantelli, E. L. (1973) Neglected characteristics of collective behavior, *American Journal of Sociology*, 79(November), 665–685.

Zacharias, G. L., MacMillan, J. & van Hemel, S. (Eds) (2008) *Behavioral modeling and simulation: from individuals to societies* (Washington, DC, National Academies Press).

Mass action and mundane reality: an argument for putting crowd analysis at the centre of the social sciences

Stephen Reicher

School of Psychology, University of St Andrews, St Andrews, UK

In this paper I challenge the view that crowd action derives from a loss of identity, that it is mindless and that crowd phenomena are asocial. I argue instead that psychological crowds are based on shared social identification, that crowd action is highly socially meaningful, and that crowd phenomena are fundamental to the understanding and analysis of society. More specifically, I argue that crowds are important to social scientists in terms of (1) informing us about the social understandings of groups, especially marginalised groups; (2) understanding the processes by which cohesive and empowered groups are formed; (3) understanding the processes by which social change occurs; and (4) understanding core cognitive and emotional processes in social groups. I conclude that the study of crowds needs to become far more central in the social sciences.

Introduction

While I was in the midst of writing this paper, I was phoned by a Canadian journalist who was writing a seasonal piece entitled 'Why I want a cattle prod for Christmas'. Her complaint was with people who insist on standing at the entrances on crowded trolley buses and blocking people from getting on or off. From this beginning she had branched out into a more general piece on the annoying and irrational nature of crowds. So she had brushed up on Gustave Le Bon's seminal nineteenth-century text *The Psychology of Crowds* (1895/1947). And now she was talking to me.

We spoke at some length. I explained the difference between 'physical crowds'—a set of people who are co-present in the same space at the same time—and 'psychological crowds'—a co-present set of people who see each other as belonging to the same social category (a crowd of Catholics, a crowd of anti-cuts protestors, a crowd of England fans or whatever). I illustrated the difference with the example of commuters squeezed into a train carriage, who start off as a physical crowd: substantial in number but each psychologically separate, each avoiding eye contact with others, each uncomfortable with the touch of others. Then the train breaks down, and in time there is a psychological shift from the physical crowd to a psychological crowd of aggrieved commuters. People begin to look at each other, they begin to talk. Sometimes they might share sandwiches as they wait. Even in Britain. I used this illustration to make the core theoretical point that people in psychological crowds do not act irrationally. Rather they act meaningfully in terms of shared social identities. They act on the basis of shared group norms. They act for the shared group interest and not for their specific individual interests. The upshot of this is that psychological crowds are particularly adept at organising themselves, in coordinating with others and in achieving optimal group outcomes. What is irrational—or, more properly, dysfunctional—is to act as a psychological individual in a collective setting. Then multiple actors competitively pursuing divergent individual interests may lead to suboptimal outcomes such as clogging up the entrances so no one can get in or out.

All these are points that I shall elaborate below. The journalist listened politely to what I had to say. Then, at the end, she asked if I had any particular example that summarised my view of crowds. I suggested perhaps those caught in tube trains during the 7/7 attacks in London who supported and helped and aided each other in dire and dangerous circumstances. Or, perhaps, the demonstrators of December 1989 in Timsoara who opened their shirts to Ceaucescu's Securtitate forces and challenged them 'shoot, for what value is life if Romania is not free.' She listened, and then in a tone which told me with certainty that my persuasive efforts had been in vain, she responded 'interesting, yes, but do you have anything a little more *light-hearted*?'. My place was not to change the underlying story. It was to add some colour to an account that fits with the dominant representation of crowds as something noxious, something that is possibly dangerous, but ultimately as something that is an entertaining diversion and a distraction from the serious matters of everyday life—a representation that predominates both in academia and in the wider culture (e.g. Carey, 1992; McPhail, 1991).

Perhaps I should not have been surprised. A number of years before, fed up with the number of times my words about crowds had been misused by journalists, I agreed to one further request for commentary but only on the grounds that I would write the piece myself and any changes would be agreed with me. So I wrote the strongest and clearest attack that I could on the idea that crowds act irrationally and asocially. However I forgot to agree one thing. I left it to a subeditor to choose the headline. My piece was published under the banner 'Psychologist explains Mob Madness!'.

But even so, one carries on and one lives in hope. And perhaps there is real reason for hope when a prominent social science journal like this devotes a special issue to 'the crowd'. That in itself suggests some recognition that crowds are not just a bizarre aberration (I once referred to crowds as 'the elephant man of the social sciences') but might actually have important things to tell us about the nature of society and social processes in general. That has been my overarching aim in over 30 years of studying crowd phenomena. It is my specific aim in this paper. In the following sections I will argue, first, that crowds reveal to us the understandings and aspirations of social groups—particularly those generally without voice in our world; second, that crowds consolidate, cement and empower those groups; third, that crowds not only configure but also reconfigure the groups that structure the everyday workings of society; fourthly and finally, that the study of crowds reveals the processes which constitute us as social subjects who both make and are made in social relations.

Crowds and the nature of social categories

It is no coincidence that my Canadian contact was reading Le Bon. His crowd text (Le Bon, 1895/1947) has been characterised as the most influential psychology book of all time—something that not only analysed but helped form the mass politics of the ensuing century and more (Moscovici, 1981). In a nutshell, Le Bon contends that people become 'submerged' in crowds and lose their individual identity and gain a sense of invincible power. As a consequence, they lose their ability to make principled judgements and decisions and become subject to contagion—the inability to resist any passing idea or emotion. In particular they succumb to suggestions that come from the collective unconscious. Because this is an atavistic substrate (in effect, what remains below when our 'thin veneer of civilization' is stripped away), so the power of crowds is yoked to primitive and barbaric impulses.

To cite one infamous passage from Le Bon's book, which sums up his politics as well as his psychology:

> it will be remarked that among the special characteristics of crowds there are several—such as impulsiveness, irritability, incapacity to reason, the absence of judgement and others besides—which are almost always observed in beings belonging to inferior forms of evolution—in women, children and savages, for instance. (Le Bon, 1895/ 1947, pp. 35–36)

Psychology has often been accused of sexism, of ageism and of racism. It takes a truly great psychologist to achieve all three in a single sentence.

There are many grounds, both analytic and normative, on which to contest Le Bon's account. But perhaps the most fundamental is that it gives a profoundly misleading picture of what crowds do. It is simply wrong to suggest that crowd action is generically mind*less* and meaning*less*. Indeed those who have taken care to look at what people do conclude precisely the opposite. Crowd action is remarkable for just how meaning*ful* its patterns turn out to be.

Consider food riots. If one were looking for atavistic action, surely this would be a prime contender. Surely people go hungry, get desperate, storm the food stores and make off with what they can get. Yet, as E. P. Thompson makes clear in his study of several hundred English food riots in the 18th century, this is *not* what happens (Thompson, 1971). Riots did not usually occur at times of greatest dearth. They happened when food stocks were rising again. Moreover, they tended to happen around specific events, notably the transport of grain out of a locality. And when they did happen, people did not simply run off with produce. Rather, they tended to seize the grain, to sell it at a popular price, to hand the money and often even the grain sacks back to the merchants.

These, then, were highly patterned events. Moreover, the patterns reflected shared understandings of proper social practice. Thompson points out that the riots occurred at a time of transition from feudal to capitalist social relations, and that each vision of political economy was associated with its own notions of how social relations should be conducted. For the merchants, a market economy dictated that commodities be taken and sold where they command the best price. But they confronted a population who subscribed instead to a 'moral economy' based on locality. From this perspective, life might involve hardship, but local produce was there to serve local needs. These two economies conflicted precisely at the point where grain was being transported out of the locality to the market. The food riot—both in when it occurred and the forms it took—was in fact a way in which people enforced their vision of a just society.

Thompson goes further. He argues that these shared notions of rights and customs underlay 'almost every eighteenth century crowd action' (Thompson, 1971, p. 78)—and since his seminal work, a whole host of historical studies have shown that this conclusion need not be limited either in space to England or in time to the eighteenth century (e.g. Davis, 1978; Feagin & Hahn, 1973; Reicher, 1984; Smith, 1980). Take, as one example, Reddy's (1977) study of textile crowds in Rouen over two centuries. He concludes that 'the targets of these crowds glitter in the eye of history as signs of the labourers' conception of the nature of society' (p. 84). Putting all the examples together, we can abstract a more general message: the targets of crowds glitter in the eye of history as signs of the participants' conception of the nature of society.

The inability of Le Bon's approach to account for, or even acknowledge, the socially meaningfully patterning of crowd events reflects a fundamental individualism in his core constructs. Le Bon considers a sovereign individual self to be the sole basis of reasoned action. The loss of the individual self in the crowd therefore leads to the supposition that crowd action is necessarily uncontrolled. By contrast, the last thirty years of psychological research on group processes has been dominated by the notion that the self is not unidimensional but is rather a complex system that encompasses different levels of abstraction (e.g. Tajfel & Turner, 1979; Tajfel, 1982; Turner et al., 1987; Reicher et al., 2010). Thus we can and often do think of ourselves in terms of what makes us unique as individuals compared to other individuals (personal identity). But we can equally think of ourselves in terms of what makes us unique, as members of one social category, compared to other social categories (social identity). Moreover, when we act in terms of any given social identity, our behaviour is not dominated by idiosyncratic beliefs and values but rather in terms of the beliefs and values associated with the relevant category. In other words, social identity is the psychological mechanism through which social meaning systems come to structure the psychological field of the individual.

These notions are directly applicable to crowd settings. For, as research into a variety of crowd settings from urban riots to student protests to celebratory crowds to football fans has shown, the defining moment in the formation of a psychological crowd is the emergence of a shared social identity amongst participants (for a review, see Reicher, 2001). Contra Le Bon, people do not *lose* identity and *lose* control in the crowd. Rather, they *shift* identity and shift the basis of control.

This is not to suggest that crowd behaviour is automatic and preordained. What makes crowds distinct from other groups is precisely the lack of routinisation. Crowds lack formal membership or formal structures. They often face novel and ambiguous situations. It is therefore necessary to interpret the implications of general categorical understandings for appropriate action in context: what do we do now as socialists, as anti-fascists, as Catholics—or whatever the relevant category happens to be. As emergent norm theorists have pointed out (Turner & Killian, 1987), the role of informal leadership (or 'keynoters' as Turner and Killian term them) is very important. But, such leaders do not have free rein to suggest what they will. Their influence depends upon their ability to translate 'who we are' into 'what we should do'. As we have put it elsewhere, they need to be skilled 'entrepreneurs of identity (Reicher & Hopkins, 2001; Haslam *et al.*, 2010).

So, while crowd behaviour emerges out of an active and contested process of interpretation, and while there may, in consequence, be some variability in the actions of crowds, these actions still occur within strict limits which derive from the contours of social identity. It is this which ensures that crowd actions trace out in the world the conceptual frameworks of social groups. Or rather, it is this which instigates people to act in terms of their social belief systems. But of course, the instigation to act and the ability to accomplish action are very different things. In many situations, group members may wish to act in terms of their social identities but will desist from doing so for fear of disapproval or punishment from powerful outgroups (Reicher *et al.*, 1995; Klein *et al.*, 2008). However in crowds, shared social identity amongst many people empowers them to do things that they might shy away from in everyday life. Thus, for instance, in my first ever study of a crowd event—the St. Pauls Riot of April 1980 (Reicher, 1984)—a young man explained to me that, as a black person, he had always wanted to strike back at the police and now he was finally able to do so. So, while we may have finally reached a point where there is agreement with Le Bon—concerning the experience of power in crowds—my conclusions concerning the social implications of this are the polar opposite to his. Power does not abet mindlessness. Power abets the full expression of social identities.

In one sense, I am getting ahead of myself here. The feeling of empowerment in crowds is not something simply to be asserted. It is something to be explained. That is the focus of my next section. For now the point I want to underline is that perhaps uniquely in crowds one can gain access to the understanding of those groups who tend not to leave written records but rather speak eloquently in the language of the street. In his great study of the revolutionary crowds of 1789, the historian Georges Lefebvre writes that 'in the crowd, the individual, escaping from the pressures of little social groups which form his everyday life, becomes more sensitive to the ideas and emotions which stem from larger social categories to which he also belongs' (Lefebvre, 1954, p. 277, translation by the author). In short, perhaps it is only in crowds that we become the subjects of history. For any social scientist who wants to understand social ideas the crowd is a precious resource. We should not allow pathologising theories to dress down the crowd as mere dross and encourage us to discard its significance.

Crowds and the consolidation of social categories

The power of crowds does not derive from size alone. After all, if people fail to align their actions and act in pursuance of different—even incompatible—goals, then individual efforts are less likely to be additive than to cancel each other out (Reicher & Haslam, 2006). In short, collective empowerment is a function of the number and the coordination of participants. How, then, does shared social identification bring this about?

At this point, we need to distinguish between two subtly but importantly different senses of 'shared social identification' which feed into different but complementary antecedents of collective coordination. On the one hand identity is shared in the sense that a set of people define *themselves* in terms of the same category membership. This engenders a *cognitive* shift whereby crowd members adopt a common perspective on which to base thought and judgement. We can term this the *representational* sense of shared identity.

On the other hand, identity is shared in the sense that a set of people believe *each other* to define themselves in terms of the same category membership. This engenders a *relational* shift whereby crowd members cease to view fellow participants as other and hence orient to them as intimates. We can term this the *meta-representational* sense of shared identity.

Shared identity in the representational and meta-representational senses do not necessarily correlate with each other as the ongoing work of Fergus Neville shows (Neville, 2010). It is perfectly possible to participate in a crowd as a member of a given category and not recognise others as fellow category members—or even to stop recognising oneself as a category member if these others are what the category is in practice. For instance, people might turn up at a protest against a far-right group, all of them seeing themselves as anti-racists. However some might feel that those who *do not* confront the racists are not true anti-racists, while others might feel that those who *do* confront the racists are not true anti-racists. Both may thereby become disillusioned with the anti-racist category which they previously embraced.

The sense of 'we are in this together' is far from automatic. It is an accomplishment—and how it is accomplished through effective leadership, inclusive chants, shared practices and so on demands further study. Yet when it is accomplished it has profound consequences.

There is a growing literature on the various aspects of intimacy which flow from thinking of oneself and others in terms of the same category membership (for reviews, see Haslam & Reicher, 2007; Reicher & Haslam, 2009). Amongst other things, people are more likely to trust and respect people they see as 'one of us'. They are more likely to see their decisions as just and less likely to experience their decisions as coercive. They are more likely to help others and also more likely to expect help from others.

Even at the most basic, embodied and visceral levels, the sense of sharing identity with others impacts on social relations so as to facilitate co-action. It is hard to pull together with others if you cannot stand being near them. And there is much literature to show how people seem to have a clear need for 'personal space' and can be quite literally nauseated when it is violated. But in recent work, we have shown that people seek greater physical proximity with others when they are ingroup members (Novelli *et al.*, 2010). In a set of ongoing but as yet unpublished studies, we also have evidence that people find the touch and stench of other human bodies less disgusting when they are the bodies of ingroup members. This fits with much observational evidence that people will easily grasp, hug, even embrace others in the pursuit (or celebration) of group goals when ordinarily one might recoil from them.

In passing, it is worth noting that this account has profound implications for a relatively new and growing field which seeks to model the behaviour of crowds in both mundane settings (pedestrian flow in buildings and streets) and mass emergencies (e.g. Helbing *et al.*, 2000). There are, by now, a variety of such models (Challenger *et al.*, 2009) based on somewhat different underlying mathematical algorithms. But the problem lies less in the mathematics than in the underlying psychological assumptions. There has been a tendency to treat people as individual units each of whom has a fixed set of spatial preferences and goals.

Recently, there has at least been a recognition of the need to factor group memberships and relationships into such models (e.g. Moussaïd *et al.*, 2010; Singh *et al.*, 2009). But while the analysts may be willing, the analysis remains weak. For these analysts, the group is a set of people bound together by previous existing interpersonal ties. This leads to the idea that crowds are made up of multiple small groups of intimates. There is no recognition that a crowd can be formed of strangers who are united by the salience of their common category membership. Equally, there is no recognition that the nature of the psychological groups in a crowd event (and hence of the preferences and goals of crowd members) is not fixed, but rather may vary as a function of who else is present, of the way events unfold and of the social meaning and significance of particular sites and spaces.

The irony is that, far from acting as distinct individuals, or in terms of pre-existing ties, emergencies are contexts par excellence in which people come together as group members and act in support of fellow group members. A number of years ago, John Drury and I started a research project with the hope of showing that people are better at dealing with emergencies when they act in terms of social rather than individual identity. While we had some success when using virtual reality simulations of emergencies (Drury *et al.*, 2009c), a problem arose when we looked at actual emergencies. We found it remarkably hard to find instances of people acting as individuals and trampling over others (either metaphorically or literally) in their attempts to save themselves. Even where prior social identities did not exist, the shared experience of something as overwhelming as a life-threatening disaster created a powerful sense of shared group membership and this was accompanied by powerful examples of the types of intimacy that have been discussed above. People helped and supported others even at considerable risk to themselves. They were far more likely to sacrifice themselves for other people than trample over them (Drury *et al.*, 2009a, 2009b). The notion of mass panic, then, is largely a myth. It may be commonplace in the narrative of Hollywood disaster films. But in real life, disasters serve as prime examples of the type of the 'shift to intimacy' which occurs in psychological crowds.

Here we encounter a critical question: is the intimacy, the solidarity and the cohesion of crowds a fleeting thing which evaporates as soon as the event is over? Or are these more long-lasting things and do crowds play a part in creating the everyday solidarities which allow social categories to achieve cohesion? Even if the former were true, it would still mean that crowds would have much to contribute to our understanding of the processes by which social solidarity can be produced. That is to say, by observing the emergence of solidarity in unstructured collectivities we can isolate and examine the basic conditions of effective human co-action. Already, from my brief sketch above, it should be clear that these include elements which have been generally ignored both within and beyond psychology—notably the importance of embodied factors and the role of shared identity in breaking down the barriers to us being together and doing things together.

But, albeit still preliminary and limited, there is evidence to suggest that collective intimacies may survive the moment of assembly, and so the crowd may not only contribute analytically to our understanding of solidarity but may also contribute substantively to enduring social solidarities in society. Studies of extended social movements suggest that the expectation of social support that derives from previous actions feeds into people's willingness and confidence to take part in (or even initiate) future actions (Cocking & Drury, 2004; Drury & Reicher, 2005). Studies of mass pilgrimage suggest that participation in the religious event increases commitment to faith groups, to religious practice and to seeing society in general as organised in sympathy with the values of one's faith (Cassidy *et al.*, 2007; Prayag Magh Mela Research Group, 2007).

In addition, there is some suggestion from our ongoing studies of St. Patrick's Day and Easter Sunday Parades in the North and South of Ireland, that collective participation may impact upon social solidarities in other more indirect and unexpected ways. Notably, crowd events seem to serve as important agents of socialisation whereby young people are bound into key social categories such as the nation. Parents take their children along to events in order to teach the next generation 'their history' and, through the excitement and pageant of the spectacle, to make them enthusiastic and proud of their national identity (O'Donnell & Muldoon, 2011). What is more, in the act of bringing different generations together in the same event—either actually (as grandparents, parents and children stand together) or in the imagination ('your grandfather stood here long ago, just as you are standing here now, and in the future your grandchildren will stand here too')—so crowd events can help bind families together as a tight group that extends across time (Reicher, 2008). This interweaving of category, family and socialisation is perfectly expressed in the words of the Protestant Orange Order's emblematic song, The Sash. The last two lines of the chorus run: 'My father wore it as a youth in bygone days of yore/And on the Twelfth I love to wear the sash my father wore.'

These ideas are clearly in need of further investigation, but they point to the many ways in which crowds impact beyond the crowd itself. Yet, for all this richness, there is still a severe limitation in what has been presented thus far. All the studies refer to the impact of crowds on crowd participants. Yet, even in the most mobilised of communities, only a small percentage of people actually join crowds. Many, many more watch on. And so we now encounter a further critical question: do crowd events only impact on actual participants, or can they also affect observers as well?

In answer to this question, I will again draw upon historical evidence. But first, it is necessary to make a general claim about the relationship of crowds to broad social categories. Benedict Anderson famously described the nation as an 'imagined community' (Anderson, 1983). His point was that we can never actually get all the people as a country together and see them as a material entity. Rather, we have to imagine ourselves as part of a nation by imagining others like us behaving and thinking in the same way at the same time. For instance as we open our morning paper and read of some great national tragedy we imagine others reading the same news and sharing our sorrow—or else sharing our joy at news of some great national triumph. Well, for present purposes, it is possible to extend Anderson's argument in two important ways. First, Anderson's logic does not only apply to nations but to any large-scale social category: one cannot assemble all the Catholics in the world in one place, or all the women, or all the black people, or all the socialists or even all the Manchester United or Liverpool or Tottenham Hotspur fans. Many, perhaps most of the categories which concern us are 'imagined communities'. Second, there may be many ways through which we are able to imagine ourselves as a community and through which we infer the nature of our community.

I want to suggest that crowds play a critical role in this regard. In effect, *crowds are the imagined community made manifest*. Just as psychological crowds consist of people who see themselves in terms of their category membership, and just as crowd members recognise each other in terms of their shared category membership, so they are recognised by onlookers as a manifestation of a category to which they too may belong. England fans watch England fans watching a game of football at the World Cup; Catholics watch Catholics watching the Pope in St. Peter's Square. And what those crowds do, and how those crowds are treated by others tells the onlookers as well as the participants much about who they are, what they are prepared to do and how they stand in society.

For instance, it is arguable that the US urban uprisings of the 1960s and 1970s in the United States and of the 1980s in the UK were critical in creating self-conscious and empowered black communities (Benyon, 1984; Feagin & Hahn, 1973; Kettle & Hodges, 1982). Recent UK student protests against government cutbacks (and, more specifically, against a resultant rise in university student fees) seem to have galvanised wider action by demonstrating that there is a critical mass of people who are angry enough at what is happening and willing enough to act together as to make a broad and effective anti-cuts coalition a viable proposition. Obviously, since these are ongoing processes, this is largely speculation, but we can look backwards to see similar processes in action.

Breen (2010) points to a specific mobilisation which he identifies as critical to the history of the American revolution. In early September 1774, a rumour arose that British troops had attacked the New England population, killing a number of inhabitants and even 'cannonading the town of Boston, and massacring the inhabitants without distinction of age or sex' (cited in Breen, 2010, p. 138). This led to a widespread mobilisation of American insurgents led by an aging general, Israel Putnam. Putnam and his peers discovered that the rumours were false before they reached Boston, and they then quietly returned home. One might think that this could have proved a debacle, demonstrating the poor judgment of Putnam himself and the delusions of those who opposed the crown. However the actual consequences were quite the opposite. The size of the mobilisation became a source of success, the very fact that large numbers of people were prepared to mobilise against English outrages gave people a sense of group solidarity. Each small community that took action saw that they were united with other communities and that they had strength as a broad American insurgency. As Breen (2010) himself puts it:

> It was in these adventitious circumstances that the insurgents of America initially became conscious of their membership in larger communities built upon shared identities. Crisis encouraged political imagination on the group ... (and) helped weave local experiences into a larger and much more compelling narrative of a united cause. (p. 151)

And when, eight months later, British troops did actually kill 'fellow Americans' at Lexington, Putnam rode again, the populace mobilised with him and the war of independence began.

Translating this account into the conceptual terms provided above, we can see how, first, the collective event creates shared social identity amongst different participants, allowing them to see previously disparate groups as one and leading to both the experience and the expectation of mutual support and coordinated action. But we can also see how this critical mass had a sufficient gravitational pull as to draw others into its ambit, making them feel empowered and effective as category members.

If this is so and if it reflects a general phenomenon then it speaks to the iconic importance of crowds in creating and binding together the groups that create social reality. It is not just that individuals become subjects of history in the crowd but that crowd events are key moments in creating social formations. Once again, we ignore crowds, or else treat them as exceptions to normal social process at our peril and at considerable explanatory cost.

Crowds and the creation of social categories

Thus far, I have emphasised the way in which crowd events serve to consolidate already existing social categories. But even in advancing that case, I could not help but stray into addressing how such events serve to create categories—in the sense of bringing into being categories which did not previously exist; in the sense of changing the meaning of existing categories; and also in the sense of leading people to recategorise themselves in such a way as to make notional (or marginal) categories real and socially significant.

Breen, for instance, contends that the mobilisations of insurgents in New England in 1774 did not just bind Americans together and empower them, they also led insurgents to see themselves *as* Americans against British troops and the British Crown (whereas previously they had protested against specific measures as patriots). This was critical in the transition of a protest movement into a secessionist movement. As Archer (2010) puts it in his analysis of the British occupation of Boston a few years previously, before there could be a political revolution there had to be a *revolution of identity.*

It is not incidental that the consolidation and the creation of identity, even if analytically separable, should be so intertwined in reality. If we accept that social categories are only possible to define in their relations to other categories (Tajfel & Turner, 1979; Turner *et al.*, 1987)—then necessarily group empowerment and the changed relations to other groups that this entails will change the nature of the group itself.

I referred above to a young man in the St. Pauls riots who, as part of the crowd, was able to enact his prior hostility to the police. Crowd members were able to do this and more. The police were driven out of the area for several hours. People took control of the area and decided who came in and who did not. They also decided which institutions belonged to the community and which oppressed it—the latter coming under prolonged and concerted attack which left a bank, a post office and several large showrooms in ruins (Reicher, 1984). The impact of these acts was clear the next day. St Pauls identity, defined largely in relation to black experience, had previously been characterised in terms of subordination and repression. Now it was defined in terms of agency, of strength and of self-assertion—and this was clear in the acts and even to assertive postures of the locals as police pairs nervously walked by on patrol.

But intergroup relations are not just an outcome of the change process, they are at the heart of the process by which change is produced. For the action of outgroups can bring people into relations in new ways, give rise to unprecedented forms of social power and hence create identities that had not previously been imagined. To use the St. Pauls case for one final time, what instigated the riot was when the police raided the Black and White Café. The significance of this was that, in contrast to the targets of previous raids, the cafe was used by all sections of the local population and seen as both a symbol of and a resource for the existence of an effective community. All saw it as an attack on them and responded together. Together they had the power to impose themselves over the police and to redefine their place in the world.

This reflects a recurrent pattern of change which we have found since across a range of studies using a range of different crowds and which we have come to describe and analyse as the Elaborated Social Identity Model of crowd action, or ESIM (e.g. Drury & Reicher, 1999, 2000, 2009; Reicher, 1996; Stott & Drury, 2000, Stott *et al.*, 2001; Stott & Reicher, 1998). The pattern has four phases:

- First, there is a heterogeneous crowd (by which we mean a single physical assembly in which there are a variety of different psychological groups, some more radical than others, but generally with the majority seeing themselves as 'respectable citizens' with respect for the police and the law).
- Second, an initially powerful outgroup (often the police) see the crowd as a whole as being dangerous and act so as to impose their own control over the crowd—in the process depriving crowd members of what they consider to be their legitimate rights.
- Third, the crowd become united through an experience of common fate and a common sense of grievance. This makes even those who were previously moderate open to voices counselling radical action. It also empowers crowd members to challenge the restrictions placed upon them by the (police) outgroup.
- Fourth, this action confirms the original outgroup sense of crowd danger and fuels on ongoing process of escalation.

John Drury's extended study of an anti-roads building campaign in the East End of London (Drury & Reicher, 2000, 2005; Drury et al., 2003) provides a striking example of these processes. The campaign was initially divided between more moderate local protestors and more radical environmental activists who came to the area. But in time this distinction was erased as the police were seen to treat everyone equally as dangerous and to deny them their rights of protest (and also to fail to protect them against dangerous acts by the contractors). This set in motion a whole series of changes, especially for the locals.

They initially positioned themselves as liberal–democratic subjects exercising their democratic rights but, having been positioned as 'oppositional' and 'anti-state' by the police they began to see the world in oppositional terms and accept their own positioning as being opposed to (and repressed by) the state. As a consequence they began to redefine their own values and aims in life. They began to see other oppositional groupings such as striking miners and the Ogoni tribe in Nigeria—to whom previously they had felt no connection—as part of a common category. They even began to redefine the point of their protest and what constituted success. Whereas previously they simply wanted to preserve their local community and village green, now they wanted to challenge the entire government roads building programme and its imposition on the population. Hence whereas success previously meant stopping their green being concreted over, now, even after that happened, the campaign could still be counted as success if it mobilised people against the government and exposed the illegitimacy of their policies.

It is important to stress here that we are not suggesting that crowds always, or even often, lead to social change. Many crowds are relatively routinised. In most crowds, outgroups do not 'misrecognise' crowd members but rather acknowledge and even affirm their self-definitions. For change to occur there must be a relatively rare combination of an asymmetry between the way crowd members define themselves and the way they are defined by the outgroup, the willingness and the ability of the outgroup to impose their definition upon the crowd, and sufficient empowerment of the crowd to allow them to challenge the acts of the outgroup.

The point, then, is that the study of the crowd is useful not only in showing us that change does occur (and hence warning us against the essentialisation of social categories). It also helps us to understand how change occurs, the conditions under which it occurs and also the interconnections amongst the various dimensions along which change occurs. At the risk of sounding repetitive, here is yet more evidence that the study of crowds needs to be taken seriously.

Crowds and social processes

In the brief space I have left, I now want to use the foregoing account of the social phenomena involved in crowd events to address some basic matters concerning the processes underlying those phenomena—and I will consider issues relating to both how we represent our world and how we feel about our world (in more conventional psychological language, both cognition and emotion).

We can start by asking what sort of concepts of self and social reality are necessary in order to make sense of how these can be changed through crowd events. There are two parts to the answer. The first has to do with self and is already implicit in the argument that group identities change through a change in ones social relations and the implications of these relations for how the group acts: if, for instance, the authorities are on one's side then they can be reasoned with (and one can be reasonable). If, however, they are an antagonistic foe, then they have to be fought against (and one has to be a fighter). Put more generally, identity needs to be seen as a representation of one's position in a set of social relations along with the proper and possible actions that flow from that position (Drury & Reicher, 2009; Reicher, 2001). What are often abstracted as traits or norms of a group should rather be conceptualised as ways of manoeuvring through the world as one sees and experiences it.

The second has to do with social reality and is already implicit in the argument that the process of change is initiated through being repositioned by outgroup action. People begin to define themselves as oppositional because, in reality, they find themselves in opposition. But that reality is constituted by the understandings and actions of the outgroup which then confront crowd members in material guise: lines of riot police and police vehicles, who prevent them from going where they wish; police horseback charges which force them to disperse. What is distinctively clear in crowds is that representation and reality are not separate orders but rather are different temporal moments in an unfolding process. The representations of one group form their actions and then constitute the context in which the other group forms its representations, act and constitutes a context for the first group to act again. This process may be more obscured in mundane reality where we often find the actions of others sedimented into institutions where human agency is obscured, where the products of that agency confront us as natural phenomena and where social change is taken off the agenda. If we want to put the possibility of change back on the agenda, then crowd research suggests that we need to adopt a historical and interactive approach to social phenomena.

One issue now remains—and it is a big issue. I have dealt at considerable length with representations and norms and how these relate to crowd action. I have done this to challenge the classic idea that crowds are irrational, to show how they are mean-ingful and that they create as well as reflect social meaning systems. Yet all this is very cold. It runs the danger of missing something fundamental about crowds, which is stressed in the classic theories and which helps explain their continuing hold. Crowds are emotional affairs. Crowd members are passionate about their groups, which is why they can kill or even die for them. Any approach which ignores this is clearly inadequate and even risks failing to explain how crowds can make history. What is more, the passion of crowds can serve as a more general basis for understand-ing of investment in groups as Freud (1921) himself clearly understood. And, it might be added, understanding of group investment is one of the main things that other social scientists want from psychology (why do people cling to groups when all the structural and cultural analysis might suggest they should do otherwise?) but on which psychology fails to deliver.

The classic approach sees passion as resulting from the loss of self, the loss of reason and the loss of conscious agency—in such circumstances primitive enthusiasms can run rampant. Our work suggests otherwise. When asked, what makes people so excited about crowd action is that, for one of the few times in their lives, they feel empowered to enact their identities. Within the event itself they can live according to their own values and act according to their own beliefs—what we term 'collective self-objectification' (Drury & Reicher, 2009). Through the event, they are able to shape the wider world in their own terms. For once, they do not have to live in a world made by others, they make the world for themselves. In other words, in crowds, people become the *subjects* of history. The crowd (that is, the social category united and in action) constitutes them as effective social beings. And that, I suggest, is why people invest so heavily in the crowd. It explains the conditions under which people invest in groups more generally. And it also explains why crowds are such pas-sionate affairs.

Conclusion

This paper is possibly the longest response to a journalist's throwaway comment in history—or at least in *my* history. While I doubt that my Canadian contact will ever read it, at least I hope to have convinced those who have read this far that crowds are weighty phenomena that deserve sustained analysis. Yet still, the more I think about it, the less satisfied I am with my response. For if crowds raise profound issues, that is not to deny that they can equally be light-hearted and fun. Indeed one of the things that makes crowds compelling for participants and analysts alike is that they are frequently combine high politics and hilarity, seriousness and subver-sive humour, at one and the same time. It is fun to walk down a street, singing, banging drums and improvising ribald chants. Riots are generally riotous. The street carnival is generally political and street politics is often most effective when it is most carnivalesque (Kenney, 2002; Thompson, 1991). Often, then, the richest crowd phenomena have the aspect of frivolity.

Had I not been so thrown by her request for a light-hearted example, I might have told that journalist a story of the one time I ever went to the Wimbledon tennis championships. It was at the end of a rainy first week, so they let the general public onto the show courts that are normally reserved for a select audience. These more refined folk were concentrated at one end of the court, their blazers and panama hats (it was quite a while ago) contrasting with the jeans and t-shirts of the rest of us. I cannot recall exactly who was playing, but I do remember that, at one stage, the proceedings became very tedious. So, to entertain itself, members of the crowd began a Mexican wave. The wave flowed round three sides of the court, but those at the select end declined to join in such a vulgar spectacle. The rest of the crowd made jocular remarks called on them to participate. Though, at first, these calls failed, the wave continued round the court, each time pausing for the exact time it would have taken to pass through the inactive end. After a while the popular calls got louder, the elite began to falter. Then finally, to a massive cheer and much laughter from all around, they joined in whole-heartedly.

The incident said much about class in contemporary Britain, about the clash between 'low' and 'high' culture, about the pressure upon the elite to conform (on the surface at least) to popular democracy and about how the apparent victory of the masses can leave privilege intact. But equally the whole affair was a laugh and it was expressed through laughter. Even (or perhaps particularly) when crowds are light-hearted they have so much to teach the student of society. This paper is a plea to take note.

References

Anderson, B. (1983) *Imagined communities: reflections on the origins and spread of nationalism* (London, Verso).
Archer, R. (2010) *As if an enemy's country* (New York, NY, Oxford University Press).
Benyon, J. (1984) *Scarman and after* (Oxford, Pergamon).
Breen, T. H. (2010) *American insurgents, American patriots* (New York, NY, Hill & Wang).
Carey, J. (1992) *The intellectuals and the masses* (London, Faber & Faber).
Cassidy, C., Hopkins, N., Levine, M., Pandey, J., Reicher, S. D. & Singh, P. (2007) Social identity and collective behaviour: some lessons from Indian research at the Magh Mela at Prayag, *Psychological Studies* [Special Issue: Social Psychology of Collectivity], 52, 286–292.
Challenger, R., Clegg, C. W. & Robinson, M. A. (2009) *Understanding crowd behaviours: simulation tools* (Easingwold, The Cabinet Office Emergency Planning College). Available online at: http://www.cabinetoffice.gov.uk/sites/default/files/resources/simulationtools1_0.pdf/.
Cocking, C. & Drury, J. (2004) Generalization of efficacy as a function of collective action and intergroup relations: involvement in an anti-roads struggle. *Journal of Applied Social Psychology*, 34, 417–444.
Davis, N. Z. (1978) The rites of violence: religious riot in sixteenth century France. *Past and Present*, 59, 51–91.

Drury, J., Cocking, C. & Reicher, S. D. (2009a) Everyone for themselves? A comparative study of crowd solidarity among emergency survivors, *British Journal of Social Psychology*, 48, 487–506.

Drury, J., Cocking, C. & Reicher, S. D. (2009b) The nature of collective resilience: survivor reactions to the 2005 London bombings, *International Journal of Mass Emergencies and Disasters*, 27, 66–95.

Drury, J., Cocking, C., Reicher, S. D., Burton, A., Schofield, D., Hardwick, A., Graham, D. & Langston, P. (2009c) Cooperation versus competition in a mass emergency evacuation: a new laboratory simulation and a new theoretical model, *Behavior Research Methods*, 41, 957–970.

Drury, J. & Reicher, S. D. (1999) The intergroup dynamics of collective empowerment: substantiating the social identity model of crowd behaviour, *Group Processes and Intergroup Relations*, 2, 381–402.

Drury, J. & Reicher, S. D. (2000) Collective action and social change: the emergence of new social identities, *British Journal of Social Psychology*, 39, 579–604.

Drury, J. & Reicher, S. D. (2005) Explaining enduring empowerment: a comparative study of collective action and psychological outcomes, *European Journal of Social Psychology*, 35, 35–58.

Drury, J. & Reicher, S. D. (2009) Collective psychological empowerment as a model of social change: researching crowds and power, *Journal of Social Issues*, 65, 707–725.

Drury, J., Reicher, S. D. & Stott, C. (2003) Transforming the boundaries of collective identity: from the 'local' anti-road campaign to 'global' resistance, *Social Movement Studies*, 2, 191–212.

Feagin, J. R. & Hahn, H. (1973) *Ghetto revolts* (New York, NY, Macmillan).

Freud, S. (1921) *Group psychology and the analysis of the ego*, International Psycho-Analytical Library No. 6 (London, George, Allen & Unwin).

Haslam, S. A. & Reicher, S. D. (2007) Social identity and the dynamics of organizational life: insights from the BBC Prison Study, in: C. Bartel, S. Blader & A. Wrzesniewski (Eds) *Identity and the modern organization* (New York, NY, Erlbaum), 135–166.

Haslam, S. A., Reicher, S. D. & Platow, M. (2010) *The new psychology of leadership* (London, Psychology Press).

Helbing, D., Farkas, I. & Vicsek, T. (2000) Simulating dynamical features of escape panic, *Nature*, 407, 487–490.

Kenney, P. (2002) *Carnival of revolution* (Princeton, NJ, Princeton University Press).

Kettle, M. & Hodges, L. (1982) *Uprising!* (London, Pan).

Klein, O., Spears, R. & Reicher, S. D. (2007) Social identity performance: extending the strategic side of the SIDE model, *Personality and Social Psychology Review*, 11, 28–45.

Le Bon, G. (1895/1947) *The crowd* (London, Ernest Benn).

Lefebvre, G. (1954) *La revolution française* (Paris, Presses Universitaires de France).

McPhail, C. (1991) *The myth of the madding crowd* (Chicago, IL, Aldine).

Moscovici, S. (1981) *L'Age des foules* (Paris, Fayard).

Moussaïd, M., Perozo, N., Garnier, S., Helbing, D. & Theraulaz, G. (2010) The walking behaviour of pedestrian social groups and its impact on crowd dynamics, *PloS ONE*, 5(4).

Neville, F. (2010) The united crowd: shared identification and the experience of collective action, Paper presented at the ISPP Annual Conference, San Francisco, CA, USA, 2010.

Novelli, D., Drury, J. & Reicher, S. D. (2010) Come together: two studies concerning the impact of group relations on 'personal space', *British Journal of Social Psychology*, 49, 223–236.

O'Donnell, A. & Muldoon, O. (2011) National celebrations and the socialisation of national identity. Unpublished manuscript, University of Limerick.

Prayag Magh Mela Research Group (2007) Living the Magh Mela at Prayag: collective identity, collective experience and the impact of participation in a mass event, *Psychological Studies* [Special Issue: Social Psychology of Collectivity], 52, 293–301.

Reddy, W. M. (1977) The textile trade and the language of the crowd at Rouen 1752–1871, *Past and Present*, 74, 62–89.

Reicher, S. D. (1984) The St. Pauls riot: an explanation of the limits of crowd action in terms of a social identity model, *European Journal of Social Psychology*, 14, 1–21.

Reicher, S. D. (1996) 'The Battle of Westminster': developing the social identity model of crowd behaviour in order to explain the initiation and development of collective conflict, *European Journal of Social Psychology*, 26, 115–134.

Reicher, S. D. (2001) The psychology of crowd dynamics, in: M. Hogg & S. Tindale (Eds) *Blackwell Handbook of Social Psychology: Group Processes* (Oxford, Blackwell), 182–208.

Reicher, S. D. (2008) Making a past fit for the future. The political and ontological dimensions of historical continuity, in: F. Sani (Ed.), *Self-continuity* (London, Psychology Press), 145–158.

Reicher, S. D. & Haslam, S. A. (2006) Rethinking the psychology of tyranny: the BBC Prison Study, *British Journal of Social Psychology*, 45, 1–40.

Reicher, S. D. & Haslam, S. A. (2009) Beyond help: a social psychology of social solidarity and social cohesion, in: S. Sturmer & M. Snyder (Eds) *The Psychology of Prosocial Behaviour* (Oxford, Blackwell), 289–309.

Reicher, S. D. & Hopkins, N. P. (2001) *Self and nation* (London, Sage).

Reicher, S. D., Spears, R. & Haslam, S. A. (2010) The social identity approach in social psychology, in: M. Wetherell & C. T. Mohanty (Eds) *The Sage handbook of identities* (London, Sage), 45–62.

Reicher, S. D., Spears, R. & Postmes, T. (1995) A social identity model of deindividuation phenomena, *European Review of Social Psychology*, 6, 161–198.

Singh, H., Arter, R., Dodd, L., Langston, P., Lester, E. & Drury, J. (2009) Modelling subgroup behaviour in crowd dynamics DEM simulation. *Applied Mathematical Modelling*, 33, 4408–4423.

Smith, D. (1980) Tonypandy 1910: definitions of community, *Past and Present*, 87, 158–184.

Stott, C. & Drury, J. (2000) Crowds, context and identity: dynamic categorization processes in the 'Poll Tax riot', *Human Relations*, 53, 247–273.

Stott, C., Hutchison, P. & Drury, J. (2001) 'Hooligans' abroad? Inter-group dynamics, social identity and participation in collective 'disorder' at the 1998 World Cup Finals, *British Journal of Social Psychology*, 40, 359–384.

Stott, C. & Reicher, S. D. (1998) How conflict escalates: the inter-group dynamics of collective football crowd 'violence'. *Sociology*, 32, 353–377.

Tajfel, H. (1982) *Social identity and intergroup relations* (Cambridge, Cambridge University Press).

Tajfel, H. & Turner, J. (1979) An integrative theory of intergroup conflict, in: W. G. Austin & S. Worchel (Eds) *The social psychology of intergroup relations* (Monterey, CA, Brooks/Cole), 33–48.

Thompson, E. P. (1971) The moral economy of the English crowd in the eighteenth century, *Past and Present*, 50, 76–136.

Thompson, E. P. (1991) *Customs in common* (London, Merlin).

Turner, J. C., Hogg, M. A., Oakes, P. J., Reicher, S. D. & Wetherell, M. S. (1987) *Rediscovering the social group: a self-categorization theory* (Oxford, Blackwell).

Turner, R. H. & Killian, L. (1987) *Collective behaviour.* (3rd edn) (Englewood Cliffs, NJ, Prentice-Hall).

Index

Note:
Page numbers in **bold** type refer to **figures**
Page numbers in *italic* type refer to *tables*
Page numbers followed by 'n' refer to notes